'Her story is an object lesson to any youngster, rider or not'
Daily Telegraph

'The text gallops through Funnell's life story with engaging candour'
Independent

'The prose zips along . . . and with it all the highs, lows and bits in between that make for the rider's lot. Not rags to riches, but an inspiration to those who aspire'
Horse & Hound

'The read of the year . . . by turns inspiring, moving and funny, this book shows that all of Pippa's triumphs have been earned'
Eventing magazine

'A highly engaging and deeply revealing account . . . It is an inspirational story, thanks to the frank manner in which Pippa describes the hardship, setbacks and self-doubts which plagued her chosen career . . . The book reveals a well-rounded individual who avoids being self-congratulatory, despite her incredible success'
Irish Field

'Gripping, dramatic and touching . . . a fascinating insight into what life is really like on the international eventing circuit . . . This is a story of struggle and success and of the horses that made it all possible, told with the gritty determination of a driven individual to become a true national champion . . . This book is interspersed with funny moments, private personal moments and the inevitable lows associated with horses. It will inspire all who read it'
The Scottish Farmer

'Her achievements on the equestrian scene in the past few years are undeniable. A double European Champion and Badminton winner, she is an authoritative figure on the circuit and an inspiration to young riders'
Waterstone's Books Quarterly

Pippa Funnell is the first woman to become eventing's world number one. She was born Pippa Nolan in 1968 and, with her first horse, Sir Barnaby, went from pony-club level to Badminton, en route winning the European Young Rider title in 1987. Her numerous victories include back-to-back European Championships in 1999 and 2001, and back-to-back Olympic silver medals in 2000 and 2004. She is the first (and so far only) winner of the Rolex Grand Slam, in 2003, and has won Badminton three times in 2002, 2003 and 2005. In 2003 she was the *Sunday Times* Sportswoman of the Year. In 2005 she was awarded an MBE in the Birthday Honours List. Pippa is married to the international show jumper William Funnell and lives in Surrey.

Kate Green, who worked with Pippa Funnell on the writing of the book, is a freelance journalist who has covered most major three-day events, including the Olympics, for *Horse & Hound*. She was editor of *Eventing* magazine for ten years and has co-written five other books with leading riders Andrew Nicholson, Ian Stark, Blyth Tait, William Fox-Pitt and Pippa Funnell. Kate lives in Berkshire and works for Blenheim Horse Trials.

PIPPA
FUNNELL

The Autobiography

ORION

An Orion paperback

First published in Great Britain in 2004
by Orion
This paperback edition published in 2005
by Orion Books Ltd,
Orion House, 5 Upper St Martin's Lane,
London WC2H 9EA

Revised edition

3 5 7 9 10 8 6 4 2

A CIP catalogue record for this book is
available from the British Library.

ISBN 0 75286 519 6

Printed and bound in Great Britain by
Clays Ltd, St Ives plc

www.orionbooks.co.uk

To Ruth McMullen and Sir Barnaby,
without whom none of this would have been possible.

Contents

Acknowledgements

Many thanks must go to Susan Lamb from Orion for spending over a year trying to persuade me to write this book. After the results I had in 2003, Susan made me realise it had to be done and so, with the aid of my agent Jonathan Marks from MTC, an agreement was made. Running on a very tight timescale due to all my Olympic preparations, the team at Orion have done a great job working out times to suit me. Kate Green has also done a fantastic job as my ghostwriter. Having worked on my first book, *Training the Young Horse*, she knew exactly what she was letting herself in for: endless late nights at Cobbetts Farm tirelessly writing about my life.

During my thirty-six years, a great many people have been influential or have helped and supported me through the highs and lows and I am eternally grateful to them:

William, not just for being a wonderful husband, but my best friend as well. Whether it's because he is fairly laid back he always looks on the positive side of things, and many a time it has been his encouraging words and his sense of humour that have picked me up when I have been down. Also for the endless help with improving my jumping.

My mother, father and brother Tim, for always being there for me in all aspects of my life. I realise how privileged and lucky I am to have such a close, wonderful family to laugh with and cry with. It is amazing the strength it gives me knowing that they are always there for me, no matter what.

Becky Coffey, not only for keeping me organised with sorting out the bills and entries, but for all her support over many years at pretty much every event. She is a very dear friend and special person.

All of my owners, without whom my career would not have been possible, for supplying me with many fabulous horses.

My sponsors, who have helped enormously in relieving my financial pressures and supplying me with top-quality products.

Duncan and Clare Inglis, Lizzie Bunn, Chris Warren, Wally and Clare Wales and, of course, Tina Cook, for being such wonderful friends.

All my staff over the years, who have continually grafted away, loving and caring for all the horses. They have all been an essential part of my backup team.

There are so many people – old friends, new friends, staff, trainers and, of course, other horses – who haven't been mentioned, but every one of them has played a role in helping me get to where I am today.

But my greatest acknowledgement has to go to my dear beloved horses and dogs, every one of them holds a special place in my heart. I thank them for the endless pleasure they have given me over the years.

Thank you all.

PIPPA FUNNELL

The Autobiography

Prologue

'As the final part of the treble came down for Zara Phillips, the audience roared and, as she heard this, Pippa, who was standing isolated in the middle of the collecting ring, clapped her hands to her face, weeping with relief…

'Her first words on flopping thankfully into a chair with a glass of champagne in one hand, a Rolex watch in the other – and a quarter of a million American dollars in the bank – were: "I really don't know how I've kept my head through this. So many people have been behind me – my husband William, my mates – and I so wanted to do it for them…"

'A dream finale greeted the record crowd who poured into the last day of the Burghley Horse Trials in the expectation of seeing history in the making. They were not to be disappointed…'

[From *Horse & Hound*, 11 September 2003]

Anyone who watched me in the seconds following my momentous realisation that I had won the Grand Slam of eventing might imagine that an experience like that turns you into a completely different person. But it doesn't and hasn't. I now know that the feeling of winning something so crucial lasts only a split second compared to the lifetime of striving for that moment.

I find it hard to explain how the actual moment of winning

feels. The most accurate description of that time, on a hot Sunday afternoon at Burghley in 2003, would be a state of shock. I couldn't take the enormity of it in at all. After shock, comes overwhelming relief and gratitude to my horses. It sounds arrogant, but I felt as though the hopes of the entire sport were resting on my winning the Grand Slam because the possibility of anyone actually doing it had always seemed so remote, yet here I was with it within my grasp, if only I could hold everything together.

I always have something to prove to myself; I don't get a kick out of winning unless I feel my performance has justified it. I don't know whether my tendency to over-analyse is a blessing or a curse, but often at the time of winning I am still thinking about what I could have done better, or what needs to be improved before the next competition.

But practicalities set in quickly. In eventing and, I am sure, in other sports, there's no chance to dwell on the win because you're always on to the next thing. In this case, it was a flurry of presentations and press conferences, followed by packing the lorry and a 200-mile drive home. The next day I had horses to ride, breeches to wash and a lorry to clean and repack because I was going to be living in it for the next two weeks. I had other competitions to go to which, as far as everyone connected with them were concerned, were just as important as the Grand Slam.

The wonderful thing about success in eventing is the way it radiates out. On the Monday morning after my first Badminton win on Supreme Rock in May 2002, the horse's owner Emma Pitt was greeted by her newsagent in Fulham excitedly waving a newspaper with our picture in it. And right over in a tiny hamlet in West Cork, Rocky's breeder, Lindy Nixon-Grey, was in tears of excitement watching on television the horse she knew as a foal winning the world's biggest event .

Although the Rolex Grand Slam looked like my moment of glory, other people got enormous pleasure and reward from it – owners, trainers, breeders, as well as staff, family and friends – and, at times, that can feel like a huge burden to carry. The flip side is that the same people will be gutted when there's a disappointment – a mistake made when you're in the lead, or (and this, for me, is the absolute worst part of my work) having to make that horrible phone call to an owner to tell them their horse is lame. That's why winning is so special; I always want to win for all those people involved as much as for myself as it makes up for the many low moments.

Never did I think it would be such a long road. When I was in my mid-twenties, and the international career I had set my heart on as a teenager seemed about to go belly-up amid feelings of failure and self-doubt, it was only fear of wasting those years of hard graft, combined with my enormous hunger for that elusive success at the top level, that made me stick with the sport.

I feel strongly that if all this could happen to me, then it's possible for many others too. For my early life was no different to hundreds of other pony-mad children. I tasted early success and then it all threatened to go horribly wrong – at times it was only the thought of the amount of hard work others had put in that made me determined to keep going.

And, now, I have to reassess my life again. After the Athens Olympics I started to rethink my priorities because of the guilt I feel about how little time I have to give to the important people in my life is causing me sleepless nights. My owners are fantastic. They have all been with me for many years, and I like to think that the whole thing has been rewarding for them, but I know that if they have a complaint it is my lack of communication with them. This has got worse, because at the end of a long day's riding I have got other things to do, like being a wife. It's the same for Mum and Dad and my brother Tim – I don't see them nearly as much as I would like, and it's getting me down.

Also, after twenty years in the game and a few falls, I am stiff when I wake up in the morning. My body takes longer to recover and I have to be more choosy about which horses I ride. And, after a relatively quiet season in 2004, I realise that I love being at home. I have no plans to close the door on a sport about which I am passionate, but William and I do want to have a family, and I am thinking about how I can use my experiences to help others. For what has happened to me has made me realise that anything is possible in life, if only you can somehow hold on to your dream throughout even the lowest points.

I
Early Days

My dream of becoming a full-time event rider didn't take shape until I was fourteen and got my first horse, Sir Barnaby, who was to take me further than I'd ever dreamed was possible. By then, I'd been taken to watch at the big events, Badminton and Burghley, and I was in awe of riders like Lucinda Green, Ginny Leng and Mark Todd. When I groomed at events for friends who actually *talked* to these people, I would be completely mesmerised by the magic of the whole atmosphere of eventing and its camaraderie.

Looking back, though, there were earlier signs of the rider – and the personality – I would become. I was a self-analytical child who was constantly striving to improve. I lived for riding lessons and Pony Club rallies: my favourite class was 'best rider', because I would have to concentrate hard on my own performance, and I took it all terribly seriously, keeping a diary of my results at gymkhanas and how my pony had gone.

I also learned very quickly that if you spend time creating a relationship with an animal, it will do many things for you. Even as a small child, I had a strong relationship with my ponies; they weren't just tools for winning rosettes, I loved being with them. They were my special friends.

In fact, my eventing career began long before I was born, thanks to a horse called Majador, whom my mother, Jenny Brown, acquired when she was a teenager. Much to her father's horror, her grandmother, who was mad on racing and betting, bought her a locally bred wild two-year-old off the racecourse. Majador (Teddy) was an impossible horse at first, and Mum spent a lot of time on the floor gazing up at him. While she was away in Switzerland for six months, Mum sent Majador to be trained by Ruth McMullen, who taught at the Enfield Chace Pony Club, of which Mum was a member. Mum remembers how Majador was transformed as a result of his time with Ruth. Not only was it the start of a lifelong friendship, it was the foundation of my riding career.

Another great friend of Mum's was Dinny Nicholls. She later married the well-known show promoter and BBC commentator Raymond Brooks-Ward. Uncle Raymond became my godfather and they provided my first pony when I was just six. But in many ways the most influential friend of Mum's, as far as my life is concerned, was Margie Coffey, as it was through her that Mum was introduced to my father, George Nolan, when she was working at the British Show Jumping Association. The Coffeys are Dad's cousins, and Margie's younger sister Becky was also a great friend of Ruth's. Becky comes to most events, and having spent so much time with Ruth is a useful pair of eyes on the ground, and many times she has been a shoulder to cry on. She now does all my bills and helps me with all my correspondence. She's a special character, and is immensely popular with the other riders, too.

That first pony, Pepsi, was a little black hairy thing of about 11.2 hands who had been ridden by Raymond's sons, the twins Simon and James, and Nick. As we didn't have stables at home,

Mum kept her horse, Smokering, with family friends, the Minchins, about a mile away from our house in East Sussex. Pepsi moved in here too, and every night after school I would go round to see him. Pepsi lived out in a field with a big barn with all the Minchins' ponies. That first winter seemed terribly cold and, being only small, I struggled hugely in the mud, falling over time and again as I tried to help carry bales of hay. As I attempted, fruitlessly it seemed, to brush Pepsi's shaggy coat clean of mud, I dreamed of owning a big bay horse who was clipped and wore rugs and bandages and lived in a stable with a deep, clean bed of straw.

My best friend was Ally Minchin – we were at Mark Cross Primary School together – and we had a lot of fun with our ponies as children, hunting with the Eridge and going to Pony Club rallies and lots of gymkhanas. We and our friends would go out riding for hours – we went miles to rallies and meets – because in those days parents were not so worried as they are today.

Pepsi could be awkward, and sometimes took me unawares: I can remember on the way home from one good day's hunting being so cold that when Pepsi stuck his head down I fell straight out the front door. On another occasion out hunting, when I was with Ally's mother, Angela, Pepsi refused to go through a stream; Angela got on him to sort him out, at which point he put his head down, the saddle shot forward and Angela ended up in the stream.

Ruth McMullen was responsible for finding my next pony, Flighty, when I was nine. I wasn't the sort of child who was brought up with the traditional aged Shetland. All my ponies were young (even Pepsi was only about eight) and Flighty, 12.2 hands and not quite four, had only just been broken. He was smashing-looking but naughty; he bucked me off endlessly and once trod on my fingers, but I was quite undaunted and would just get back on again. Every so often Mum would get on him to square him up, but she got bucked off as well. I did every sort of competition with Flighty, who could have been a good show pony if I hadn't found showing boring – wearing hair-ribbons wasn't my style at all!

Flighty was kept in the side of a logshed at the Minchins'. This was very exciting: now I had a pony I could keep in during the winter and who wasn't always going to be covered in mud. It seemed a big step forward. That little logshed was my first stable, and I learned from an early stage that how well you look after your pony has nothing to do with having super facilities – it's all about horse management, and Flighty never went short of love and care.

Throughout my schooldays, my parents made a lot of sacrifices in terms of both time and money to enable me to have ponies. Every new purchase that made life easier was a milestone; it was a particularly big day, for example, when we got a trailer. I'd longed for ages to have our own transport, and our first show in the trailer was a red-letter day.

I was very tearful when at eleven I grew out of Flighty and he had to be sold; I felt as though half my heart had been ripped away. He was replaced by Jeremy Fisher, who was 13.2 hands and again came from Ruth. Jeremy was a difficult pony and quite sharp, a contrast to Flighty whom I used to have to kick into fences in traditional Pony Club style. When I first got Jeremy I made the mistake of kicking him too, with the result that he would take off flat out.

I learned a lot from riding Jeremy because he used to twist badly over his fences, especially at uprights, and this took quite a bit of sitting and I realised I had to use my eye to place him at the right point of take-off. One day out hunting he twisted so hard that I came off and lost half my front teeth, which had to be capped. This was the beginning of my lifelong terror of the dentist. I hated having injections for fillings and wearing 'railway tracks', and the teeth-capping was the start of a phobia about needles and injections that I still suffer from. Blood I can handle – but the sight of a needle makes me go cold.

It was with Jeremy that I got the hang of the idea that it was possible to make a horse nicer to ride. He had a habit of going along with his head up in the air, and I worked hard to improve him. I didn't necessarily know what I was doing, but I tried. I would get terribly frustrated with him and lose my temper, but it wasn't long before I realised that getting after him would set him back two weeks; Jeremy taught me a lot about patience. At that stage, Ally had a good pony called Musketeer, who was a fantastic jumper and never refused, and she was winning all the jumping classes we entered. Even though she was my best friend, this would get me down because, by contrast, Jeremy was a difficult pony. But it also gave me the hunger to improve. I kept a show diary, in which I analysed every single performance, keeping a record of the results and making comments about Jeremy's performances. I wrote things like: 'Behaved much better and kept his head down for the *whole* show'; or 'Jumped well, but got a bit upset in thunderstorm'; or 'Eliminated at fence 5, got very scared but the band was playing'.

We have always been a really close family and in the winter, when there weren't shows, we would have Sunday lunches together, something which is almost unheard of today as we always seem too busy. But, looking back, I now realise that an awful lot of our family weekends revolved around what I wanted to do, which was to go to competitions with my ponies. This was hard on Dad and my brother Tim, who regularly found themselves abandoned at weekends.

Tim, who is two years older than me, gave up riding early on; the Eridge branch of the Pony Club, to which we belonged, disapproved of tetrathlon for some reason and, as this would have been the only thing that would have kept my sports-loving brother riding, he packed it in. I adored Tim, but I suppose I was an annoying little sister and we did fight as children: he would pull me along by my hair. Still, when he went away to prep school at Marlborough House, I was devastated.

My father was totally unhorsey; his sports were ocean racing, including the Fastnet Race and many cross-Channel contests, and rugby: he played for London Irish and later on Beckenham and Crowborough. It was many years before he realised he would have to find a role within eventing if he was ever to see the female members of his family, but once I had moved away to work and competitions were the only places he could see me, he took up commentating. He started off at Mum's horse trials and did it so well that it snowballed from there.

Dad has always been a lot of fun as a father – he is a great one for telling stories and jokes, and could keep my friends amused for hours – but I also respected him hugely. Whenever I had an argument with Mum – and I was prone to tantrums, especially about things like having to wear a skirt – I'd stomp upstairs in a temper and fling the window open, then hide under the bed, hoping it looked as though I'd jumped out. I was always packing my bags and threatening to leave the house, but Mum would bring me up short by saying, 'Wait until your father gets home.' That would stop me.

We weren't a family that went on loads of holidays – in fact, the first time I went abroad was on a junior eventing team –

but I do remember fabulous times in Cornwall with the Brooks-Wards, who had a house near St Just-in-Roseland. Tim was mad keen on fishing and, inspired by Dad's love of sailing, loved the water. I have often thought that if I hadn't chosen a life with horses, I might have done something on the water. It has the same buzz and element of uncertainty.

Mum and I have always had a lot in common. My October birthday usually fell during the Horse of the Year show at Wembley and, because Mum worked there every year, it was my treat to stay with my grandparents Annie and Billy, whom I adored, and go to the show. (Dad's parents were a bit older and his father died when I was very young, so we didn't know him quite so well.) Even when I was little, I remember watching Ruth in the show hunter classes and being hugely impressed and inspired because she was so evidently at the top of her game. She always seemed to win. Without really understanding what I was watching, I now realise that I was influenced by her methods from an early stage.

After Mum left the BSJA she worked at the South of England Showground at Ardingly – the horse trials she runs there has now celebrated its thirtieth anniversary – and at half-term I used to help her lay out the rosettes for the big annual show.

Mum and I still have an amazing relationship; we can really laugh, sometimes crying with it. She is the sort of person who will get into a major panic over little things like losing her car keys, but when a serious drama looms she deals with it better than anyone. Mum never forced me to ride or look after my ponies; I just loved doing it. But from my earliest years she instilled in me the importance of a smart turnout – she was always immaculate herself when she went hunting – and I took great pride in cleaning my tack as well as grooming my ponies.

When I was still a small child, Mum had a serious riding

accident which affected me deeply. She broke her back badly in a hunting fall: she jumped a gate which hadn't been shut properly and, as it swung open, her horse hit the top. I remember going with Dad and Tim to visit her in hospital and being quite disturbed by the whole experience. Mum's accident didn't put me off riding, but it was a traumatic time and I became rather clingy.

As Dad was working, he couldn't cope with looking after Tim and me as well, so we stayed with the Minchins and with Annie and Billy. But although I loved my grandparents and was quite at home with the Minchins, this episode had the longer-term effect of turning me into a kid who loathed staying away from home. So when I was ten and went to Wadhurst College it was as a day girl, which suited me perfectly – not only because I didn't want to board, being still unhappy about leaving home after Mum's fall – but because it meant I could carry on riding.

Though I didn't much enjoy the academic side of school, I loved sport. I was mad on lacrosse and played for the county as captain of the Sussex team. It was a big thing for the school to have someone in the county side and the sense of achievement this gave me whetted my appetite for more.

I wasn't too bad at exams because luckily I'm the sort of person who can read through things and memorise them – two weeks later I wouldn't remember a thing, of course – but I still didn't enjoy the classes. I was probably mildly naughty, and would be the one to think up the tricks, but get someone else to do them because I have always been nervous of real trouble and tended to bottle out of anything really daring. The sort of things I got told off for were bad deportment, squidging the heels of my shoes and thinking it trendy to have my fingers poking through the holes in my jumper.

I have never been gifted with languages – I was useless at Latin and German and certainly no good at French. On the day of my French O-level oral exam I was up in a loft smoking with some mates. When the cleaners turned up underneath us, we didn't dare come out of the loft and had to miss the exam. Needless to say, I failed.

I had a great bunch of friends at school, but Ally was still my best buddy, and so I was distraught when her father went to work in Kuwait and she was sent to boarding school; it was the first time we had been split up. I never minded getting up early before school so I took on looking after Musky for her and would ride him before school with Jeremy, riding one and leading the other, to get him fit for Ally for the holidays.

I particularly loved the Easter holidays because of the hunter trials and the hunting, and I would be gutted if anything was cancelled because of bad weather. When that happened, we would take the ponies down to the beach at Camber Sands and jump the breakwaters, blissfully unaware that there were massive pools underneath.

In the holidays there were occasional trips to Ruth's yard in Norfolk, which was then a very long journey. Once my friend Sophie Howgego and I spent a week there. Another time at Ruth's I met Charlotte Hollingsworth (now Bathe) who was to become a great friend. I always had a lot of fun at Ruth's and would long for my next visit.

When I was fourteen, I started to grow out of Jeremy and Mum became concerned as to where my first horse was going to come from – obviously a horse costs more, and eats more, than a pony. But Ruth was on the case; she had a five-year-old of 16.1 hands called Sir Barnaby, who had just started eventing with her head girl Kerrie Daykin, and Ruth thought that he would be a suitable step up from Jeremy for me. So – taking

Jeremy, who was bound for a new home in Norfolk – I went to meet Barnaby at Dick Stillwell's, a well-known trainer of top show jumping and eventing riders, where Kerrie was on a course. I had a preconceived idea that Barnaby was steel grey and I was so excited about this new horse that I rushed off down a row of stables to find him. But it was winter and dark and I couldn't work out which horse he was; when Ruth pointed out this dark roan to me, I thought he seemed absolutely enormous and was rather nervous about the jump in size. Jeremy, Barnaby and I then went back in the lorry to Ruth's, from where my pony could go on to his new owners. Next day I had to say goodbye to him and, inevitably, there were tears. Barnaby, meanwhile, was tied up ready for a lesson and when Jeremy had gone I turned around to find him standing up on his hind legs looking for his friend. I was horrified and couldn't think how I would manage this great big horse. All I wanted was my pony back.

A few days later I took Barnaby home. That Christmas he was clipped, and I remember thinking that finally my dream had been realised: I'd got my clipped dark horse. Easily the best Christmas present was a day rug with red binding and a matching surcingle.

More then ever now I was aware how many sacrifices my parents were making so that I could ride competitively. There were rows, many of them sparked off by Dad and Tim being left at home while Mum and I went to competitions. I used to block my ears against the arguments; but I did have a sense of guilt and knew that my hunger to succeed was making me selfish. The same feeling often strikes me still.

During my first winter with Barnaby I jumped him at Ardingly, which was when I first spotted William Funnell. He had already left school, being two-and-a-half years older than me, which at the time seemed quite an age gap; but, having just started to take more of an interest in boys, I used to go home and dream about him. That didn't last for long, though!

It was at this time that I really got into eventing – I had read Lucinda Green's biography *Up, Up and Away*, which totally inspired me – and now the dream was starting to take shape. Previously, I hadn't focused on which discipline I wanted to go into; it could easily have been show jumping up until then.

Although I'd now decided what I wanted to do, life was still manic because by this point I was school games captain, often playing matches at weekends; and I'd also discovered boys and parties. So I had a lot to fit into my life. I rode before school, going for a quick hack around the block the moment it was light enough. Then Barnaby would be turned out, Mum would arrange for him to be caught in the afternoon and I'd sort him out for the night when I got home from school.

Barnaby was now living opposite us, with Fenella Fawcus's parents. Fenella had four horses, and I was hugely in awe of her; she'd ridden on the junior eventing team and I couldn't believe that we had someone who had ridden for Britain as a neighbour. Clea Hoeg, now married to Vere Phillipps, was working there then, which is how we first met.

Getting to know Barnaby seemed an uphill task at times. His propensity to shy terrified me on the roads; we lived on a commuters' rat-run to the station and I would be hacking out at just the wrong time of the morning. One day he spooked at a milk crate and went into a car. This scared me, but it also made me realise that I couldn't just sit on him and do nothing: I had to confront the issue. Barnaby also had a serious buck, but Jeremy and Flighty and the hunting had taught me to stick on and I didn't come off him as often as people expected me to.

I was on all the Pony Club teams with Barnaby, which is

how I first came across William Fox-Pitt, who was a member of the West Street branch and therefore in the same area. I remember him riding big horses and looking gangly still in his jodhpur boots, as we all were. Making the transition to long black boots was a milestone for everyone – and not just for the sake of looks. The first time I wore them Barnaby jumped sideways into the water and I caught them on a nail on a post, ripping a pair of boots that Mum had owned for years. She was upset, but without the boots my leg would have been a mess.

I remember the summer of 1984 for being a particularly happy time. I was fifteen and we had lots of great family friends, all with children of mine and Tim's ages. It was this year that I met my first serious boyfriend, Paul Bartlett, who also evented, at the annual summer holiday tennis tournament, where my partner was Mark Pougatch, who now works on Radio Five Live and has remained a close friend since.

Tim left school that summer and went travelling, working on a big ship going around the world. Even though we still argued like cat and dog, I was distraught at the thought of not seeing him for a whole year. I passed eight O-levels, though not with particularly good grades – and then the arguments started at home. Dad was adamant that I should stay on at school and take A-levels; he thought the horses were just a phase and that if I left now I'd regret it later on. I was miserable because my friends had left to go to sixth-form colleges or to do various courses and if I did go back it wouldn't be the same; I was also obsessed with the idea of leaving school and going to Ruth's to train, because I was absolutely convinced that I wanted a life with horses. I was very pig-headed and, beginning my lower sixth year against my will, even devised ways I might be able to get myself expelled. I also spent a lot of time thinking up examples of people who had been to university and then ended up in dead-end jobs. And I delighted in pointing out that the career-aptitude test I took concluded that I should be a bus conductor! Looking back, I can, of course, see my father's point and I think I'd feel the same about my child now, but at the time I was immovable.

Poor Mum didn't know which way to turn. She had to support Dad, but I think part of her would have been happy for me to opt for a life with horses there and then. Eventually a compromise was reached: I agreed that after one season with Ruth I would do a secretarial course so that I had something I could fall back on. On this condition I would be allowed to leave school at the end of the spring term in the lower sixth. I couldn't wait.

When I was sixteen I started affiliated eventing. My first outing, in the spring of 1985, was a novice class at Crookham and, amazingly, I won, with a double clear despite a poor dressage. I remember beating a couple of quite famous names in the section and it completely inspired me. One of the special things about our sport is that, with young horses being brought on all the time, even at grass-roots level you can compete against the top people – there are probably young people who get a serious buzz from beating me now, and it gives them incentive and hope.

My next competion with Barnaby was the horse trials at Brigstock, where Mum took me with all my kit, and from there I went on with Ruth to Norfolk to start my new, grown-up, working life.

2
Hard Work to Build the Foundations

I was in for something of a shock at the start of my Norfolk life. By this stage I liked to think that I understood horses. I'd ridden a few for other people and had had good results on Barnaby and, though I certainly wasn't over-confident I couldn't believe it when Ruth wouldn't let me out of a walk for two weeks. I had an impending junior trial in which I had to enter the dressage arena in canter and then halt – quite a big deal – and the prospect of being so (as I thought) unprepared reduced me to tears.

But this is when it hit home that if the foundations aren't laid correctly, you can't build the house. In other words, if the basics aren't there in riding, everything that happens subsequently is built on a false premise. Ruth's insistence on getting the basics right, especially balance and straightness – we spent hours riding on the lunge without stirrups – instilled in me the realisation that this was how it would have to be with every horse for the rest of my life. I imagine it's the same with any sport – after all, with tennis or golf everything goes back to the correct swing or grip.

I was in tears after every lesson for the first few weeks at Ruth's. I would hide it from the others, of course, but I was so demoralised. In fact, the whole thing was much harder going than I had expected after the fun of my brief visits in the past. We worked twelve-hour days, from 7 a.m. to 7 p.m. – at least. I missed the laughs I had had with Charlotte Hollingsworth and that crowd, who had moved on. It was a long, hard winter, so everyone was not the happiest and there was a lot of bickering. My abiding memory was of being tired, hungry and freezing.

We lived in a massive old house called Little Palgrave Hall near Swaffham in west Norfolk, which Ruth rented from Peter and Valerie Mason. It stood on a hill and was one of the coldest houses I've ever been in. The only forms of heating were the Aga and the fire, if we had time to light it. There never seemed to be enough hot water and the bedrooms were so massive they could have fitted ten beds. On top of that, I had been used to Mum's excellent food, and here it wasn't the same.

The stables were laid out quite randomly. There were five lovely old-fashioned indoor stables and a yard of four boxes, all the others were dotted around and in the middle of everything there was a little sand-school for lungeing. This was a nightmare because it would get very wet and deep, and the giant wheelbarrows which we used had to be dragged through it. Mucking out was hard work and the muck-heap seemed miles away, so we would try to get as much as we could into the barrows on each trip. It was back-breaking. And because we were on a big arable farm, there was a rat problem. We would talk at the tops of our voices and clap and bang the bins to try to scare them off, but I was still terrified of going out in the pitch-black early mornings.

As the newest there, I struggled. I didn't always understand what Ruth was going on about and I felt I was going backwards. My dressage was horrendous, and when we competed Barnaby and I were consistently last in that phase. I'd get loads of noughts because he would buck and be so naughty that the movement wouldn't happen. But because he was so consistent in getting fast, clear cross-country rounds and would go clear in the show jumping, he was always placed overall. So, though I was often deflated and demoralised after the dressage, I always finished an event with a smile on my face.

I looked forward desperately to the events – not just because I so badly wanted to succeed, but because I'd see Mum and Dad, and often my grandmother Annie. And, most importantly, they would bring me food!

If those times felt hard for me, they weren't easy on Barnaby either. I had another horse to ride, Harvest Sunshine at novice level, who belonged to Anne Brickell, whose son Scott now helps build the course at Burghley; but as Barnaby was the only horse I was eventing properly, I probably ran him every weekend. Nowadays my older horses run a maximum of six times a season, whereas poor Barnaby did about eighteen that year!

When I applied to be part of the junior (under-eighteen) system I was invited on a training course with Gill Watson, who is still trainer to the juniors and young riders and to whom many of us owe such a good start to our careers. I was so excited – I really thought I'd arrived. Gill was based at Tony Cuthbert's stud at Aston Rowant in Oxfordshire, where Gary Parsonage was then her head lad. The others on the course were Georgina Anstee, Sally Bateson, Rowland Lloyd-Thomas, Jason Verey – and Polly Lyon (now Williamson), of whom I was in awe because she was trained by Rachel Baylis. Rachel had just won the European Championships on Mystic Minstrel and was a big heroine of mine. We were put up in a

B&B, and I had to share a big double bed with Polly. Thankfully we got on very well.

I think I probably got on the course because Ruth knew Colonel Allfrey, the chairman of selectors, and because I'd done well at Pony Club level, but Barnaby went so badly that Gill must have wondered what she'd got – we still laugh about it now. The jumping was fine but the dressage was a nightmare. I was definitely the weakest link on that course, but I loved it and I enjoyed meeting people with similar ambitions. Although I hadn't made a team at that stage, I felt part of something and it inspired me even more to get selected to ride for Britain.

My first three-day event, the junior national championships at Windsor, was a big milestone. I was very excited and couldn't believe I was finally doing a three-day event; Windsor was like a Badminton for juniors. I thought the course was the biggest thing I'd ever seen and I hadn't a clue what I was meant to be doing each day but, luckily, Ruth's head girl Kerrie Daykin was riding Becky Coffey's horse Mr Jackpot that year and she helped me with the roads and tracks and steeplechase. We weren't stabled on site then – nowadays it is a rule at a three-day event – so we had to box up every day from Windsor Forest stud where all the competitors were stabled.

We went clear across country, but afterwards discovered that Barnaby had hit his stifle; we iced it, but I didn't realise that I should have trotted him up that night and the next morning he was very stiff. In my ignorance, I continued with the idea of presenting him at the final inspection, even though I could see he would probably fail. But just as I was about to trot him up, a team of carriage horses came past and he was so lit up that he stormed up in front of the judges and sailed through the inspection.

I finished eighth; but although I was of course elated at being placed, I was frustrated by our poor dressage score. I didn't enjoy that phase at all then, and nor did Barnaby; he would look quite pretty, but I didn't know how to get him engaged and the moment there was any sort of distraction, he would misbehave.

I was longlisted for the junior national team that year because Barnaby had been placed so often, but his dressage wasn't good enough to make the team and, after he blew up in front of the selectors at the final trial at Dauntsey, I didn't even get an individual slot. This was terribly disappointing because 1985 was a home European championships, at Rotherfield Park, at which Britain, as host nation, was allowed twelve riders instead of six.

However, this did mean I could go to the Pony Club Championships instead, and there Barnaby excelled himself in the dressage. We finished second individually behind Tina Reeve, and the Eridge team was third. My team-mates were Guy Cosgrove, Debbie Cox and Victoria King, who also had her horses at Ruth's.

The other major event I did that summer was the British Novice Championships at Locko Park, where we finished eleventh on a not very good dressage mark. There were some classy horses in this competition: Lucy Thomson won on Red Gold, Ian Stark was second on Glenburnie, Jane Thelwall (now Wallace) was third on King's Jester and Mary Thomson (now King) was eighth on King Boris. A really special moment was when Lucinda Green came up to me and said: 'What a nice little horse.' I couldn't believe that my heroine had spoken to me in real life! Remembering it now reminds me to make the effort to talk to younger riders, because I know just how it felt to be over-awed.

At the end of the season I had to fulfil my promise to Mum and Dad and go home to do my secretarial course in London. Although I loathed the course, I had to admit that my first year at Ruth's had been tougher than I expected, and I was ready for a break. I was longing for a taste of London life as well, so I would stay up there a couple of nights a week with various friends, one of them being Tetta Neville. She has a wicked sense of humour and we had a lot of fun.

On the other nights I had to go home, frantically revising my Pitman script on the train, because I was trying to earn some money by working four nights a week as a waitress in a pub called The Vine at Cowsley Wood. The Vine insisted that we served the vegetables by silver service, and many sprouts went flying during my time there. We also had to wheel out the sweet trolley, and you had to memorise what all the wretched puddings were called. One evening when it was very busy, I pushed the trolley too close to a table and a whole load of creamy trifle went down the back of a man's jacket. I couldn't bring myself to tell him and rushed into the kitchen crying with laughter, pleading to be a washer-up instead. I realised then that I was not cut out for a catering career. I also realised that, much as I was loving London and seeing my friends, I wanted to stay in the countryside and work outside.

We had a fantastic family Christmas, as always, thanks to Mum and Annie who put on a wonderful spread, and after that I found I was really looking forward to getting back to Ruth's and the horses.

That second year in Norfolk, 1986, was altogether much happier. I had new horses to compete: a mare called Shanlaragh (Tilly) owned by Annabel Adams, an old friend who was starting at Norwich University; and, though Paul Bartlett and I had split up by this stage because of the distance between us, we remained friends and he sent me his horse Airborne, a 17.1 hands eventer with lovely paces who had already gained novice points. I also got my first sponsorship, through Uncle Raymond, with Modern Alarms, who gave me a lump sum of money. Coincidentally, their colours were yellow and black, the same as my Pony Club colours, and I have worn them ever since. And Ruth had a new head girl, Gill Hardacre, who had ridden on a junior team some years before; not only was she a lovely person, she was also the most fantastic cook, which meant we now got decent meals in the evenings.

So things were looking up; and they got even better when the boys arrived: Ben Case, Guy Cosgrove and Richard Aldous. We had a tradition that when anyone new started work they had to be chucked into a smelly old water tank; they also had to be tied to an old trolley called Jemima Trolley, no matter what the weather. When Richard arrived, we kindly stripped him of all his clothes and left him tied to Jemima in the middle of the garden.

Ruth had a wonderful old wooden Oakley lorry which she used to tow a caravan in which we all slept when we stayed over at events – often about four or five of us crammed in together. The caravan was Ruth's pride and joy, but to the rest of us – for that very reason – it was the subject of much mirth. One very windy day it became detached from her car and ended up upside down in a field with all the contents flying around inside it. Ruth was distraught, but we found it hilarious. On another occasion it simply got left behind – I remember going outside after the rest had left for an event and seeing it sitting in the yard with all the vital stuff in it.

Two caravans were lost in two years. We were driving through Brandon when Ruth stopped to go around some cars in the middle of the village and I was woken up by a bang.

Ruth never usually swore, but she did on this occasion, exclaiming: 'A bloody lorry's gone into the back of me!' I got out to discover that the caravan hadn't just got hit, it had concertina-ed into nothing.

Ruth lived in the house with us and I don't know how she coped, because she tends to go to bed at about eight in the evening and gets up at 4 a.m. We used to have some rowdy nights with a few drinks and when she went off teaching early in the morning we'd have a lie-in. Once she came back earlier than we expected; luckily someone spotted her coming down the drive (we were only just getting up at this stage) and we had to climb out of the sitting-room window and run around the back to the stables so we could pretend we'd been up for hours.

We used to go down to the local pub called The Ostrich, where Friday nights were packed out and we met loads of Norfolk people. The school holidays were good fun too, bringing Sasha Skinner and Victoria King to come up and stay because they were doing junior trials. Sasha's mother Judy later gave me a horse to ride.

Ben had a rather tame relationship with Victoria King; one night we'd had a party and Ruth came up to me the next morning in a real state because she'd found a dress at the bottom of Ben's bed. Eventually I had to admit to her that we'd all swapped clothes and had dressed Ben up as a girl. In fact, it was my dress!

I had a brief romance with Richard, but we argued like mad, and when he threw a pitchfork at me I went right off the idea of having a relationship with someone I worked with. But it was all fairly light-hearted and Ben and Richard were more like brothers to us girls.

I now had two horses with which to try for the junior team. Airborne was ninth at Windsor and Barnaby went to

Punchestown in Ireland for an unofficial team competition. This was my first time ever out of England – apart from a day trip to Boulogne when I was tiny – and it took for ever. We drove from Norfolk in the lorry with the caravan on the back and it took about five hours to get across Wales. When we got to Holyhead it was so windy and wet that we couldn't sail; so we stayed in some awful stables nearby with horribly dusty straw bedding. I stayed in a B&B and poor Mum slept in Ruth's lorry. It was a nightmare.

I don't know whether it was the dusty stables or the drawn-out journey, but Barnaby was not himself at Punchestown. At the last steeplechase fence he fell and just lay there. Nothing like this had ever happened to me before and I felt so guilty I didn't run him across country – thereby earning me a huge telling-off from the selectors because I was part of a team. I was made to feel dreadful and that I'd let everyone down. It couldn't have been a worse first experience of going abroad, and the journey home felt very long indeed.

However, despite this disaster, I still got chosen for my first British team, alongside Simon Haslem, Polly Martin (later Phillipps) and Sue Cope, to contest the Junior European Championships at Walldorf in Germany. Because the championships were being held in Germany, a nation that specialises in that phase, the selectors reckoned that good dressage would be needed and Airborne got the nod. I couldn't believe that they chose Airborne, who had such limited form and was still a novice in points, whereas Barnaby had never had a single cross-country fault, apart from his fall in Punchestown, and was well into advanced points.

I don't remember an awful lot about the trip to Germany, except that we got loads of team goodies, which seemed a huge bonus. But I do remember the cross-country course that confronted us at Walldorf: to my horror, it was set in woods and was very winding, and the first thing that came into my head was: 'Why on earth didn't I have Barnaby?' Bob Baskerville, our team vet, reported in *Horse & Hound* that 'handy ponies excelled in this very twisty course'.

Even though it was my first time on a team, I was chosen to be the fourth and last member to run, a position which often carries extra pressure if something has gone wrong for one of the earlier riders. We knew that Simon Haslem's horse had strained a ligament and wouldn't be able to jump next day, so the pressure was very much on me to get round, because you have to have three members complete the competition or else the team is eliminated. My instructions were to go 'fast and clear'. Bob wrote: 'Pippa Nolan faced a difficult task on the big and long-striding Airborne; riding him must have been like navigating the Serpentine in an oil tanker without running down the ducks. She achieved a skilful clear, but with time faults.'

The Germans, always strong in dressage, won team gold and we got bronze, while Polly won the individual silver on Krugerrand. Sue finished eighth and I was nineteenth. I felt very proud to be representing Britain and to get my first medal, and the whole experience was, in contrast to Punchestown, a great thrill.

In October I took Barnaby to Chatsworth for my first senior three-day event. You had to be eighteen to compete at this level and my birthday fell on the Saturday, cross-country day, which caused a bit of a hoo-hah because of course I was only seventeen when the competition started. In the end I was allowed to run.

Chatsworth, a big, three-star course, felt like a serious test; but I had a fantastic ride, and with a clear round in the show jumping as well, we finished fifth; Anne-Marie Taylor won the event on Bolebec Miler. But the excitement of my best ever result so far was somewhat spoiled because I couldn't understand why Mum had disappeared on the Saturday night, my eighteenth birthday, and didn't come back to watch me in the show jumping. Dad and Tim had given me the excuse that she had to go back to work urgently, but after the competition was over and we were back at the lorry Dad broke the news to me that Annie had died suddenly, collapsing with a heart attack. For the first time in my life I felt a real loss. Tim and I had been really close to our grandmother; Annie had been very supportive and helped in so many ways through my teens, both financially and simply by constantly being encouraging, and I felt particularly sad as I hadn't seen so much of her since moving to Norfolk. So, while Chatsworth was obviously a fantastic end to the riding season, in our family life it was a very sad time.

After taking a month off over Christmas, I went back to Norfolk for the 1987 season, my first in young riders (under twenty-one category). This year I had plenty of horses to ride: Gill wasn't that keen on breaking youngsters and, as I was rather a toughie and didn't mind getting bucked off, I did much of the breaking. We had Bell Boy, Metronome and Heron's Flight, all bred by Ruth out of her mares and sired by Home Boy, plus Better Judgement and Cartoon, who was known as Leggy because he was so tall and long-legged. His owners and breeders, the Rawsons, were friends of Mum and Dad's and their daughters Debbie and Juliet were friends of mine. So I was riding up to eight or ten horses a day, all different types.

Some of these horses belonged to owners who are still with me today; in fact, many of my owners stem from those Norfolk days. Susie Cranston sent a pony for schooling and her daughter Sophie came for lessons; Susie was later to become one of my key owners with Cornerman. Richard and Sarah Jewson, whose children were taught by Ruth, were the first owners for whom I rode professionally – and the first horse I rode for them got the relationship off to a great start. He was a little cheap and cheerful horse called Wallis, who had a deformed eye and looked a runt but was a lovely mover and a good jumper.

That year Justine Ryder (later Ward) came to work at Ruth's as an extra pair of hands; she became a really good friend, although at first our relationship was rather stormy and we argued a lot. Justine soon started going out with Charlie Ward, a local farmer, and Gill had meanwhile struck up a relationship with Jeremy Mason, whose parents owned Palgrave Hall. My own social life had improved too, as not only did I have a car – a brown Mini handed down from Tim – but I had started going out with Ben Case's elder brother Adam, whom I had met when seated next to him at the Brooks-Ward twins' twenty-first birthday party. Adam, who rode in point-to-points, was at the Royal Agricultural College at Cirencester, which meant we went for weeks without seeing each other, but I met some great people through him. Norfolk is sometimes thought of as a cliquey county where it's difficult to get to know people, but as Adam and Ben had always lived there, I didn't have that problem. Wally Wales, Adam's best mate, is still a good friend; when he later married Clare Gribbon I was a bridesmaid, and I am now godmother to their son Harry. Suddenly I started to have a really fantastic time; I felt a part of Norfolk life rather than an outsider, and began to feel genuinely happy there.

Ruth was very long-suffering, although I'm not sure that she ever realised some of the things we got up to. She had a bit of a thing about curfew and there were fixed times by which we were supposed to be in: as I was older than Justine, I was allowed to be out an hour later. One night Adam had asked me to a smart dance and Justine had been asked to another party with Charlie, but as there was an event the next day we didn't dare ask Ruth about going out. So I scrumpled my evening dress up in a plastic bag and slipped out to meet Adam, while Justine crept off to Charlie's, from where I'd arranged to pick her up at five the next morning. The trouble was that when the time came, I couldn't wake her – eventually I was throwing stones at the window and shrieking because I was so scared that Ruth would be up by the time we got back. In fact, by then the house lights were on, so we thought we'd just have to get straight on with getting the horses ready as though we'd never been away. The only snag was that we were an hour too early. So when we walked into the house – only to bump straight into Ruth – I made up a story about being so worried about oversleeping that I'd got up early. I still don't know if she knows what happened.

Ruth would be horrified to think that we were scared of her, and we weren't really because she rarely got cross, but we had so much respect for her that we didn't want to upset her. At the same time, though, I knew I wanted a social life.

I had daily lessons with Ruth on her young horses; in fact by this stage I was doing more riding than Gill, who had become engaged to Jeremy, so her priorities changed. She was very much in love and looking forward to her next life and, as a result, I was riding all hours and sometimes felt exhausted. We had a blacksmith called David Fuller who sometimes didn't turn up until about five in the afternoon and I can remember Justine and I sitting in the corner of the shoeing box until 11 p.m., feeling absolutely shattered and thinking: 'Why do we do all these hours?' But as much as we questioned it among ourselves, we loved what we were doing and I felt completely driven. I had a huge respect for Ruth; she is an amazing lady who would help anyone. She never said no, which is why we had so many horses to do. But despite the long hours, we felt privileged to be working for her. I also felt that I was getting somewhere with my riding; every different horse was a bonus, giving me a bit more experience. I felt I was creating personal relationships with all these horses and spent as much time as I could with the younger ones. Ruth got cross when I taught Metronome to wave a front leg for a Polo because he started to hang this leg limply in the air at inconvenient times, such as in showing classes and at vet's inspections.

Ruth has always had a true connection with all of her horses, and a wonderful quiet manner, and I knew I wanted to emulate this. At last her teaching seemed to be sinking in and I felt that I was now understanding how to feel what was going on underneath me when I rode. I was fascinated watching Ruth ride during lessons. By now she was older and bounced around more in the saddle, and I would think: 'She's doing everything she tells me not to do, yet the horse has switched into another gear and is going quite beautifully.' Ruth could get a tune out of every horse she sat on, and eventually I realised that it was because of her balance: she never interfered with them and so they always went in wonderful lightness and self-carriage. More than anything else it was that – watching Ruth riding and achieving an instant rapport with the horse – which inspired me.

In 1987, having qualified at Chatsworth, I was all set for my first Badminton. This was really exciting: as for so many young riders, taking part in this great event had long been my dream, but also because Ruth, who had come from the showing world, had never had a horse at this level. *Horse & Hound* quoted me as saying that my aim was to get around and that I was optimistic because Barnaby was good across country. Of course, I hadn't a clue about fitness – I have no idea whether he was fit enough – and we were described in the form guide as having little advanced experience: 'A brave horse ridden by a jockey who will go for it – could do well if they don't come a cropper.'

The countdown seemed momentous and I was overcome by a gut-wrenching feeling of excitement mixed with terror, as though it was a sort of judgement day. And then the rain came down, and the phone call came saying that Badminton was cancelled. I was shattered, but in hindsight it was a blessing because there was no way I was ready.

My immediate ambition switched to getting into the British young riders' team for the European Championships, and with this in mind I entered Barnaby in the National Young Rider Championships at Bramham, the remaining major spring fixture. We were lying third after the cross-country, but the next day I went into the show jumping arena and missed a fence, thus getting us eliminated. It was an awful moment; I have never been so mad with myself. I thought: 'I've asked Barnaby to do all of this and now I've let him down.'

Later, I was watching the seniors and, as the overnight leader, Richard Walker, came into the ring, I told myself to look on the bright side – at least I hadn't been in the lead. And I thought: 'Wouldn't it be awful if he did the same thing.' Unbelievably, he did. I felt devastated for Richard and we talked about it afterwards, but at the same time it made me feel a tiny bit better. I was still longlisted for the team but no one was cross with me – there was nothing they could say.

The final trial for the European Championships was at Rotherfield Park, a decent advanced track; and it was here that I had my first ever cross-country fault on Barnaby. It was a nasty fall, I was sore afterwards and there was doom and gloom in the camp as I felt I'd wasted our good performances across country at Chatsworth and Bramham and blown my chances of making the team. I wanted to go straight home that night because it was such a low moment, but we had to stay because the selectors wanted me to trot up Barnaby the next day. Ruth and I thought there was no hope, but to my surprise the selectors said I was on the squad because they were happy enough with my form. I cheered up instantly.

Bialy Bor in Poland, where the European Championships were held, was the trip of a lifetime. Giles Rowsell, who was great fun as *chef d'équipe* of the young riders' team, drove out in a Range Rover and we also took two lorries. On the way we stayed in an army base in Germany, which was a fairly hilarious experience as six young girls staying at an army barracks inevitably attracted a bit of attention. We came to an agreement with the officers that if anyone came home with a medal, she would get to drive an army tank on our return journey.

Poland was an eye-opener – in 1987, of course, the Iron Curtain was still very much in place – and really made me appreciate the Western world. It was quite an experience driving through the Corridor; there was masses of protocol to get through on the borders and we had to cross into Poland on the Friday night because no vets would come out at the weekend to check the horses' papers. The event stabling wasn't open until Monday, so we stayed the weekend at a beautiful old stud. On the way, we had passed horses and carts and real old banger cars – it was like going back to the 1950s; and yet the top-level sports facilities they had were just out of this world.

The children in the village were fascinated by us; we must have seemed like something from outer space. They seemed to latch on to me and also to Ted, one of the lorry drivers. If I was going from the lorry to the stables, they all wanted to help me, and if I didn't have enough stuff for them each to carry, they would empty out my grooming box so they all had something to carry, like a brush. It was amazing how well we communicated with no common language.

A Polish translator who had been sent to look after us explained that two of these children wanted to ask Ted and myself back to their home for tea. We went to their two-roomed bungalow where we were offered vodka and disgusting-looking wild mushrooms in pickle. Ted and I looked at each other and thought 'no way', but we knew we had to get them down, as this was obviously a delicacy they were proud of. I had noticed there was no mother around; when we got up to leave, the father suddenly grabbed hold of me and broke down in tears. I didn't understand what was going on, but the kids started crying as well. Eventually we managed to get out. The translator told us that this poor man's wife had died and he'd been an alcoholic who managed to get off the booze; they had no money and because the kids had latched on to me, he was hoping I could be their new mother. It was the most heart-wrenching incident and made me appreciate more than ever what I had at home.

When we got to the event and walked the course, Christopher Schofield, who was chairman of selectors, announced the team as Katie Parker, Judith Copeland, Susanna Macaire and Ruth House. I was disappointed not to be on it, but understood the reasoning as I hadn't been able to prove myself with another outing since the fall at Rotherfield

Park. Sarah Kellard was the other individual.

Barnaby did a fairly reasonable dressage test and was lying seventh at the end of that phase. I was quietly excited because seven is my lucky number. He then sped around the cross-country and took the lead. Meanwhile, the team had blown out as two of them didn't complete, and suddenly the entire British effort was riding on me. It was the first time I'd sensed such expectation; I was now the only chance of a medal and we'd come a long way not to come home with anything.

It was, therefore, very special when I won the individual gold. I was ecstatic; I couldn't believe that I was suddenly the under-21 champion of Europe. Really special, too, was seeing the pride in Mum and Dad's faces when I won, as they had driven out independently; I hoped they felt that all their efforts had been worthwhile. And, of course, I felt so emotional about Barnaby because of what we'd been through together; I couldn't believe he'd taken me from Pony Club to winning a championship.

Big celebrations took place that night; a lot of vodka was consumed and the shower rota went right out of the window – suddenly showering had become communal with the Italians, who had won the silver medal. They were an all-boy team, with the exception of Lara Villata – and all very good-looking; we British girls had been flirting with them all week! And, on the way home, I got to drive the army tank. This had been one great trip.

There were more celebrations at home, as Ruth hadn't been in Poland – in fact she never came on any of my trips abroad, and I always felt a bit lost without her. This was also our last party at Palgrave, because at the end of that year Gill married Jeremy with Justine and I as bridesmaids. They were to move into the main house, so, sadly, Ruth and the rest of us had to move. I was also sorry that Ben and Richard were leaving, both headed for careers in racing.

The rest of us moved to a yard at High House, Westacre, which was three miles away and belonged to Captain Harry Birkbeck and his wife. Set on an estate in wonderful parkland, it was the most beautiful house, with an old-fashioned yard which had ten excellent stables and a lovely old oak-panelled tack room. As I was already riding so many of the horses, it seemed an obvious solution that I should become head girl for Ruth. Justine and I moved into a little semi-detached cottage a mile and a half away – and Ruth, probably much to her relief, to another cottage.

Suddenly we were independent, Justine and I; we were nineteen years old, we could entertain, and our boyfriends could stay the night. Adam had left Cirencester by now and the two of us went out a lot with Wally and Clare. It was also blissful going over to Adam's parents, Robert and Amanda. They became like my second parents and suddenly I felt looked after again; they cooked nice food for me and their house was warm. It was a happy time.

As well as the ten stables at High House, we had four more up the road at Yard Farm, a quarter of a mile away. Ruth had cut down on numbers and there were ten fewer horses than we'd had at Palgrave – all eventers, bar the odd racehorse – making life a good deal more manageable.

Riding out was quite nerve-racking, though, as we came out of the stables straight on to parkland and I'd have to sit very tight. I used to ride and lead across the park, which was pretty hazardous as you had to open gates and there were cattle grids. I would lead Barnaby off another horse, they'd buck and I'd lose Barnaby; he would go careering off, get the rein caught and then suddenly, thank heavens, stand still until I caught him. He was an amazing little horse for self-preservation; in everything he did showed a pony's instinct. However cheeky he got, there wasn't a nasty bone in his body and I always felt completely safe on him.

In 1988 I had another crack at getting to Badminton, and this time we made it. I felt very sick. With Bramham and Bialy Bor behind me, I had another year's experience under my belt, but that only served to increase my nervousness. I was only eighteen-and-a-half; few riders now tackle Badminton before the age of twenty-two.

Barnaby was stabled in the overflow farmyard at Badminton, and I was quite relieved not to be in the main stable yard and to be slightly removed from the main buzz of it all. Badminton is like a theatre, in that behind those stable gates is offstage, quite relaxed and normal. The moment I first rode out through the gates into the park, on to 'centre stage', the magnitude of it hit me; I wondered what on earth I was doing. Do I want to be here? No, I don't! I was disappointed by my feelings, which had more to do with fear than excitement.

I hadn't been to Badminton for years, not since I was a tiny kid, and it struck me as soon as I arrived that the cross-country course was a completely different ballgame from anything else I'd seen. The ditches were massive, far bigger than I'd imagined, and around the Vicarage Ditch area there seemed to be endless yawning holes. The course was one huge problem after another and at every fence I looked for an alternative, even if it meant trotting down into the ditch.

The course designer, Colonel Frank Weldon, was famous for producing 'rider-frighteners', and this was his last year before retirement. One of his feature fences was the Normandy Bank, a step up on to a bank with a bounce off and a massive great drop after it. I discussed this fence with several riders I looked up to, and they all said: 'Whatever you do, don't let your horse shuffle on top of the bank or you'll be in trouble. You've got to be committed.' Well, Barnaby shuffled everywhere, and I couldn't think how we would stay in one piece. This problem preoccupied me.

Ruth came to help me with the dressage, but I was fairly off the pace after this phase. Half of me thought it was hopeless carrying on, but the other half said: 'You've got to; this is what the sport's all about.'

On Saturday morning I was relieved to see many of my fellow competitors, some of whom had been riding at Badminton for years, looking just as sick as me, all of us dashing continuously back and forth to the loo. Many of them told me that it wouldn't get any better with age or experience.

The steeplechase phase felt like a doddle compared to the enormous test Barnaby and I had in front of us. In those days, on the roads and tracks phase you rode down the Avenue, and it was when you turned on to that that it hit you. There's Badminton House in the distance, and swarms and swarms of people. Gradually, you get closer and closer, half excited and half dreading the next twenty minutes. Being met by a mounted runner who escorts you into the ten-minute box (the area where you wait before the cross-country) is a huge relief because finally you have someone to talk to after the loneliness of the roads and tracks; at last you can escape from the reality of the situation – and I wanted to stay in that ten-minute box for ever.

I don't know who put more trust in whom, whether I believed Barnaby could do it or he believed I could do it, but there was something special in our partnership that day. He looked before every fence and I could feel by the way he was going that it was a seriously big question for him, but in my ignorance I kept kicking and he kept going. Each fence we cleared was a bonus, until we got to the Vicarage Ditch, a wide ditch in front of a rail. It was one ditch too many; Barnaby stalled on the point of take-off but, bless him, he still jumped, though he hit the rail hard with his stifles, catapulting me out of the front door.

Adrenalin and an ambition to complete made me get back on. I still had to jump the wretched Normandy Bank, where Barnaby proved everyone wrong by shuffling a small stride but surviving, and we completed the rest of the course penalty-free.

My parents were so relieved, especially Mum who was hiding in a car with the radio on at full volume. Next year she tried Valium and thereafter a wonderful herbal remedy.

Thankfully, Barnaby was unharmed by our fall and was able to trot up and show jump on the final day. I felt that I had achieved what I set out to do – completing my first Badminton and conquering the biggest course in the world – but at the same time I was disappointed. I kept analysing the fact that we could have gone clear. But, despite the terror, I was hungry to do it all over again.

That year the European Young Rider Championships were at Zonhoven in Belgium. It was to be the first time I rode in a team with William Fox-Pitt; the others were Polly Lyon and Susanna Macaire. I felt quietly confident, having Badminton and the 1987 title behind me, but much to my disappointment Barnaby had a little relapse in the dressage, got distracted and lay way down the order. It was another of those moments when I hated him; there were many times I hated him after dressage because I'd feel that he'd let me down after all the work Ruth and I had put in. I knew on this occasion that my individual medal chances were blown and I was gutted, but I was part of a team and I had to kick on.

On the cross-country the water was quite tricky. Barnaby did one of his 'ditters' on take-off, which caused a debate as to whether I'd refused, because in those days the horse was allowed to hesitate on take-off as long as he didn't step back. The fence judge gave me twenty penalties for a stop, but Giles put down the deposit for an objection because our gold team medal position hinged on those twenty penalties. All the fence judges had to be recalled and my stop was taken away. The team duly won the gold medal, I was eighth individually and Polly Lyon won the first of her two young rider titles, on Highland Road.

That winter I went on my first holiday abroad, to Tenerife with Adam. I was really excited about going to the sun, but three days before we left I developed a horrendous rash on my chest, with huge red blotches. The doctor told me not to lie in the sun, but I ignored him and probably looked as if I had a disgusting skin disease. In the end, though, the weather wasn't great; there was also a lot of construction work going on, so it wasn't the most picturesque setting. However, it was a good holiday and lovely for the two of us to have some time together. Probably the most amusing bit was when Mum picked us up from the airport and forgot where she had parked the car – it took us an hour to find it!

Again I spent Christmas at home, though these days, without Annie, it was a bit subdued. The horses were on holiday in Norfolk and it was bliss to have a break from them. I had lie-ins and caught up with my old mates.

The spring of 1989 brought my second Badminton, and – as everyone had warned me – I felt just as sick, going through exactly the same experiences in the build-up. It turned out to be a major anti-climax. For the first time in his career, Barnaby refused. There was a big silver birch parallel under some trees and several horses running in the middle of the day stopped there, perhaps flummoxed by the shadows and light. Barnaby actually planted his feet and said no. I surrendered and we walked home.

Ginny Leng (later Elliot) won that year, on Master Craftsman. I remember watching her dressage – she was such a perfectionist and made it look so easy. I felt that I'd never be like her. Despite my own successes, I felt that the top riders had a professionalism that I could never achieve. This is never going to happen for me, I thought; I simply couldn't see my name up on the scoreboard with them.

But, because of our consistent one-day record, Barnaby and I were still put in the team for my final year in young riders, for the championships in Achselschwang, in Bavaria. This was the first year I got to know Tina Gifford, because she and I and William Fox-Pitt were all in the squad, with Daniel Hughes, Tim Randle and Belinda Cubitt, and it became obvious that this was the start of a special friendship for the three of us.

On the journey, we stopped first at William Fox-Pitt's home in Kent and then at Helena and Pete Weinberg's show-jumping yard in Germany. William's mother Marietta insisted on letting the horses out every three hours and the journey seemed to take for ever. When we arrived, I went for a ride through the woods and I remember seeing signs saying 'Beware of Rabies', which terrified me.

Barnaby behaved more consistently in the dressage this time and produced quite a good test. I was one of the last to go across country and no one before me had achieved the optimum time – Tina, riding as an individual, had got lost on the roads and tracks and incurred a huge number of time penalties, and all the others were having time penalties on the cross country, too. Gill, however, had every confidence in

Barnaby's nippiness. I had a counting-down type of stopwatch, which, unbeknown to me, she had set thirty seconds behind. Every time I looked at it, I thought I was down on time, but I was actually thirty seconds ahead – so I made the time, one of only two riders to do so. This put me into the individual lead, but I had a show-jumping fence down on the last day, which dropped me down into individual silver behind the Swedish rider Stefan Lidbeck; we still won the team silver, though.

There was also a proper senior three-day event going on in Achselschwang at the same time. Charlotte Hollingsworth was out there riding in it; so was Mark Todd and also Blyth Tait, who had come over from New Zealand for his first season competing in Europe on Messiah. I think this was one of the first times I'd socialised with international senior riders and it made me feel grown up; I realised I was looking forward to riding against them.

I was sad to grow out of young riders; I loved being part of a team and I was aware that I had been cushioned by the system. There was always someone to turn to for advice, especially Gill Watson, who was brilliant at her job. I'd also had some great results, which had brought me quite a lot of attention and media coverage for a young rider.

At the same time, though, I was raring to get on and be part of a senior team; the whole team spirit and the experience of bonding with people who were all working towards the same thing was a special feeling and I knew I wanted to be a part of it again, as soon as possible. Little did I know that it would take me ten years.

3
Sir Barnaby

I was pretty optimistic at the start of my senior career. In the spring of 1990 I had a string of about ten horses, which in those days was a lot – only about four or five riders in the country had that many horses then, though nowadays this would be considered quite a modest number.

I had Barnaby for Badminton, Ruth's home-bred horse Better Judgement for Bramham, plus Cartoon, Metronome, Heron's Flight, the McIntyres' Marshland Amigo and, running alongside him, Man About Town, owned by Judy and Jeremy Skinner, plus some youngsters.

I didn't have too many illusions about getting on to the senior British team at this stage, because the established riders of the day were the likes of Ian Stark, Ginny, Lorna Clarke, Mary King, Rodney Powell and Karen Dixon, but I was still hopeful of making an impression.

My first year in seniors was preceded by my parents giving me a smart black-tie twenty-first birthday party at Ardingly, at which Uncle Raymond made a speech. It was a pea-souper of a night and an awful lot of people were late, though I had been worried that they wouldn't be able to make it in the conditions.

I remember thinking then that, much as I loved life in Norfolk, I seemed to be missing out on several of my friends' twenty-first parties because of the distance. The competing alone was creating a lot of early mornings and late nights, getting up at the crack of dawn to plait and coming home late to find lots of horses to do. I was also doing an awful lot of the driving to events now, as Ruth had sold a horse called Bell Boy to buy an under-the-weight lorry which didn't need an HGV licence. At times I was shattered – it took an hour just to get out of the county and two hours to get to the M25. I had no plans to leave Norfolk and I was happy in my relationship with Adam, but somehow I couldn't see myself living there for the rest of my life; instinctively I knew that change wasn't far off.

This may or may not have had something to do with the fact that over the winter, while helping Mum with the indoor shows at Ardingly, I had met William Funnell again. Whenever I bumped into him, I found him highly amusing, but I certainly didn't have the over-awed feeling that I had had when I was a teenager. It didn't enter my head that anything would happen between us, or even that I wanted it to.

In February, though, I got chatting to William at an indoor show at Mill Lodge, our local equestrian centre where I would take a lot of horses for jumping. He said that if ever I was stuck for stabling when eventing in the south of England I should let him know. Funnily enough, three weeks later I was due to ride at Tweseldown horse trials and I duly booked myself into his yard in Surrey.

I arrived with a puncture in the back wheel, which was embarrassing as I hadn't noticed. I could never change a tyre on a car, never mind a lorry, and, on this occasion at least, William didn't either – he called his mechanic out!

William offered to take me out to supper at the Italian

restaurant in Cranleigh. As I changed in the lorry, I felt a little nervous at having a one-to-one supper with someone I didn't know that well. But it was an entertaining evening, relaxed and easy, and I realised William had a massive sense of humour. After dinner we went back to his local, The Parrot at Forest Green.

When we got back, William asked me in for coffee and said that as it was cold I could stay in the spare room. Straight away I thought: 'Oh no, he's a show jumper!' and went back to sleep in my lorry. I woke with a dreadful hangover, but thinking what a good evening it had been, particularly as I had been so apprehensive beforehand, and, looking back, there was clearly some chemistry at this stage.

William had been born and brought up on a farm in Challock, Ashford, Kent, so, like me, he became involved with horses at a very young age. His father, John Funnell, is a farmer and has also been a great hunting man, being Master and Huntsman for both the Tickham and Surrey Union hunts. His mother, Dawn Mason, is involved with helping children with special needs. William's parents split up when he was seven years old. William's elder brother, Nick, makes the Claydon Horsewalkers. He is married to Bea and has two delightful girls, who are both mad keen on their riding. His younger brother, David, is married to Sheila and they have two young boys. He runs a pet crematorium, so he spends his life dealing with distraught animal lovers.

I next saw William at Mum's horse trials, the South of England, where there were also show-jumping classes taking place. As I was having problems with one of my horses' jumping, I asked him for advice. He replied: 'Only if I can take you out to dinner tonight!' This was awkward because, as Mum had so few chances to see me, I thought she'd be upset.

But she was very good about it and off I went to dinner with William, his best friend Duncan Inglis, with whom he'd jumped on pony teams, and Duncan's girlfriend Clare Taylor. William had warned them that I was an eventer so they were to treat me gently (we're always thought to be posh little rich girls by the show jumpers!). I, on the other hand, was really nervous, realising I was being assessed by his greatest mates, but it turned into a great evening.

Next month Barnaby and I went to our third Badminton and by now I could understand what the more experienced competitors meant when they told me that the nerves don't get any better. There's something about Badminton which makes me want to turn around on the M4 and flee straight home; so much hangs on a Badminton performance and, no matter what else changes in the sport, it's still the ultimate test. Everyone has a yearning to do well at Badminton, but also an awareness that it's the place where dreams can be shattered.

As usual, I stayed in the lorry and Justine came with me to help. Mum would stay in a caravan and feed us and Dad, who by this stage had started commentating at events, would walk the course and think it helpful to tell me there were 650 strides between fences two and three!

Barnaby did one of his better dressage tests that year. I had also learned not to let the tension get to me and had begun to take a more carefree attitude, thinking: 'I'm going to give this a go' instead of: 'It's going to go wrong'.

One of the most important lessons Barnaby taught me is that the worst thing a rider can do is nothing, sitting frozen by fear that the horse will explode. No matter what a horse does underneath you, when you're doing a dressage test you've got to get on and ride them.

I had now been at Ruth's for five years and finally cottoned on to what she meant about having the horse straight. I had always been a 'thinking' rider, but I had become more so, and my flatwork was definitely starting to go in the right direction. Ruth taught us to be disciplined in the dressage; if we were supposed to canter at a particular letter or marker, then it should be at that letter – not a stride earlier or later. She was a perfectionist and generous in her time for me. Also, as I was riding more horses, so they were teaching me too.

That year also marked my first clear round at Badminton. Admittedly we took several long routes, but Barnaby was so nippy that we didn't lose much time. At the Quarry, near the end of the course, there was a step down and a bounce over some rails down a steep slope, as if horses were jumping down into a hole. Barnaby 'dittered' around on the edge and then jumped from a standstill, but thankfully didn't take a step back which would have meant twenty penalties. He always liked to see where his feet were going.

I was elated; I felt as if I'd conquered Mount Everest. Never mind that I looked like a kid out of Pony Club with my legs kicking, elbows flapping and pony-tail bouncing – style didn't come into it and we scrubbed our way around, but because of the belief I had in Barnaby, it never occurred to me that he would stop and I never gave up kicking.

We were lying seventh – my lucky number – and I was nervous because I knew my show-jumping round would be live on TV. We went clear and rose to fifth place, which meant I got the best under-25 prize and a saddle. More thrilling, though, was being presented with my first little silver horse. These are presented to the top twelve at Badminton and are among the most coveted trophies in the equestrian world.

I quietly hoped that I might be longlisted for the British team and was half waiting for Jane Holderness-Roddam, the chairman of selectors, to come up to me. She did, but it was to say 'well done' – and, actually, to tell me that I wouldn't be longlisted. I was a bit gutted because I felt my little horse deserved the recognition. Of course, I now know that this was terribly naïve of me; I can see exactly why Barnaby wasn't selected for senior teams because his way of going didn't fill watchers with confidence. Yet he did the job, and so I resolved to wait another year. Having 'cracked' Badminton, the 1991 European Championships at Punchestown became my next big goal.

Meanwhile, other developments preoccupied me. William had asked me to go and watch him at the Royal Windsor Horse Show, which would involve taking a rare day off. I had found myself thinking about him a lot, not in a totally besotted way but certainly with a buzz of excitement. It made me question my relationship with Adam and I knew that at some point soon I would have to face up to changing things.

At Windsor it hit me how much I respected William as a rider. There is no way I could get involved with anyone who got rough with their horses and whom I didn't admire as a rider. That occasion was the start of our life together – but, thrilled as I was by the exciting newness of it all and by being madly in love, I was sick at the thought of telling Adam it was all over.

This was one of the hardest things I've done. I knew it would be difficult, but I had no idea – perhaps because he hadn't made it clear or because I hadn't interpreted him correctly – of the strength of his feelings. The hurt I caused was dreadful, made worse because I adored his family and friends and felt I was letting everyone down.

I was soon to go through another growing-up experience. At Bramham in June I had the ride on Better Judgement – known

48

at home as Orville – a lovely big horse, whom Ruth had bred. He was 17.2 hands, with a gentle giant personality; I'd broken him in and ridden since he was a baby. He was giving me a brilliant ride across country until we got to a big ditch and trakehner out of the wood, about five fences from home.

The second Orville landed, I knew he had broken down and pulled him up immediately. He had to be trailered off the course and it turned out that he had ruptured the deep flexor tendon on a front leg.

Orville was on box rest for two months and every day I gave him loads of attention. This was before tendon-scanning machines were used widely and I didn't know a lot about horses' legs so it was a really steep learning curve for me. We knew he wouldn't event again; we hoped, though, to get him sound enough to do another job. But after another investigation in Newmarket, Ruth was told he would never come sound again and she decided to have him put down. He wasn't the sort of horse who enjoyed living out in a field; he was a big horse and needed pampering.

I felt awful for Ruth because she adored him. I also felt hugely guilty as it was the first time a horse I'd ridden had suffered a serious injury. There were lots of tears and I had a bit of a scene with Ruth because I wanted to be the person there when he was put down and thankfully she wouldn't let me.

The worst thing was that he'd developed a habit whereby if I went into the stable with him and sat down, he would lie down beside me. He did it on the awful occasion when I went into the stable to say goodbye to him, and the others had to physically drag me out. I drove off to William's for the rest of the day and watched him jump, just to get away from it.

But I learned from this horrible experience. I learned from the sensible way Ruth handled it and I learned that you have to be paranoid about horses' legs. Since then I have always checked my horses' legs regularly for warning signs of weakness.

Metronome was qualified for the British Intermediate Championships, which were then held at Locko Park, and he finished third. He was another big softy of a horse, beautiful looking and a flashy mover. He was so polite he could have come into the house, and he adored people; to ride, though, he was quite strong and spooky and difficult to hold. I had to remember to soften and relax if he shied, otherwise he would get even stronger with me. Ruth occasionally hinted that Metro was too big for me, but because I adored him and had always ridden him, I was selfish and couldn't bear the thought of anyone else riding him.

Despite being by the same sire, Home Boy, Heron's Flight was quite different in nature. He was a sensitive young horse and would be worried as to what you were doing on top of him, half looking back at you all the time. Heron was timid and you had to ride him quietly, but he tried so hard to please.

This batch of horses had all had the same upbringing, yet they were all so different in character and really made me appreciate that horses are individuals. If Barnaby wasn't upright and engaged on the flat, he would use it as an excuse to be naughty; Heron, by contrast, would use the same situation as an excuse to back off and be lazy and hard work to ride. I learned that when I got on each horse I had to remember how that individual thought, which was an invaluable lesson. But I also learned a lot from being on the ground with a horse; it's just as important to know a horse's character in the stable as when you're on it.

My next major event was the British Open Championships, which was the start of Barnaby's three-year run as a Gatcombe specialist. It was our second visit – we'd won the best under-25 prize the year before – and I was quite hopeful because I knew that the course at Gatcombe, which is unusual and requires a nippy horse, was just his style.

The British Open is a high-pressure, high-profile competition where everyone wants to do well; many of the top foreign riders used to do it as a prep run for Burghley, including the Americans who were then based at Gatcombe. The cross-country phase runs in reverse order of merit and there is huge excitement and tension as the competition isn't won until the last horse has run.

This year I finished second behind Mary King on King Boris. Mary was another rider disappointed not to have been selected for the World Equestrian Games in Stockholm, where the team won silver behind New Zealand. Mary was quite hard done by at times in those days. Many times she deserved to ride on a championship team but was passed over. It always impressed me to see how she just kept going until she eventually got there. She is one of the riders I most admire for her perseverence, her hunger and her professionalism. I looked up to Mary hugely then because she was another rider who had struggled. She'd had some horrible falls, worked incredibly hard to come through a bad patch and was winning some major competitions. Now that I know her better, I know she is a real competitor – a winner – and a lovely person.

In September, Barnaby and I tackled our first Burghley. I have always loved this event. It has a more welcoming feel than Badminton; even though it is the same level it feels less crucial, and because it's at the back end of the season everyone is more relaxed. The course itself, too, seems friendlier somehow, even though the terrain is more demanding on horses than at Badminton. So, although when I walked the cross-country course I was thinking of Barnaby and still looking for long routes because a lot of the direct routes frightened me, it didn't seem so daunting as Badminton. There were some difficult fences, but more let-up fences in between, which, even though they were big, would allow a horse to regain its confidence. The Trout Hatchery has always been imposing, like the Lake at Badminton, because you know that there will be crowds of spectators there, hoping you will get wet.

The other fence to fill me with horror was Centaur's Leap. It is still the biggest ditch I've ever seen in front of a fence. It is not only incredibly wide, but deep as well – you could drive a car down it. And sure enough, probably because I over-rode it, during our cross-country round Barnaby jumped *into* the ditch instead of over it and we fell. I got back on and we completed without further penalties, but when I'd finished I realised he'd cut his head. A swelling had come up so we got him X-rayed. Fortunately it was just a bit of minor concussion, but obviously we couldn't complete the competion.

At the end of the season I went to Stoneleigh for the first of four annual visits to the High Performance Horse Sale. This was a brilliant sale devised by Jennie Loriston-Clarke for owners and breeders to show off their young sports (competition-bred) horses, and spent a couple of weeks up there with other riders preparing the horses to ride in front of customers. It was a good experience and gave me my first taste of dealing. A horse called Current Magic wasn't sold and so I approached the owners and made an offer, buying him with some of the prize money Barnaby had won. I sold him six months later and made a little bit on the deal, which felt like a great achievement.

That winter I had six weeks off and spent it with William at his home base, Cobbetts Farm, probably much to my parents' disappointment as they loved having me at home. It wasn't much of a break from horses, but I loved being with William and getting to know him.

We went to Spain with Duncan and Clare for five days because Duncan's father had a house there. It was a hilarious trip. Much to the men's horror, we forced them to go shopping. William treated me to a smart matching handbag and vanity box, so Clare made Duncan buy her something nice too. Then we were sitting in a restaurant having lunch and I said jokingly that I'd seen a car being towed away and wouldn't it be funny if it was ours? Quite a lot of wine later, we discovered that indeed it *was* ours – or, rather, Duncan's father's – but all Clare and I were worried about were our new bags. We had to get a taxi to the compound to pick the car up, and by the time we'd paid to get it out, we hadn't got a bean. Unfortunately, in our merriment we'd completely forgotten about the motorway tolls and had to turn the car upside-down looking for loose change. We were crying with laughter. Clare is very attractive and somehow she persuaded the man in the booth to let us through – I think he was just thrilled to get rid of us.

It was on that holiday I discovered that drink can make William talk in his sleep. One day we'd been fishing and that night he woke me up by jumping up and down at the end of the bed. I turned on the light and he said: 'It's there! It's there! The fish is alive!'

How William and I sustained such a long-distance, part-time relationship I will never know, but I suppose the fact that we did proved there was something strong and worthwhile there. We spoke on the phone two or three times a day and aimed to see each other once a week. This had to be midweek, because we were both busy competing at weekends, and involved either my driving to Surrey, which could take three hours, or his coming to Norfolk. I couldn't leave Norfolk until after work and I had to be back for 7 a.m., but William, being self-employed, was more independent; so, as Ruth fortunately liked him and approved of his riding, he often arrived by midday and would help me jump some horses. Justine and Charlie got on well with William, too, and I was lucky to have stayed very close to Adam's friends Wally and Clare.

William and I were both so busy that we didn't have much chance to watch each other compete, but I remember going to watch him at Kent County Show. There was a barbecue in the evening and I drove down for it. This was the first time I'd met his close jumping mates. They gave me an enormous amount of stick, especially Tim Stockdale, but I managed to hold my own.

Although I was very happy to have so much time with William that winter, as it drew to an end I could feel the excitement mounting about the 1991 eventing season – and by then I was really looking forward to seeing the horses again. I also had my first dog, Fingers, a scruffy, hairy little Jack Russell puppy bred by Mum. We'd always had family dogs, but having one of my own was very special. Mum warned me to be careful with Fingers around the horses, but when she was ten weeks old she got trodden on and broke her front leg. I've never heard yelping like it and I felt dreadful. But after a few weeks in a plaster, with front leg stuck out straight in front of her, she was fine. She came everywhere with me and hardly ever left my side.

The human population at Ruth's was increasing, too. That spring Terry Boon came to work with us from Cornwall, where his father was huntsman of the Lamerton. He was just leaving school and had written me a letter asking for a job; I persuaded

Ruth to let me phone him because I felt we needed more help, and he sounded so charming on the phone that we took him without an interview. Marie-Louise Thomas – known always as Bumble – had been with us for a year by now. Both she and Terry have turned out to be great riders and a credit to Ruth. You can really tell the Ruth McMullen stamp on a rider.

I was disappointed when an overreach ruled Barnaby out of Badminton 1991. It was decided to take him to Luhmühlen in Germany, a three-star event in July, which would be my first senior three-day event abroad. Terry groomed for me and we travelled with Robert Lemieux and Nicky Coe, who had won Badminton the year before on Middle Road and was married to the Olympic athlete Sebastian Coe. Now that I was no longer being mollycoddled by the young rider system and was out on my own without my parents or Ruth, I got to know a lot of the riders much better. That's the great thing about trips abroad: they tend to be a bonding experience. Rodney Powell, who had won Badminton that year on The Irishman, was there; so were Ian Stark, Tanya Cleverley, and the New Zealanders Andrew Nicholson and Blyth Tait. I was stabled next to Karen Lende (later O'Connor) and she had a Gameboy which I spent hours playing. Karen promised me that if I won, she'd give it to me.

It was very hot and there was a swimming pool nearby with a really high diving board. I had always thought that Ian was one of the bravest riders and I wasn't surprised when he straightaway dived off it. Blyth and I went up there with the intention of following him, but weren't so brave and, rather humiliatingly, had to climb back down past a load of kids who were happily clambering up and hurling themselves off.

I'd be lying if I said that there wasn't a fair amount of drinking and partying. One night in the hotel our *chef d'équipe*, who was a tough ex-army guy, burned his lips on flaming Sambucca and got the most horrendous blisters around his mouth.

Luhmühlen was the first time I'd jumped a track built by the renowned German designer Wolfgang Feld, who was known for building decent courses. I thought it was big, but I was quite confident because it was twisty and through the woods. Barnaby was brilliant on those sort of courses, so nippy that I'd have to lift my legs up to avoid getting them bashed on trees when he cut the corners. True to form, he gave me a fantastic cross-country ride. Taking a step down from four-star level seemed to give us both confidence. I've always been paranoid about what people think and hate the idea of making a fool of myself, but because there were fewer spectators at Luhmühlen, and no one I knew, I wasn't affected by such negative feelings – and it showed.

Next day we show jumped clear to win my first senior three-day event – a huge thrill. Blyth was second and Andrew third and, waiting for the presentations, we all got very excited as a carriage laden with prizes came out. Unfortunately, these were all for the German National Championships: all I got as a trophy was a little white china horse, which looked as if it had cost ten pence on a bric-a-brac stall. It was a bit of a let-down. On top of that, the Germans were allowed to go first in the lap of honour. But Barnaby got to wear a garland and, best of all, Karen stuck by her word and gave me the Gameboy.

At dinner that night, Rodney Powell wound me up by saying that I'd have to pay for dinner. Eleven of us got into a jacuzzi with the massive bottle of champagne I'd won. There weren't enough glasses, so we sent Rod to fetch some more, and by the time he got back we'd finished the champagne – so we filled the bottle up with spa water, which, of course, he drank. He was right about footing the bill, though, which was painful.

Luhmühlen was an important trip for me; I had been the baby of the group and everyone had been really kind. Now I genuinely felt part of the system – and very keen to go abroad again. I didn't have long to wait: the next overseas trip a few days later was to Breda in Holland with Heron's Flight for his first three-day event. We had a nightmare crossing from Harwich to Hook and Heron hated it. He pawed the ground the whole time and I had to stay with him in the lorry. Now I always travel the short Dover–Calais route.

Once the journey was over, I took the opportunity once again to 'broaden' my social life – and this time nearly blew the whole event as a result. I spent the night before dressage drinking vodka and schnapps in a lorry with a couple of real party animals, Ken Mahon, an Irish rider, and Anna Hermann (now Hilton), who is Swedish. My test was early the next morning, in bright sunshine, and I felt so sick I could barely see. I longed for dark glasses and vowed I would never get in that state again. Somehow we finished tenth, but I don't remember much about how we did it.

I won my first car this summer when Cartoon – 'Leggy' – took the national novice title at Locko Park. Toyota had been sponsoring a points accumulator through the season and, as the title carried double points, I went to the top of the leaderboard and won the use of a smart Land Cruiser for a year.

Then it was Bramham: this year I took Metronome and, for the first time, found myself in the lead at the end of the dressage phase at a senior competition, which was a big thrill. I was still in the lead after cross-country with a show jump in hand over Ginny Leng on Welton Chit Chat. Show jumping was not Metro's best phase anyway, and on this occasion matters were made much worse by a thunderstorm and pouring rain. I have always been terrified of storms and became completely disconcerted, with the result that I had three fences down and finished out of the top ten. This was the first time I'd been last to show jump and tasted the awful disappointment of dropping right out of contention. But, because of the way Metro had gone across country, the natural progression was to take him to Burghley that September.

This would be the first time I'd had two horses at a four-star event, the other, of course, being Barnaby, with whom I experienced déjà vu at Gatcombe when we were again second to Mary – who this time did earn her place on the senior team. On the day at Burghley, Barnaby and I carefully trotted *through* the ditch at Centaur's Leap, but we still finished fourth, and Metro was fourteenth. I felt on a huge high with my first double of clear rounds at a four-star competition, and that Thursday I couldn't wait to open my *Horse & Hound* to read what I felt were bound to be glowing reports. Instead, I discovered that both Lucinda Murray (now Fredericks), who was fifth, and I had come in for a slating from Mark Phillips in his column. He described us as 'two young ladies who won't be reliable at top level until they go back to basics and learn to ride across country properly'.

I was shattered. I have never minded constructive criticism, but at a time when I was just finding my feet in the senior ranks this kind of dismissal was very damaging to my confidence. It felt like a public dressing-down and I was crushed because I knew a lot of people would read it. I think if Mark had known how I felt, he would never have written it; but to this day he thinks he did me a big favour. Although I can now look back and see what he was getting at, with my cross-country riding style as it was, I'm not convinced that at the time it did me any good.

Again I spent part of the winter with William – but this time when the day came for me to return to Norfolk I felt like a child reluctantly going back to boarding school. With our relationship strengthening all the time, I was dreading seeing less of William. As the oldest of Ruth's team, I did most of the cleaning and cooking in the cottage. It was desperately cold and there was always a fight for the bath; often we shared what hot water there was. Working such long hours made me less enthusiastic about housework in the evenings and the cottage got filthy, although I couldn't bear the thought of William seeing it like that so I always cleaned it when he was coming round. It's not easy, living and working with the same people, and, though we all got on, I often needed to escape. I was particularly grateful to Clare and Wally at that time for letting me stay with them on numerous nights.

Duncan and Clare got married that winter in Barbados. They decided they didn't want a big wedding, so it was just the four of us, and we had a fabulous holiday – my first trip out of Europe. I loved it, especially the water skiing. Clare and Duncan got married on the beach and the wedding itself was very romantic, with the sea and beach in the background.

Inevitably, I suppose, Duncan and Clare's marriage had the effect of making me wonder what would happen with William and me. William had a great head lad then called Jason Mather and, during one of our many conversations, Jason said to me: 'Why are you going back to Norfolk? You know this is a permanent relationship.' But William wasn't exactly forthcoming about his feelings and I wasn't prepared to leave Norfolk without a commitment from him. In my head, I knew I had a lot going for me up there, surrounded by the horses, great owners, Ruth and my friends. I was only twenty-three and marriage seemed a huge step. But the parting was definitely getting harder.

That spring of 1992 I was aiming for Badminton with the two horses who had done so well at Burghley: Barnaby and Metro. In the event, it was memorable for all the wrong reasons. The rain came down continuously, making the ground treacherous and drenching everyone's spirits. Metro only got as far as fence five, the big ditch after Huntsman's Close, where he said 'no thank you' and I retired him. Barnaby was giving me a great ride until we got to the Ha-Ha, two fences from home. This was a stark sunken road in the ground with a one-stride distance in the bottom. (Nowadays it is more inviting, being preceded by rails.) I had asked various people's opinions about how to jump it and they advised me to get Barnaby right back to a trot and just let him pop gently in. My gut instinct was to ride him into it faster because I knew he would naturally prop and slow himself down, but I was talking to people who had actually won Badminton. Now I know that they were talking about what they'd do on their particular horses, as all riders do.

Barnaby dithered on the edge of the Ha-Ha and I heard the fence judge say, 'First refusal.' I felt awful. We'd done a good dressage test and I later worked out that I could have finished third. It was a hard lesson; no matter what advice you are being given, remember that it's you that knows your horse.

Clearly after that I was not going to be remotely considered for the Barcelona Olympics – another senior team would pass me by – but at least I came home with my two horses safe and sound. Three horses died at Badminton that year. I felt devastated for Karen Lende, who absolutely adored Mr Maxwell; he was put down after injuring his neck. Toddy was first out on the course on Face The Music who broke his leg, and poor William Fox-Pitt had a terrible fall into the Lake with Briarlands Pippin, who broke his neck and lay there in the water in front of everyone. In addition, Ian had a nasty fall with Glenburnie when trying to jump the Ha-Ha in one go. There was a sober atmosphere in the stable yard that night, and it made me realise that the most important thing was that my horses were all right. On a positive note, what did come out of that Badminton was a realisation in the sport that more needed to be done to take-offs and landings in wet weather to make the footing safe.

On the Sunday night, William asked me to go home with him. I said no because I thought I should go back and see to Barnaby, and he looked disappointed. I wasn't sure why he minded, but I did clock it, so I changed my mind and told Ruth I'd be back in the morning.

We drove to William's in separate cars and, as I went under a railway bridge, a train came over the top at the same time. I always make a wish in those circumstances and I wished that William would propose to me.

We went to the curry house in Cranleigh and had a nice supper. I couldn't work out why William kept going on about not needing a cleaner any more and other odd things, but when we got home he suddenly asked me to marry him. I said: 'Are you joking?' And he replied: 'Yes, I am actually.' But he produced a ring! It was a bit tight but I was determined to get it on and, with a bit of soap, it fitted. Words could not describe my feelings at that time.

Next morning I woke up in a panic because Ruth was expecting me back in Norfolk early. I rang Mum to ask if we could meet her and Dad in a pub for lunch and she was puzzled why I hadn't gone back. Instantly I thought: 'Well, she must know why we want to see them – oh God, she doesn't approve.' But, of course, they were thrilled about our engagement.

It was quickly decided that I should see the rest of the year out in Norfolk, talk to the owners of my horses and make sensible plans. Despite the euphoria of being engaged, I realised it wasn't just a case of me moving into William's house: we had to organise the merging of two separate businesses, and we decided that we should have a whole year together before getting married.

Things continued to go well, as during the next month I was third on Cartoon at Windsor and won Bramham on Metro. His stop at Badminton had been a huge disappointment, but at least its having come so early on the course meant he could be rerouted to Bramham. He excelled there, giving Ruth a special moment: the first three-day event at this level that she'd won as a breeder. Sandy Pfleuger (later Phillips) was second and I was also seventh on Heron. Toyota was sponsoring Bramham and they let me keep the Land Cruiser for another year, which put the icing on the cake at an already happy event.

Then in August it was third time lucky for Barnaby at Gatcombe, where he finally won his own national title. It was a precious moment when I realised my name would be on the trophy along with the likes of Ginny, Toddy and Mary.

But the day was marred by an awful tragedy. On the Sunday morning I heard that Uncle Raymond had died of a heart attack down at his house in Cornwall. Not only his family and friends, but the whole equestrian world were in shock, because he was such a personality and had played a big part in promoting the sport. He was a huge, enthusiastic character and has been greatly missed.

I was already feeling down because, on top of everything else, I had squandered a promising dressage placing by dropping to a seemingly hopeless tenth place with a show jump down, which was unusual for Barnaby as he was so consistent in this phase. The terrible news about Uncle Raymond and the general atmosphere of gloom made it hard to focus and I wasn't much interested in going across country. But Barnaby was his usual speedy self and we had the fastest time of the day which, amazingly, propelled us to the top of the leaderboard.

I felt very emotional when the time came for me to be interviewed for television and it was Hugh Thomas at the microphone instead of Uncle Raymond. I remember saying: 'No offence, Hugh, but I wish it was Raymond standing here interviewing me' – and he agreed. I knew that Raymond had enjoyed following my eventing career and was proud of me; as he had three boys, I think I was something of a surrogate daughter to him.

That autumn I took Heron's Flight to his first four-star event, Burghley, where he finished sixteenth. I was rather pleased, but I remember Ginny's mother Heather Holgate commenting that you never know whether you've got a four-star horse until its second time. She was so right. With hindsight, Heron hadn't enjoyed it much, and I'd had to ride him strongly; but as usual he had tried hard to please.

A week later at Blenheim Leggy was third and Amigo ran out but still qualified for Badminton. Leggy had been in the lead after the cross-country but show jumping was never his strongest point – his long legs dangled in all the wrong places – and we had two fences down, dropping to third behind Rodney Powell on Limmy's Comet.

Leggy was a lovely-looking horse, great to ride on the flat and a charming personality – he always thought everyone had something for him. Riding dressage tests on him was very rewarding, as he had a good dressage brain, but although he was bold, he wasn't the most careful jumper. People thought I was always having stops on him; in fact he never refused with me, but he did give me some serious falls: if I wasn't winning on him, I was coming off. I'd walk a course and think: 'That fence has Leggy's name all over it.' Then he'd catch me unawares by jumping that one fine and hitting something else. Eventually I became scared, which was disastrous.

Another horse who frightened me was Man About Town. Ruth had found him for the Skinners, who wanted to carry on owning an event horse after their daughter Sasha gave up. He was a fabulous mover and a really good jumper but, boy, was he strong. At his first three-day event, Osberton, he carted me through the string both on the steeplechase and on the cross-country, where I lost my steering and careered into the spectators.

I tried all sorts of bits and gadgets with which to hold Man About Town, but I think the problem was more in his head than anything. I had a horrendous fall from him at Weston Park. He took off down a hill to an elephant trap and I had nowhere to turn him as there was a wire fence in the way. He ended up upside-down in the ditch and cast against the post; fortunately I was thrown clear, but it shook me. Shortly after that he injured a leg and, while on box rest at the Skinners', got navicular. He had an injection into his navicular bursa, tragically got an infection and died. I was shattered because despite his headstrong behaviour, like all my horses, I'd got attached to him.

Marshland Amigo, who ran alongside Man About Town, was sent to Ruth by Janet and Ian McIntyre for schooling, after they discovered that the horse they had bought as a hunter was impossible to hold. He had a wonderful strong front, but quite a weak back. I always see the good in every horse, and I fell for him. He was another challenge, and the more I worked on him, the more I felt he would be fun to event; so I persuaded the McIntyres to let me keep him.

There were subtle signs that some of the horses I was riding weren't right for me, but I adored them so much that I couldn't bear to part with them. I was stubborn and couldn't admit defeat with a horse, even if it was crystal clear that I was going nowhere. I was also selfish in that I didn't want to see anyone else riding any of 'my' horses, and I was determined that they would all move to Surrey with me.

Barnaby won all his advanced one-day starts in 1992. He was fifteen now, and I felt he had done enough four-stars, so instead I took him to Boekelo, a three-star three-day event in Holland.

It was a disaster. For a start, the weather was terrible and we sat for days at Chris Hunnable's Towerlands Equestrian Centre in Essex waiting for the storms to abate. In the end, it was a case of flying or missing the event, so a couple of RAF planes were commissioned to fly the horses over. As I was a lorry driver and had all the kit, I still had to go by ferry, so couldn't travel with Barnaby. It was the first time I'd had a horse flown and I was worried sick, my mind full of visions of scenes from the film *International Velvet* in which a horse has to be put down because it panics on a plane. I didn't even get to see Barnaby load and apparently he wasn't happy; he sat down during the flight.

At Boekelo, Barnaby didn't feel 100 per cent, but I still ran him across country because we'd come such a long way that I felt I had to. But he wasn't going well and I had to pull him up, thus learning the important lesson that you should never run a horse across country if it doesn't feel right.

When I got back from Boekelo my mind was full of what on earth I should wear at the Animal Health Trust Awards 'do' to which I'd been invited in London on the Monday night. I was flapping around in the cottage in Norfolk when I got a phone call at 12.30 p.m. saying where was I? It turned out that not only was it a lunchtime event – I hadn't even read the invitation properly – but I had been voted *Horse & Hound* Personality of the Year by readers. Some of them had been invited to the lunch to meet me.

I was mortified. It was such an honour to have won and, by not turning up, I had given the impression that I didn't care. Simon Brooks-Ward collected the award on my behalf and I wrote a letter to *Horse & Hound* apologising profusely.

It was a good year for awards, in fact. I was fourth in the prestigious Land Rover FEI global rankings – fourth in the world! – behind Blyth, Mary and Bruce Davidson; and I also finished at the top of the national points table for the first time, which at the age of twenty-four was quite an achievement. I was presented with the Tony Collings award at the Horse Trials AGM and, importantly, I also won a Volvo car, which I sold in order to buy a lorry in readiness for going solo.

Another big honour – though an absolutely terrifying one – was an invitation to be on *A Question of Sport*. William drove me up to the Manchester BBC studios and watched the session. I was on Bill Beaumont's team and, it being the first time I'd met a top-class rugby player, my overwhelming memory of that evening is being astonished by the size of him! My fellow team-mate was the cricketer Robin Smith while the boxer Duke Mackenzie and footballer John Aldridge were on Ian Botham's team. I think I got all my eventing questions right, but I was absolutely clueless about everything else.

The year ended with my traditional duties at Olympia as a rosette girl, something I did for years alongside Jane Milligan and Lucinda Hanbury. Here too there was an award: I was honoured to win my first BEWA (British Equestrian Writers Association) trophy, an accolade conferred by the journalists who vote for their leading rider each year and present it at their annual lunch at Olympia. I love Olympia, with its Christmassy atmosphere and fantastic international show jumping, but 1992 was rather poignant without Uncle Raymond.

That year a new trophy was presented: the Raymond Brooks-Ward Memorial Trophy, to go to the most promising under-25 rider across the disciplines of show jumping, dressage and eventing. Everyone connected with Uncle Raymond and the show had gathered in the arena to pay tribute, along with his widow Auntie Dinny, and I was there in my role as rosette girl. Then, suddenly, the last horse to come into the arena was Barnaby, led by Mum. It turned out that I had won the trophy. Of course I burst into tears. Nick, Simon and James Brooks-Ward presented it to me, along with David Broome. It was a very emotional moment on which to end 1992.

It had been a year full of achievement and I felt pretty positive about my future in eventing. Little did I know that it would be so much harder than I expected.

4

Independence

T hough I was very sad to leave Ruth after eight amazing years, I was thrilled to move in with William at Cobbetts Farm at the end of the 1992 eventing season. At last I had a home of my own after eight years of communal living. It meant an end to those wearying hours of driving and the beginning of a proper life together for William and me. This was going to be permanent, and I couldn't believe it.

I have never forgotten how lucky I am that William sacrificed so much to buy a property at such a young age; he was only nineteen when he bought Cobbetts Farm with his then girlfriend, Shelley Redbart. A danger of working in the horse world is that riders get stuck in a pattern of pouring money into renting and improving other people's yards. This can only be dead money, and eventually you wake up and realise you've got nothing to show for years of hard grind. If I hadn't met William, the same thing could have happened to me.

He knew he'd rather have a mortgage than pay rent, but it was still a struggle, especially after he and Shelley parted eighteen months previously, and finances were a bit rocky around the time I moved in. Fortunately, a real opportunity to mend them arrived when William was asked to supply horses for the film made of Jilly Cooper's novel *Riders*, which is set in the show-jumping world. William provided six horses and he and Duncan went off to France for three weeks' filming. They loved it; they gave the actors riding lessons on their days off and William was extremely chuffed to be asked to double for the smoothie lead part of Rupert Campbell-Black! Duncan doubled for Michael Praed, who played Jake Lovell, and when he got appendicitis William borrowed a black wig and doubled for that role as well. William couldn't believe the size of the cheque he got for three weeks' work; it got us out of a big hole.

Despite the security of my engagement to William, the financial side of going it alone did worry me. I couldn't rely on William to prop me up – he had his own business to run – and, unlike him, I hadn't a clue what it meant to pay bills or wages. Although I hadn't earned much at Ruth's, I'd never paid rent, electricity bills or any other expenses. All my attention was focused on producing horses, rather than running a business, and the thought of financial responsibility was daunting.

For a start, I needed to buy loads of equipment. All I owned was one saddle – I didn't even have a dandy brush! Ruth gave me a dressage saddle, Mum gave me a pair of clippers and Becky Coffey offered to come and do my entries. The Volvo money meant I could buy the lorry – I had been having sleepless nights about how I was going to transport myself to competitions – and Modern Alarms kindly gave me their sponsorship money up front.

A big confidence-booster was being assured of owners paying livery fees, because the McIntyres, Rawsons and Jewsons had agreed I could keep the rides on their horses. I also had Val Attenborough's Rosebrook Illusion and Becky's mare Merry Gambler. I felt guilty about taking business away from

Ruth but, as always, the fear of being parted from horses that I adored was by far the stronger emotion. Ruth herself was generous; she knew that the owners felt that I had established partnerships with these horses and she was also prepared to let me keep the three I particularly adored: Barnaby, Metro and Heron. Their running costs were covered by my funding from Modern Alarms, which relieved some of the pressure.

Fortunately, by that stage Terry Boon was successfully riding horses for Ruth, including the promising Vital Decision. Terry had done such a good job on him that this was one horse about which I didn't have the heart to say 'my turn now'. I'm glad that he stayed in Norfolk, as Terry went on to win three young rider gold medals and Boekelo on him.

One horse I was tempted to leave behind for Terry, though, was Sarah Jewson's skewbald gelding Bits And Pieces. 'Henry', whom she had bought from the Suffolk-based Irish rider Polly Holohan, was the result of a chance union between the well-known Thoroughbred stallion Lord Gayle and a coloured foster mare who had been sent to 'cheer him up'. He had turned up in Ruth's yard the previous year as a five-year-old, and my initial opinion was: 'This one hasn't got big time written on him – it's one for Terry!' He was only 15.3 hands, didn't have extravagant movement and gave me no feeling of scope over a fence. Sarah, though, is one of the most enthusiastic and persuasive of owners, and she was excited about Henry, who had earned a few novice points with Terry; so I gave in and agreed to take him on a month's trial. I considered him no more than a Pony Club horse, which shows how little I knew then. But that spring he was quick to upgrade to intermediate level, so he stayed – and in any case, by then he had begun to appeal to me because I realised that he had a similarly generous heart to Barnaby.

And this spring was to be the end of Barnaby's career. At a one-day event at Weston Park he pulled off a shoe and so refused across country, which was so much out of character that I realised it was his way of telling me he'd had enough. This little horse, bred out of a 13.2 hands pony mare, had taken me from Pony Club to Badminton and he didn't owe me a thing. I carried on riding him for fun and he remained very much the centre of my yard.

I marked my first spring of independence by buying myself a young horse – an enterprise that is never without an element of chance, and in this instance a gamble that ultimately failed.

What A Compliment – Wattie – came from Donal Barnwell, a well-known competition horse dealer and a good friend of William's. Wattie was an Irish-bred grey four-year-old, a lovely mover and a good jumper, but after just one day with him I realised I had a lot to learn about choosing horses. I didn't know whether he'd been handled badly – or perhaps not at all – but Wattie had no trust of humans and was nervy and sharp. During the breaking-in process, I was trotting around on him on the lunge when he stumbled, I lost my balance and the horse fired me into orbit.

As a result, William decided it would be safer to long-rein him. I'd never done any long-reining before, having managed to break in all the Norfolk horses without using this process, and Wattie wasn't going to accept anything touching his rear end: he straightaway broke three lunge lines and; when William had to improvise and use some leather draw reins as a lunge line, Wattie took off. The catch on the reins went straight through William's hand, giving him an awful messy cut; he went to hospital to be stitched and that was the end of Wattie's long-reining session.

We persevered, but a few months later Wattie was

responsible for one of my most frightening moments with a horse. Our school was frozen that winter, so I borrowed a local indoor manège. As I was legged up on to Wattie, he panicked and took off, galloping straight into a harrow that was lying in the corner of the arena. He came down and I came off but, amazingly, neither of us was injured.

Wattie was partly responsible for the start of my association with an important new owner, Denise Lincoln. She lived locally and contacted me because she had a young horse she wanted me to event. I needed all the rides I could get, so I took Denise's horse on, though I quickly realised it wasn't going to be suitable for eventing. I sold it for her and then sold Denise a half-share in Wattie. I had to explain Wattie's drawbacks to her, of course, but I said I felt he had potential if only I could get his brain channelled. I later had some minor successes and Wattie nearly reached advanced level, but when it came to doing the more demanding dressage movements and I needed more engagement, he refused to go that extra distance. In the end, I had to give him up; I hated the feeling of failure, but there was nothing else for it, and eventually Wattie went back to Donal.

Throughout the spring of 1993 I was really appreciating my new home as a base from which to produce horses. Cobbetts Farm sits at the foot of Holmbury Hill in a triangle between Dorking, Guildford and Horsham on the West Sussex–Surrey border just outside the little village of Forest Green. People visualise Surrey as surburbia, commuters and the M25, but we are in the green belt, twenty minutes south of the rat race in pretty countryside.

I loved the hacking, all on National Trust land; the hills were a treat after Norfolk, and I appreciated the shelter from the trees and hedges – in Norfolk there isn't much to stop the wind.

I also enjoyed playing 'house'. When William's relationship with Shelley ended and she moved out, she took the 'girly things' with her, so that although the house was clean when I moved in, it wasn't particularly feminine – there were no curtains upstairs, for example. In fact, it was a real bachelor pad, which meant I had plenty of scope for getting it how I wanted. I'm not the most domesticated person, but I have loved having my home and slowly doing it up.

The house is more like an overgrown bungalow, with two bedrooms upstairs, two bathrooms, a large sitting room, a well-laid-out kitchen, a big office and a boot room. Outside, we have twelve acres, an outdoor school, a yard each and a flat for the staff in a converted barn at the end of the drive. William's yard is attractive and old-fashioned, with ten boxes plus six more in a beautiful old barn. My yard started with six wooden stables, to which we added another four. My first head girl was Kay Greenwood, who had worked for William before coming across to work for me. Cobbetts Farm was very much her home and she did a great job in setting me off on my first year.

In short, I had the sort of set-up of which most 24-year-olds would dream: a comfortable home, plenty of knowledgeable support, and lots of willing and optimistic owners. Sadly, this was also the start of a period of serious disillusionment with the sport for me.

The problem was my not being clear in my head about how a true four-star horse should feel; the good results I got at lower levels and in the spring advanced classes clouded my judgement. Through Barnaby, I had acquired a taste for the big time, and I was desperate to carry on being at the major events. It didn't occur to me that Barnaby and I had achieved what we did because he had a huge heart and I never gave up kicking; I didn't realise that a four-star horse should give you a much more convincing feel.

That year Heron and Metro had excellent spring advanced runs. As Metro had already won a three-star event, I was determined to have another crack at Badminton with him; and as Heron had got around Burghley, I felt he should go too.

At Badminton, Metro was well placed after the dressage, everyone was excited and I was ushered to the media tent for the usual press conference; next morning there was lots of coverage in the daily newspapers and expectation all round. By Saturday night, though, I was nowhere. I over-rode through nerves and, as a result, both horses refused across country. I've always found it hard to continue when my chances are blown and I think the horses realised that stopping equalled retirement and a quiet walk back to the stables. Giving up was the result of a lack of confidence on my part, but it doesn't do a horse's mentality any good.

When a horse isn't 'taking' you to the fence – and neither Metro nor Heron gave me that feel – the rider is kicking so much that they get in front of the horse's movement, leaving themselves in a weak position should anything go wrong. I had got into this bad habit with Barnaby. By contrast, it is that ability to cope with the inevitable glitches in a cross-country round and quickness in retrieving the situation that marks out the class cross-country riders – people like Lucinda Green, Andrew Nicholson, Mark Todd, William Fox-Pitt and Tina Gifford. I didn't realise how far behind them I was in those days. I had been gaining good results on the one-day circuit because I was riding far more forcefully than I should have been. Nowadays, a one-day event tends to be considered just a prep-run for an experienced horse – it shouldn't be a massive effort. I blame myself terribly for what went wrong with some of the horses I had then; I'd love to magic them back into my life and see what I could do with them now but, of course, I'll never know.

But I hadn't yet grasped any of this, and so on that Saturday night at Badminton I was shattered. I had taken not only my own high expectations to Badminton, but those of others too. Now there was no way I would be selected for a British team.

I went to my next event, Punchestown, in a low mood. Amigo actually went quite well, but he left a leg behind at a fence and, once more, I was unseated. Again, this happened because I was in front of the horse's movement; I wasn't in a secure cross-country position and had no chance of staying on. It was another wasted chance.

This became a hideous pattern: I'd raise everyone's hopes by leading the dressage, give meaningless press interviews about my chances while all the time feeling negative about the next day, and then go through another humiliating, crushing disaster. It was all so public, and my pride was getting badly hurt. I felt everyone must be talking about me and thinking, 'Well, we know she won't still be in the lead after cross-country.'

I had some compensation at Windsor, riding Becky Coffey's lovely home-bred mare Merry Gambler. She was one of five horses, including Mr Jackpot, bred out of Becky's mare Michelle Gambler, and I'd ridden her since she was five. Merry taught me not to give up on a horse if it hasn't got a great trot; she had no trot at first, but this pace had improved over the years and at Windsor this year she produced a good dressage test. Merry was so honest and such a good jumper that she went on to finish second, giving Becky her best result as an owner. It was a real thrill for all of us, for Becky had been such a long-time supporter of the sport and religiously came to every event with us. Sadly, Merry was dogged with soundness problems and we decided to breed from her thereafter. She has produced foals by the stallions Viceroy and Mayhill; Denise Lincoln has one of her offspring, which is an exciting prospect for the future.

Windsor was followed by another happy result when I took Cartoon to Bramham, where he was second behind my good friend Tina Gifford on General Jock. Bramham has always been known as a fun event. The Lane Foxes, who own it, are extremely hospitable and put on fantastic parties. A three-day event feels like a treat because you've just got one or two horses to ride instead of twelve, and it can be hard to remember that we're there to compete seriously and not just to have a good time.

William came up to watch and one night we retired, with Becky, to the Todds' lorry for a few drinks. Becky loves singing and the Todd children Lauren and James were into *The Sound of Music* and *Chitty Chitty Bang Bang*. Before long we were going through our limited repertoire – very loudly. Toddy was dead worried about his image, as he didn't think the strains of 'Climb Every Mountain' sounded cool emanating from his lorry, and I was equally worried that William would go back to his show-jumping mates and tell them how sad we eventers were.

The most memorable incident of the weekend was Becky's spectacular crash, when well under the influence, down the steps of my lorry. Next morning I found her groaning on her lilo, on which she always slept at the back of the lorry. Charlotte Bathe's mother, Mary Hollingsworth, kindly took her to hospital for an X-ray; as Becky returned to Bramham with her leg in plaster, she said: 'They'll laugh at me when they find out,' to which Mary replied: 'Of course they won't, they'll be really sympathetic.' Well, we took one look at poor Becky hobbling and howled with mirth.

The improved fortunes of the summer didn't last: Burghley was another four-star failure with a capital F. Cartoon slipped while I was working him in and went lame behind; this was a major disappointment and I learned the lesson of always putting studs on a horse's shoes, even the day before the event. Heron's Flight did start, but he refused to jump the water cascades fence.

But then, the next week, I went to Blenheim, a three-star event, and won it on Metronome. For many people, a win on this scale is a dream, but for me it wasn't nearly enough. What I wanted was to achieve at the top level; and not only had I not done this, I felt I was still a long way off it. Meanwhile, my contemporaries William Fox-Pitt, Tina Gifford and Charlotte had been selected for the senior European Championships in Achselschwang, along with Nick Burton – whom I had beaten loads of times, just not when it mattered. He was selected on the strength of a great Badminton result with Bertie Blunt and, thrilled as I was for all of them, I yearned to be out there with them and felt demoralised that they seemed to be so far ahead of me.

In fact, the championship was an absolute disaster for the team, but in the course of the competition Tina showed what cross-country riding is all about, and that superb round on Song And Dance Man in awful wet conditions earned her a first senior individual medal. But it all seemed way out of reach to me.

However, on another level I did have the biggest excitement of all: my wedding on 30 October, which Mum had been busy organising while I was competing. I wanted a traditional wedding in Tidebrook village church, where we went every

Christmas and where I'd sung in the choir during my schooldays, and I decided to wear Mum's dress. I loved it and knew she would be thrilled if I wore it. The reception was to be at Possingworth Manor, which belonged to Mum and Dad's friends Brenda and Roger Neville.

I had a hen night at the local pub, complete with 'gorilla-gram', and on the way home we rioted drunkenly, amassing a large collection of stolen For Sale signs, bollards and garden gnomes.

The wedding itself was more decorous, and a real family affair. I'll never forget my father's face when I came down the stairs in my mother's dress. He had tears in his eye, and that set me off. I wasn't expecting to feel emotional, but suddenly it seemed an overwhelmingly big step to take but I knew I was marrying the man I wanted to be with for the rest of my life. It dawned on me how much work my parents had put into this day.

The ceremony and reception passed in a flash – all the more so because I had a lousy bout of flu, something which tends to happen to me at the end of a season when my body seems to say: 'OK, you've got time to be ill now.'

I was anxious about the vows. My husband's full name is William Ross Norman Funnell, and all I could think of was Norman No-Mates, the character in the Sun Alliance advert. Every time I said 'Norman' in the rehearsal, I cried with laughter. On the day, I was so relieved to get over the Norman business that I swallowed down having to vow to 'obey'. I had been adamant that I wouldn't obey, but I found out later that William and Duncan had taken the vicar up to the pub and bribed him to stick it in at the last moment. To this day I regret saying it, but I could hardly make a scene about it in front of a church full of people!

We went to Barbados for our honeymoon. We spent the first week on our own, supposedly for romantic reasons, but in fact we both felt so ill with flu that though we hardly emerged from our hotel room it was for all the wrong reasons. We felt too awful to lie on the beach, and only managed one outing – to a wildlife sanctuary. As I walked down a path, there was a monkey sitting with his tail across the path and a tortoise coming the other way. As I drew level with the monkey, the tortoise trod on his tail. The monkey went berserk and chased me down the path – I had to run for my life!

We perked up in the second week, though, when Duncan and Clare came out, along with two more good friends, Chris Warren and his girlfriend Lee (now married to the show jumper John Popely), and we all went water-skiing. Chris had never water-skied before but, having been a jockey, he had great balance. As we skied past the *Jolly Roger*, a galleon full of tourists, he put the steering handle in his mouth and gave them a 'moony'. We also went deep-sea fishing and caught a barracuda. Chris dropped this into a swimming pool full of kids and you can imagine the pandemonium.

The 1994 season saw me riding with a new name – Mrs Funnell – but all the old problems. It was the worst year of my entire career: all I have to show for it on my CV is a measly seventh place in the British Open at Gatcombe on Heron.

I had entered Cartoon and Amigo for Badminton, but a fall from Leggy in the pre-Badminton advanced class at Dynes Hall unnerved me and I withdrew him, leaving Amigo as my sole ride. He stopped with me at the Quarry and I tipped over his head, landing in an ignominious Humpty Dumpty-like sitting position on the wall – a video clip which has been well replayed. Because I was in a significant position after dressage, my cross-country round was, of course, televised live.

People must have wondered why I kept going back for more embarrassment, but they tried to be kind and encouraging. Back in the stable yard that night Bruce Davidson, the leading American rider who had twice been world champion, tried to cheer me up, saying that my fortunes would definitely change.

The first year of our marriage wasn't much fun for William, with me constantly down and questioning my whole career; and yet I felt I had no choice but to keep ploughing on. I certainly wasn't in the most positive frame of mind at Punchestown; in fact at that point I couldn't imagine I would ever enjoy a cross-country round again. The weather was terrible and Cartoon, who was a promising fourth after dressage, fell when he hit a cross-country fence.

At last I realised it would be kinder to the Rawsons – and to myself – to give him up. It's difficult to admit defeat with a horse when you've built up a partnership, and I had desperately wanted to take Leggy to a four-star event myself; I knew he could do the dressage and was a brave jumper who wouldn't stop. I also loved his character and had grown attached to him. But Leggy wasn't the right horse for me; I just wasn't brave enough and my lack of confidence wasn't helping him. My problem of getting in front of the movement meant I wasn't strong enough to stay on him if he hit a fence.

But I wasn't going to let him go on to just anybody. In fact, there was only one person I suggested to ride him, and that was Andrew Nicholson, the top New Zealand rider who is renowned for his 'stickability'. Andrew had a reputation for being able to ride all sorts of horses, and there are many video clips of him sticking on in all sorts of mishaps, even under water. The partnership worked out really well – they were fourth at Burghley the following year – and Andrew was often kind enough to credit me with producing the horse. Far from being jealous, I was just thrilled, and relieved, that the Rawsons and their horse were getting the results they deserved at last.

I had another disappointing result at Bramham when Heron stopped, and then, for some reason, I stupidly returned to Burghley with Metro. Goodness knows why. But achieving a decent four-star result had become an obsession and I was incapable of listening to what the horses were telling me. And, frustratingly, the dressage was getting better and better – Ruth would drive down and help me with this – and my show jumping was improving thanks to William's input.

At Burghley, I fell off Metro at the Dairy Mound Corner and he landed on me and trod on my leg. I think it was probably agony, but I leaped back on again with William's words ringing in my ears: he felt that I was allowing the horses to get into the habit of stopping and retiring when what they needed was to feel the sensation of being made to complete the course. But my leg was too painful – it turned out that I had damaged the ligaments – and, a few fences later, I had to pull up.

So a dispiriting 1994 season ended at Boekelo – with Heron retiring, again, on the cross-country. I now realised that I couldn't go back to Badminton and Burghley to face another failure and I made the decision that I wouldn't tackle either again until I knew I could do things differently.

With Ruth's help, I made the gut-wrenching decision to relinquish Metro and Heron. It was decided that they should drop down a level and go into the young riders system with her pupils Lucy Kemplay and Blair Richardson. I was to part from Amigo too – he went to an amateur rider in Belgium. I expect Ruth would have liked to have taken the horses away from me before, but she was so loyal that she stuck to me and let me make the decision in my own time. I still feel guilty about insisting on keeping them as long as I did – really I should have given in a year earlier.

The great consolation, though, was that I had some fabulous young horses to concentrate on. The McIntyres bought Marshland Rubio ('Guinness'), a nice-looking grey horse, from Chris Warren; he was a lovely jumper with wonderful paces and a charming, playful personality – we gave him a teddy bear to play with in his stable. Then, while I was competing at Borde Hill, an event my mother ran, Anne Burnet rang me to say that her rider Tony Whipps had been balloted out of a novice section on her two five-year-olds, Designer Tramp and The Tourmaline Rose, and would I ride them for her? Designer Tramp was the most beautiful stamp of a horse, a real Thoroughbred who oozed quality and presence, and I was really excited about him. Two months later Tramp gave me the first of my six wins in the Burghley Young Event Horse final, a prestigious annual competition for potential eventers and the only thing I seemed to shine at when I was at Burghley in those days. I took on The Tourmaline Rose because Tramp was so lovely; in truth, she looked very fat and nothing like an event horse, but she had a fabulous jump.

Our winter break that year was a trip to Mauritius for the wedding of William's great friend Mark Armstrong to Dupe Powell. Dupe's parents paid for William and myself, Duncan and Clare, and another of our great show-jumping mates, Peter Charles, to go out there for a week. It was fabulous; having experienced so few foreign holidays, this was a real treat for me. One of the more amusing aspects of the holiday was that as Peter was single at that stage (it was before he'd met his wife Tara), he persuaded me to accompany him walking down the beach because he felt he looked less obvious staring at all the topless birds if I was with him. During a more serious conversation, though, Pete mentioned to me that he had a horse called Rainbow Magic – 'Sam' – who might suit me and suggested that William and I might want to buy him for Denise Lincoln, who was in between horses and looking for another one. At the time Sam was owned by Denise Stamp, who is now one of William's main owners. Pete agreed to let me have the horse to try for two weeks. I jumped him and took him cross-country schooling; he was a joy to ride and so sensible that we nicknamed him Policeman Sam. He had the most wonderful attitude and I thought he was a truly lovely horse.

The promise of these four horses made me quietly optimistic for the start of the 1995 season. I remember saying to myself that if I can't get one of these to the Sydney Olympics in 2000, then I might as well give up. None of them made it.

Ironically, the horse who seemed the least promising at this stage was Supreme Rock. He belonged to Emma Lewthwaite, who was at university with Sarah Jewson's daughter Charlotte; she was having a year out from her law degree and had contacted me for lessons. Emma's uncle, Robert Tomkinson, had spotted Supreme Rock out hunting with the Grafton and thought he would be a nice horse for Emma to have some fun with. One morning when I was away, Emma phoned William in a panic at 5 a.m.; there had been trouble at the yard where she kept Rocky and she had to move him immediately. William told her to come round straight away, and when I got back Rocky was installed. Emma went back to her law degree and I had a few rides on him.

Rocky was a big, gangly horse with loads of impressive movement that he didn't know how to handle; he would take strides out in jumping lessons and was all over the place. But you couldn't ignore his scope. I had turned him out in a paddock surrounded by a ditch in between two sets of rails: he just calmly lobbed up to it and popped over.

My priority this year was to begin the long process of building up partnerships with young horses, and it was a huge mental relief not to be going to Badminton, with all its attendant expectation and disappointment. The only problem was that because I didn't have anything to ride at top level, I was keen to hurry these lovely six-year-olds through the ranks. Anne Burnet was ambitious, too, and because Designer Tramp was so talented we decided to take him to the Windsor three-day event.

Anne was keeping her horses at her home in Sussex, where they were ridden by her head girl. She was good with the horses, but the situation wasn't ideal because I could only ride Tramp once or twice a week, and it involved a lot of running around. So when Tramp demonstrated what he had to offer by winning Windsor, it was a real thrill and boosted my confidence hugely – though I was keenly aware that it was only a two-star event, and couldn't help doubting that I would be able to sustain this level of success up to four-star level.

The big event for me this year would be Blenheim, with Bits and Pieces ('Henry'), who was back in action after a year off with a minor leg injury, and The Imposter, an advanced horse I had taken on for Nicky Fleming. Henry was a good jumper but tricky in the dressage. Ruth had impressed upon me never to lose my temper with a horse, but with Henry I was often tempted. On these occasions I would have to get off him, put him on the horse-walker, go into the house for a coffee and a cigarette, and then try again. I knew I couldn't jeopardise my relationship with him by getting angry, but he drove me mad on the flat.

RIGHT Less than a year old at my grandparents Annie and Billy's house.
BELOW LEFT Aged eighteen months
sitting on Mum's horse, Majador.
BELOW RIGHT Out hunting on my first
pony, Pepsi, with Mum on Smokering.

ABOVE My second pony, Flighty.
RIGHT On Jeremy Fisher at a Pony
Club hunter trials. (Ross Lancy)

Barnaby and I at our first senior event, Chatsworth in 1986, where we finished fifth. *(Finlay Davidson)*

Kitted out for the young rider Europeans in Poland (I'm second right) with (front row) Bob Baskerville, Gill Watson and Giles Rowsell.

The first time William Fox-Pitt and I rode on a team together, at Achselschwang in 1989.

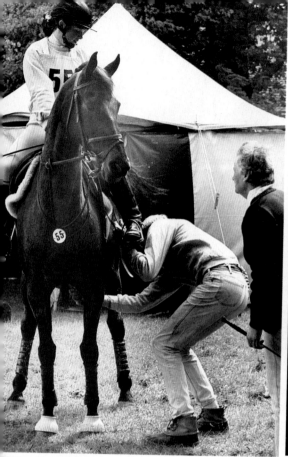

LEFT My first Badminton in 1988 – Ben Case and Ruth McMullen help me get ready for cross-country.
BELOW At my twenty-first with Simon Brooks-Ward and Adam Case and (below) my godfather, Uncle Raymond (Brooks-Ward).

Having won Bramham in 1992 on Metronome for Ruth. Bramham's host George Lane Fox is on the right. *(Event Print)*

RIGHT A New Year's Eve party at my future husband's house: Chris Warren, Peter Charles, William as Elvis and Duncan Inglis. BELOW Out hunting with William and his father John Funnell who was Master of the Surrey Union.

ABOVE Fingers and Spliff at Christmas. RIGHT In Barbados for William's best friend Duncan Inglis's wedding.

MY BIG DAY IN 1993: With Mum and Dad outside Oatridges. *(Ian Shaw)*

With my new husband.

Bits And Pieces ('Henry') gave me my first true four-star ride at Burghley in 1996 – I think my face says it all. *(Kit Houghton)*

With Henry at Badminton in 1997, where we were ninth – another wonderful ride. *(Ian Burns)*

HOLIDAY MODE:

ABOVE Skiing in Courchevel with Duncan and Clare Inglis and our godchildren Georgia Bunn and Amy Inglis.
LEFT With Blyth Tait, Anna Hilton, Carolyn Todd and Mary King in New Zealand.
BELOW Getting stranded with Karin Neiderer, Simon Hilton, Dan Jocelyn, Tanya Cleverley and Anna Hilton.

ABOVE LEFT
General Salute
wins at
Punchestown for
Sarah and Richard
Jewson. *(Equestrian Photographic Services)*
ABOVE RIGHT
Getting dressed
for dressage on
Viceroy at
Saumur.
RIGHT
Rainbow Magic, a
horse I was really
sad to part with,
in the trot up at
Burghley.
(Ian Burns)

Still, there was something special about this little horse. He was like a tiger across country, so hungry to jump the fences; yet, as Lucinda Green once wrote in the *Daily Telegraph* after she came to try him for a feature, at home he gave no feeling of scope over a fence – you didn't have the confidence that he would get over a 3 foot oxer.

Given these doubts, and my chronic confidence problem, Blenheim that year was an uplifting experience. Henry won and The Imposter was eighth. Both horses were keen as mustard across country: they took me to the fences and, for the first time in years, I wasn't walking a track looking for easy options – in fact, I was the only rider to jump all the direct options on both horses. It felt like a massive breakthrough. So even though I wasn't with my friends William, Tina and Charlotte in the British team going to the Open European Championships at Pratoni del Vivaro in Italy, where they won gold, this time I didn't mind so much because I was so excited about my young horses.

A lot of good horses start their three-day-event career at Le Lion d'Angers in France, which is a World Championships for young horses. In 1995 I took Rainbow Magic, though he was only six. Le Lion is one of the most fun events of all: there are elegant parties in the chateau and a relaxed end-of-term feeling, compounded by the demob-happy atmosphere in the bar on the overnight ferry home.

William came out with me, along with the Lincolns, for whom it was a first overseas event, and we spent a lot of time with Mark and Carolyn Todd and Andrew and Jayne Nicholson. My parents were there too – staying on an awful damp houseboat on the river. We stayed with the Todds at a famously eccentric hotel called Le Cheval Blanc. Life was always haphazard there – Hervé and Véronique, who ran it, used to have stunning and highly public rows – and eventually the place burned down, though not, thankfully, when we were there! That weekend was particularly chaotic and one evening, when supper was even later than usual, it seemed the only option was to produce it ourselves. Andrew and William took charge and disappeared into the kitchen to cook the steaks while Jayne and I waitressed. We thought this would get us a free meal, but unfortunately by the time the bill came round Hervé had woken up and we had to pay.

In the event itself, Sam and I had a minor hiccup across country but basically went well; in hindsight, I realised it was a year too early, so this was the last time I took a six-year-old to a three-day event. It is too demanding on a young horse's brain and physiology, and more important that they get the mileage at the other end of their career.

William had also had a good year in 1995. The same weekend I won Windsor he won the Eindhoven Derby on Comex and was travelling reserve for the European Championships in St Gallen, which we were very pleased to see won by Pete Charles, who was by now riding for Ireland. Comex – 'Cobby' – was a great horse for William. He had found him in Holland as a four-year-old with Tom Olysmeyer, from whom William has bought many horses, and bought him for Alan Kyson to ride. Alan broke his leg when the horse was seven, so William got the ride back, jumping forty-seven clear rounds in a row. He then sold him to our Norwegian friends Morton and Christine Aason but, two years later, the horse wasn't going that well and William was able to buy a share back and ride him again. Cobby won £250,000 for William and was a very special horse.

It seems that few couples can enjoy success at the same time – I know this has been particularly true for David and Karen

O'Connor, who have often found that when one of them wins the other has a disaster – so that Eindhoven weekend was very special for us. The advantage of being married to another rider is that we both know how it feels when it goes wrong and we both understand how unpredictable a life with horses can be; each of us feels the other's disappointment but we also really enjoy each other's successes, and the rare moments when we share equal success are special. The sad thing is that there are so few opportunities to watch each other as we both compete most weekends; I feel guilty about this because probably, on balance, William has watched me more than the other way around.

William's business operates differently from mine. I am reliant on owners keeping horses with me and, as I am completely driven to get to the top, my interest is in building up the partnerships. Buying and selling has never interested me. William would love to be the same, as he has the same ambitions, but show jumping is a completely different world from eventing. There's so much more prize money and therefore the value of the horses is greater, so he can't justify keeping many of the promising young horses he buys to produce. There's a permanent cycle of change in his yard, which is why he – and many other British show jumpers – has not always enjoyed the success at top level that he deserves. In contrast, I had a collection of promising youngsters that I envisaged keeping for their whole careers. I had reached a stage of reasonable contentment about this when catastrophe struck.

I had only just persuaded Anne Burnet that Tramp would be better off stabled with me when my head girl Kay had an awful accident with him. She was mucking him out when his leg got punctured by the metal fork. There was a risk of infection in the joint, which can be the end of a horse unless you catch it quickly, so Tramp had to have an anaesthetic so that the joint could be flushed.

I was panicking about what I was going to say to Anne, and Kay was understandably distraught. This couldn't have come at a worse time for her, as she had become very unsettled with us. Kay had suffered family tragedy in the past and Cobbetts had been a real home to her for eight years, but she was in a dilemma about her future. Grooming is a job which entails a huge amount of work with no hope of ever earning a high salary and many grooms get to a point where they have to consider their future. The awkward situation with Tramp made her feel it was time to leave and so she went, first, to the Japanese rider Takeaki Tschuya and then to Bruce Davidson, where she still is.

I was already short of a groom at the time Kay left and the sudden increase in workload caused my one remaining member of staff to walk out. I was left in an unbelievable mess with thirteen horses to look after. It was an awful period. I kept interviewing potential staff and trying to explain to them that when it was all sorted out there would be three grooms and life with me would be fine, but I didn't seem to be able to get more than one person at a time actually working on the yard, and none of them could stick the pace for more than a week. For a nightmare two months I was getting up at 3 a.m. in order to get all the horses mucked out and ridden, mostly by myself.

It was Sarah Jewson who came to the rescue; she found me Nini French, who was from Norfolk. Nini was brilliant: she became my head girl and stayed for five years.

Not surprisingly, in view of all this, in the spring of 1996 I was exhausted and run down – but I was looking forward to taking The Imposter to Badminton, as I felt it would be a pressure-free run; the horse wasn't particularly easy in the dressage but he loved the cross-country and I thought it would be a fun and restorative experience. Unfortunately, though, I was so tired that I contracted shingles. It was excruciatingly painful and there was no way I could ride. Instead I went to Badminton on foot on cross-country day, one of the most miserable and frustrating days I have endured. But although I didn't appreciate it at the time, I needed that enforced three weeks off because I was physically wiped out, and by the time Windsor came round a couple of weeks later I was much more cheerful. I was even more cheerful afterwards, because I took Guinness and he won for the McIntyres: I was delighted, because they are the most loyal and generous of owners who had put up with a lot of disappointment. Rainbow Magic was sixth, and at last I felt again that all was going according to plan with these youngsters.

Bramham with The Tourmaline Rose brought another sharp lesson, though: namely, that however competent others are, it is the rider who should take ultimate responsibility for a horse's fitness before a three-day event. Rosie had been based with Anne and, in hindsight, I hadn't been involved in her preparation. Rosie gave me a fantastic ride until three fences from home, when the lights simply went out. She felt exhausted and I had to pull her up in front of the last fence because it was dangerous. It's the only time I've ridden a very tired horse and I don't want to do it again.

This was the year of the Atlanta Olympics and, though I was obviously out of the frame, we were hopeful that William might get close; our hopes were pinned on his being the member of the Funnell family to ride at the Olympics. Sadly, it wasn't to be – he wasn't even chosen as reserve. However, I spent a great weekend watching him at the Pavarotti Show in

Modena, Italy, which was run by Simon Brooks-Ward. William was second in the Grand Prix and won £47,000; this was serious money and helped keep our businesses running.

There was much discussion about the heat and humidity in Atlanta and I felt that some of the British horses wouldn't have a hope of a medal, even if they ran at their very best. I couldn't help wishing that the selectors could have put a bit of faith in Henry. He'd stormed around Blenheim and I thought he was worth a punt, especially as the British team wasn't over-flush with top-quality horses then – Tina suffered the most awful blow when both her good four-star horses went lame – and in my self-centred opinion it was a year when they could have looked at some of the useful three-star horses.

Anyway, Atlanta was a disaster, a big anti-climax for British eventing. It triggered a depression in the sport because this was the second successive Olympics from which the team had returned home without a medal of any sort; our reputation as a leading eventing nation was dented and the Australians, New Zealanders and Americans were sweeping ahead and becoming the fashionable riders. Both Britain's training and the team tactics came in for bitter criticism and there was a clean sweep of officials: Giles Rowsell was then appointed as chairman of selectors, and Andy Bathe took over from John Killingbeck as team vet. I just felt frustrated because I knew that I had beaten some of the riders who had been on the squad and I wondered if I was ever going to get my chance.

Meanwhile, I was riding Rocky full-time; once he'd upgraded to intermediate, Emma didn't feel it was fair on herself or the horse to compete him, so I took on the ride. I loved him for his scope and loose, swinging gait, but I didn't think his brain was sharp enough. He was so laid back that he was very hard work in the dressage and struggled to hold himself on a circle at canter without breaking stride, because he was so big and weak. He had an enormous stride and found it difficult to adjust in front of a fence. So, as much as I liked him, the idea didn't enter my head that he would become such an important horse for me.

Our first three-day event run, at Blair Castle, wasn't a success – he jumped himself into trouble and had to stop. But because he was now eight, I felt I'd got to get on with it and so I took him to another two-star, Achselschwang, a month later. I love this event; it was the first time I'd been back for seven years – I'd not been there since my time in young riders – and Theo and Barbara Steinle, who run it, gave me a great welcome. They are extremely generous hosts. Barbara would come round to the lorry and ask what shopping she could get us and, as the event used to coincide with the Munich Beer Festival, a bus would be organised to take riders into town each night.

Rocky finished fourth and Rainbow Magic ('Sam') won, notching up his first three-day victory. On the way home I rang Tina – we had become close friends since my move to Surrey and we always ring each other if we've been competing at different places – to hear the great news that she had won the two-star event at Necarne Castle in Northern Ireland that weekend. Tina went on to win Le Lion as well that year, which was some compensation for her disappointment at missing the Olympics.

Part of me had been dreading my return to four-star level, but I felt Henry was ready for the challenge of Burghley in 1996. I still hadn't managed to work out a system to deal with my nerves and I was steeling myself for yet more disappointment. I'd had so much experience of the wheels coming off at four-star level that by now I was well aware that, though we'd won Blenheim, the difference between three-star and four-star is like that between a hill and a mountain if a horse isn't brave or scopey enough. But I was also confident that Henry wouldn't stop with me. He'd only done two three-day events, but he'd stormed around those and his advanced events; and Sarah Jewson was, as always, very keen.

I sometimes wonder why Sarah has event horses; she gets so excited and nervous that she can't bear to watch them jump a single fence. She had burst into tears at Blenheim when she discovered Henry was actually in the lead – she had no idea because she'd taken herself off shopping in Woodstock rather than watch! As for me, I was sick with nerves at Burghley. But Henry jumped around as if it had been a Pony Club track, and it was exhilarating. A photograph was published in *Horse & Hound* of me grinning and patting him as he galloped through the water, ears pricked. He was so extravagant and confident, especially jumping into water, that he made it feel easy and we finished fourth.

Much as I loved Barnaby, I realised that at last I'd had my first proper four-star ride. Suddenly, there was light at the end of the tunnel.

5
The Breakthrough

Despite the excitement of finally achieving a successful Burghley, I was nervous about returning to Badminton in 1997. A large part of me didn't want to go; the place seemed to hold a lot of ghosts.

The fear of Badminton wasn't just about the prospect of failing, or of losing my chances of team selection again; I was afraid because I had built up a lot of faith in Bits and Pieces ('Henry') and I was only too aware of what a comedown it is when you discover after years of work and hope that you haven't actually got the top horse you thought you had. Often, you don't find out what a horse is really made of until the longed-for day when you get it to Badminton, and if that venture doesn't come off, it can be devastating.

All my best rides on Henry had been at three-day events. He wasn't a winner on the one-day circuit – ironically, this is often a good indication of a potential international horse – because he had a 'let me at them' attitude to fences. This meant you couldn't just blast him round fast; he needed the big obstacles of a major event to make him back off and jump properly.

Henry's brave cross-country performance at Burghley,

combined with the consistency of his show jumping, had elevated him into a genuine top-level prospect, and I realised it would be a waste not to try harder to improve his dressage. He had nothing like the ability or natural paces of some of my former rides, such as Metro, but, strange as it sounds, this had the advantageous effect of relieving the pressure on me. We were never well placed after the dressage phase, relying instead on Henry's bravery across country to catch up, and this seemed to suit me better as I felt I had less to lose. Now, though, I realised something ought to be done about the dressage.

It took a lot of work. Ruth came down to lend a hand with the transformation. By the time I left Ruth's I think she had started to become immune to my faults because she had taught me so often. Now that our lessons were more intermittent, she would instantly spot what I was doing wrong. She would spend much of the time working on me, rather than the horse, re-establishing key things like straightness. I would always get extra marks in a competition shortly after a lesson with Ruth.

Henry was never going to be an amazing mover because he found it physically difficult to produce impressive paces. Therefore, the idea was to steal every mark I could with him through accuracy and presentation. But Henry was a headshaker and I dreaded our tests if the weather was hot, if the rapeseed, which bothered him, was out – and there was a lot of this around Badminton – or if there were flies, all things which exacerbate a headshaker's problems.

Being something of a party-lover, Henry also had a tendency to get lit up at events, and he would need a lot of work to get him settled. At a three-day event I would ride him around the park and lunge him for ages. There's only so much you can do on top of a horse before dressage and I'd rather be lungeing or cantering, with the weight off the horse's back, than forcing them into endless sessions of dressage in which they can become tight and sore. This is often people's downfall in the dressage phase. The difficulty in preparing an event horse for the dressage test is that it has to be fit for the speed and endurance phase that is to follow, and therefore is highly likely to be excited by the occasion. The secret is to know how much work suits a particular horse before its dressage test. Henry seemed to know he had to save energy for the cross-country, though – like Supreme Rock, he would be flat out asleep beforehand.

As Badminton 1997 approached, those people closest to me, like William, and Mum and Dad and Becky, became as apprehensive as I was, because they dreaded coping with me having another dispiriting experience. I always get tense in the countdown to Badminton – it's the worst time of the year for stress – but this time my husband managed to take my mind off it in spectacular style.

It was the Monday night of Badminton week and I had gone to bed while William was down at the pub with a show-jumping mate, Andrew Saywell. I was woken by a loud bang which, as it was a windy night, I presumed was just something blowing over outside. Next morning I woke up to find William was missing. Realising he had obviously had rather a good night, I went downstairs to find him asleep in the sitting room.

'Don't worry, darling, I'm not cross,' I said. 'Go and have a couple of hours' kip.'

I then walked through into the kitchen and found the Volvo parked, literally, in the kitchen. Apparently, there had been some sort of amusing competition in our driveway to test the braking, with the result that the car had actually ploughed straight through a wall and into the house.

I went flying back into the sitting room and yelled: 'I've changed my mind! I'm bloody furious with you!'

I rang Mum, crying hysterically. She thought something awful must have happened to the horse, but when I told her what had happened, she just roared with laughter. And at least I got a new kitchen.

I don't know whether the kitchen incident was a distraction that saved the day, but that weekend I had, for the first time, what I knew to be a true Badminton cross-country ride. It was one of the most thrilling experiences of my life. The way Henry ate up the big course, bounding through the Lake and skipping over those huge ditch fences, like the Vicarage Vee, was fantastic. He stayed in a wonderful rhythm and it was one of those rare occasions where you are actually aware at the time that you're enjoying yourself. It was a special ride and one that I still take out of my memories and think about from time to time.

We finished ninth – our dressage hadn't been that special, despite the work – but I didn't mind. It was a completion, and another little silver horse on the mantelpiece, which was good enough for me. The selectors asked me to stay behind and trot up Henry on Monday morning, after which we were put on the longlist for the Open European Championships at Burghley that September. I was ecstatic; it felt like an enormous achievement.

On returning home, it was time to sort out the kitchen debacle. Much to William's amusement, when the insurance man came to inspect the damage, he pronounced it 'a typical instance of a woman driving her husband's automatic car'! William loved this and said smugly: 'Yes, I know; she put it in drive instead of reverse!'

After that it was weeks of chaos with builders' dust

everywhere. Matters were made more complicated by the presence of our two dogs, Spliff and Fingers, and new puppy, Toes. Spliff, a Lakeland cross terrier, got on really well with Fingers, while Toes was a pretty brown puppy that Denise Stamp had bred out of Spliff's daughter. We adored her, but she drove the builders mad, picking up paintbrushes and dragging them around and walking through the paint trays.

In those days Punchestown fell on the weekend after Badminton and always came as a welcome relief. Punchestown is a favourite event for riders; after the stress of Badminton the Irish air gets to you and all you want to do is have a drink with your mates – there's loads of socialising on tap in the racecourse bars and it can be hard to remember that you're there to compete, rather than party. This one I enjoyed even more than usual because I finished second, on Designer Tramp, behind Bruce Davidson. Tramp oozed class and gave me a lovely ride around what is always a serious galloping track but, sadly, this was to be his last major success, as afterwards his career was dogged by injury.

I had travelled over in the lorry with Tina Gifford – this was really the start of our going everywhere abroad together. Spending weeks away in a lorry can be tough and, eventually, tiredness and the claustrophobia and inconvenience of camping in a small space can get to you. That's when it's essential to be with someone you know well, otherwise you'd go mad. Tina and I never run out of things to talk about and can always fill the journey, no matter what the length, with continuous chat. Her head girl, Rachel Tolley, was good friends with mine, Nini French, too, so the joint travelling would always work out really well.

Tina and I do bring out the worst in each other, though, and, as two women in an 18-tonne lorry tend to stand out among all the male drivers at ferry ports – they're always surprised to see us in the truckers' cafés on the ferries – we have had some funny moments. On one occasion we were going to Germany and needed road tax. I sent Tina to queue and when she was asked how many axles we had, she replied that she hadn't a clue and suggested 'one'. At this, all the other drivers burst into hysterics, miming a seesaw action and tapping their heads. Tina got her own back later, though, when I was having a pee in the lorry and she flung open the doors so that I was merrily going to the loo in front of all my owners.

Tina's also a good person to come home from an event with, win or lose. Once I had two show jumps in hand over her at Burgie on Jurassic Rising and I fell off and she won on Archrival. I'd have had fewer faults if I'd knocked everything over! Everyone kept ringing Tina on the way home and I had to listen to her telling them what had happened over and over again.

Of course, even while I was on a high from having had two successful three-day events, I knew I would have to come crashing down somewhere. My next outing was with Rocky to Bramham for his first attempt at three-star level, and we had two hiccups on the cross-country, which was demoralising. The problem was that he found it difficult to shorten his stride in front of a fence and so, when he found himself meeting it wrong, would have to stop.

The prospect of my first senior championships preoccupied me that summer. I felt sure that I was finally going to make it because, as the championships were in England, we had twelve places available on the squad. My friends William Fox-Pitt and Tina were dead certs for the team, and I was desperate to join them.

This was the first year when Lottery funding was awarded to

eventers, and that summer I was on the elite rider squad for the first time. We were all means-tested for Lottery funding, the money was given out monthly and, in return, we had to do a certain amount of paperwork to account for how it was spent. At the time, my husband William and I were lucky enough to have backing from British Equestrian Insurance Brokers, who took over when Modern Alarms eventually pulled out of sponsoring me because Tom Buffet, who was Raymond's contact, had left. The chief executive of BEIB, Captain Adrian Pratt, lived near my parents. He is a Jockey Club steward and has horses in training in Sussex with Richard Rowe. We've had many a good day's racing with him, not only locally at Fontwell and Plumpton but also at Cheltenham. The BEIB package wasn't huge, though, so the Lottery funding was a bonus, helping me to buy the new lorry I had needed and also to repay, over a couple of years, the money that some of my owners had kindly lent me. These loans had been a great help, but also a worry because I hate owing people money, and so the Lottery funding relieved a lot of that pressure.

I was thrilled to feel part of the British team regime at last. It was a good crew – Giles Rowsell, who was a wonderful *chef d'équipe* in my young rider days, was hugely popular; he was open and friendly, and a good leader who gave the team confidence.

I was also now receiving help from Chris Bartle, the team dressage trainer, and I found him wonderful. The most memorable piece of advice he gave me, which is something I still say to my own pupils and try to keep in my own brain, is that if the rider is tight and stiff when riding dressage it has the same effect on the horse as a tight pair of jeans would have on a gymnast. It's a great image and one which helps to relax me.

Sadly, after so much expectation, the final selection trial, at

Thirlestane Castle in Scotland, was an abysmal experience, probably because I let the pressure get to me. The water complex was a flowing stream, with the water running quite quickly, and, unusually for him, Henry just didn't want to jump into it and refused. I was feeling very nervous and didn't ride it well. I was so annoyed with myself, because the episode cast enough doubt on my performance to put me in the second six riders for Burghley, instead of the first six, out of which the championship team would be chosen.

It was during team training at Badminton House that we learned the shocking news that Diana, Princess of Wales, had been killed. After that, everything took place in a completely surreal atmosphere, and the following weekend at Blenheim – thankfully, I wasn't riding there that year – cross-country day was held on the Sunday out of respect for her funeral. The weird mood there was made far worse when an Irish rider, Sam Moore, was killed on the cross-country. I didn't know him well, but obviously we were all terribly shocked and felt awful for his family and all the Irish riders who had come over.

The one thing Henry and I needed after our disappointment at Thirlestane was a fun run around an intermediate track, but we had all been told not to run our horses again. I was therefore pretty annoyed when I saw William Fox-Pitt riding Cosmopolitan at Highclere – it suddenly seemed to me personally that the system wasn't fair. I felt that we should have been allowed to prepare for Burghley in the way that we knew most suited our particular horses. In those days, an issue like this was enough to put me in quite the wrong frame of mind to start an event, and I went into the Europeans with completely the wrong mental approach.

Thanks to Ruth and the additional input from Chris Bartle, Henry produced his best dressage test and I was well placed for an individual medal. But then disaster overtook us depressingly early on the cross-country. Henry left a leg behind at a wiggly log coming out of the famous Leaf Pit drop combination at the start of the course and I was unseated. I had struggled desperately to stay in the plate, but just as I was regaining my seat he moved the wrong way and I fell off. It seemed such a silly mishap that it was then difficult to think positively about the rest of the course, but Henry jumped around brilliantly, just like the year before.

I was shattered, but at the same time being given my senior Union Jack was a special moment because I knew that this was for life – you can wear it for ever and nothing can take it away. Henry will always be a special horse for getting me that.

There was quite a bit of drama on the cross-country that year; a Canadian rider called Claire Smith had a bad fall at the Leaf Pit, which caused a long hold-up, and Karen O'Connor was among the other casualties. Next day, the trot-up was dramatic, as Philip Dutton's horse was spun, which put out the Australian team, and both Germany's Bettina Overesch (later Hoy) and William Fox-Pitt's horses were sent to the holding box. They were lying in second and third places individually behind Toddy on Broadcast News and Britain's team gold medal hinged on Cosmopolitan passing.

Both horses were let through, though, and so Bettina became European Champion while Toddy was overall Open Champion and the British team (Mary, Ian, Chris Bartle and William) won the gold medal. This was a happy result which, I think, laid some ghosts for Mary, Ian and William, who had all been through a rough time at the Olympics the previous year.

Another result that gave me real pleasure was Tina's European bronze medal; she had just missed out on a team place with General Jock and, the year before, she'd been in the lead at Burghley, only to drop down the order with fences down. This time she show jumped clear and, as we sat and watched the last horses together, we got more and more excited as she moved up the order and got closer and closer to a medal. I was thrilled for her, but also frustrated for myself: I knew that if I hadn't had that annoying fall – a ridiculous unseating, not even a proper fall – I'd have got a medal too.

The season ended with a dreadful trip to Boekelo with Rocky and Tramp. I had a disastrous cross-country ride on Tramp, which came as a shock after his previous performances – I am convinced that it was because he was already feeling uncomfortable as a result of the problems that were to hamper his career. I felt terrible for Anne Burnet because I knew she had high hopes for the horse, as I did myself. Then it rained and rained, and I sat in the lorry and dreaded my round on Rocky. I felt so negative that I couldn't see how I was going to ride the track. Mum, Becky and Kenneth Clawson, who was to become the British team jumping trainer, tried to encourage me. They said: 'Don't be so stupid – look at the results you've had, that should give you confidence.' But it didn't; I hadn't got a shred of self-belief.

Despite my woeful mood, Rocky did go clear, but he struck into himself and was sore. My former junior team-mate Polly Phillipps (neé Martin), who was by now a qualified vet, lasered the injury to try to help me get it right for Sunday morning's trot-up. Rocky did come sound, but you could see that it was quite a nasty cut, and of course the ground jury sent us to the holding box to await reinspection when they saw it. Rocky has always been a bit of a shiverer and so, when the vet prodded his wound, he lifted his hind leg so high, as if he was in serious pain; I pointed out that he would react in the same way if the other leg was touched, but I still wasn't allowed to continue in the competition.

I was now back to a state of gloom and doom. It was nothing to do with the horses, it was how I felt about myself. I still blame myself when something goes wrong with a horse, but at that stage I couldn't accept that there might have been a reason for a horse going badly other than myself.

The only thing that went right that autumn was that I had a new generation of star youngsters. I had won both the four- and five-year-old finals of the Burghley Young Event Horse series on Midnight Magic and Jurassic Rising. Those two, along with Primmore's Pride, who didn't make the final because he had ringworm, were giving me a lot to look forward to.

Denise and Roger Lincoln had bought Midnight Magic at the High Performance sale along with Primmore's Pride ('Kiri'). I saw the picture of Kiri in the sale catalogue and he looked a cracking foal; everyone was interested in him. He was bred in Somerset by Roger and Joanna Day out of their successful Badminton mare Primmore Hill (herself by the top eventing sire Ben Faerie) by Toddy's New Zealand Thoroughbred stallion Mayhill. As the Lincolns were successful in bidding for Kiri, on whom Roger Day had bravely put a pretty high reserve, they felt it was only fair to buy a foal to run along with him as companion, so they bought Midnight Magic. He was then called Warmington Replica and was bred by Fiona Wilson by Pulsingh out of Lucy, a hunter mare owned by Michael Clayton, the former editor of *Horse & Hound*. As the Lincolns were into 'Magic' names then, and he was black, he became Midnight Magic.

These two babies both came to me as two-year-olds to break – and they just kept growing! Both horses are now over 17 hands. As I'm under 5 feet 6 inches I felt I wouldn't be able to break them in myself if they kept getting bigger and stronger. Nini, who was particularly good at breaking, helped me a lot with them.

Anne Burnet bought Jurassic Rising as a foal from Yorkshire. He was by Primitive Rising, a foremost sire of event horses, and was bred by Diedre and Bob Walker. Anne kept Jurassic Rising at home and I started riding him as a four-year-old.

That winter I was invited to New Zealand, to ride in the annual fun novice invitation class at the Puhinui three-day event outside Auckland. A big group of us came over from Europe: three Swedes, two French, Ian, Mary and myself. Tanya Cleverley came too, as a commentator – it was around the time she got together with the New Zealand rider Dan Jocelyn – and, of course, the Todds, Andrew Nicholson, Blyth Tait and Paul O'Brien had all gone home so they were there too. It was a really good time.

The Swedish rider Paula Tornqvist has had a fascinating career. She began her sporting career as a gymnast, then she was an Olympic skier, and finally, having never ridden, after being taken hunting she decided that she'd like to try eventing. She had a wonderful horse called Monaghan, a great big Irish Draught who just kept galloping. She is also a full-time professional pilot – though, having watched her manoeuvre a Land Rover and trailer, I'm not sure I want to fly with her! At Puhinui one night we were having drinks in the lorry park when Paula decided to entertain us with her gymnastic prowess; she did an amazing series of back flips down the lorry ramp, over a car and back again. We couldn't believe it.

Puhinui is a key event for the home-based New Zealand riders, who have a more restrictive calendar than us, and so for them to lend a precious horse to a foreigner was very generous. The visitors spent a day trying a lot of horses and I decided on a chestnut horse who was a very good jumper. We jumped a double clear, but the dressage wasn't very good though we did manage to contribute towards winning the fun team competition.

Afterwards we all became tourists for a spell. We stayed with Wally Neiderer, the New Zealand team vet, and his wife Karin, who kept us well entertained. Wally lent us his speedboat and we took it out on a lake for some water-skiing. Having got to the far end of the lake, we ran out of petrol. All we had were two tiny little oars and we just had to row and row. We thought we'd never get back, but then we spotted some lumberjacks on the hill that ran down to the shore. When the Swedish rider Anna Hilton shouts she has a voice like a foghorn; amazingly, the lumberjacks heard her hollering over the noise of their chainsaws and they came to rescue us.

We also had a fantastic day out on Lake Taupo with Kit and Gee Davidson, who are friends of Toddy's. We had a picnic on their boat and wonderful fishing – and another empty-tank incident: on the way home, Wally's Range Rover ran out of diesel, which reduced us all to hysterics.

New Zealand was a wonderful, carefree interlude. That winter, in fact, I was very spoiled, as one day after I got home William and I set off for Barbados for a holiday. We stayed with a great friend Sue Peacock, who used to own jumpers with William, and she really got me going with the water-skiing. I would get up at 6.30 a.m. and go out while no one was watching. It was a fantastic holiday and we became very torn between Barbados, which we love, and skiing, a sport we had only recently discovered.

We first went to the Alps with Lizzie Bunn and her husband

Nick Brown, to Courchevel 1650. Though I now love skiing, like many eventers I'm always nervous about it, worrying about breaking bones before the start of the season. Nick and Lizzie, who are great mates and who got married in the same year as us, had been several times before, which was reassuring. None the less, on the first morning, when we stupidly skied with them instead of having lessons, we were crashing into everything. We got on a chairlift, which seemed to go on up the mountain for ever, and when we got to the top Lizzie sheepishly admitted that we were at the top of a red run. I felt pretty green, but William was braver than me; his method was to go headlong and then stop himself by wiping out. We must have fallen over forty times, and by the end we were crying with laughter. It was the start of our great love for skiing and, with the aid of some lessons, we picked it up quite quickly.

Skiing is just like riding in that confidence and mental attitude count for a great deal — and back home my attitude was about to get a great boost, thanks to Lottery funding. Despite my unfortunate time at Burghley, I was still on the elite squad that winter, and I was invited to take Henry to a training session at Stoneleigh in January 1998. One of the conditions for receiving Lottery money is that riders are expected to take advice from specially appointed people like nutritionists, physiotherapists — and sport psychologists. Giles Rowsell had therefore invited a sport psychologist called Nicky Heath to come and give a talk one evening during this session. It was to change my life.

Sport psychology was pretty new then and most riders felt it was completely unnecessary; in fact, all my friends thought it was hideously embarrassing and gave it a wide berth. But I wasn't embarrassed; I just pricked up my ears. I have always been open-minded to suggestions because I feel that if anything, however minute, can help me, it's a bonus. At that stage I would have been grateful for anything that could have improved my attitude. So, after listening intently to Nicky's lecture, I went up to Giles and said that I would be prepared to be a guinea pig for sport psychology.

When I got home I mentioned it to William. He said: 'I've been saying for years that you should see a shrink!' He did, however, think it was a sensible idea, as he was aware that I had a problem with nerves and confidence.

Soon after that I went to see Nicky, who lives nearby. The first thing she did was get out a wad of paper – a huge questionnaire. I said she could chuck that in the bin straight away, because the last questionnaire I filled in told me I should be a bus conductor and was a waste of time. Instead we opened a bottle of wine.

On reflection, I don't think it was the fact that Nicky was a sport psychologist that eventually brought about such a miraculous transformation in me. I think it was that she was a completely different person who hadn't been connected with any of my disasters. She had no preconceived ideas about my riding or my mental state, and she didn't know anything about me or my history. Therefore, although I am anyway generally an open person and prepared to admit to my weaknesses, I was really able to talk to her.

Nicky wanted me to talk her through my whole system – what I did every day at home, how my marriage was, what my house was like and how I trained my horses. From there she moved to asking me about the system I used at a one-day event when I might be riding five horses in a day – what I thought, how I prepared for it – and then how this differed from the procedure at a major event.

She was very quick to get to the heart of my problems which

were, in essence, thinking too much: paralysis by analysis.

I told Nicky that at one-day events when I've got several horses to ride and a hectic schedule, my results tend to be very good. But at a three-day event with one horse, when I am normally used to riding ten horses a day at home, suddenly there's so much time to think; and I'll think far too much. I still do. I didn't have a problem with the dressage, I told her, because I'd conquered my nerves there through Barnaby. But I found myself telling her that on cross-country day I always woke up with vibes, and they were mostly bad ones. I would convince myself before I'd started that it would be a bad day. I've never taken drugs so I don't know what it's like to be stoned, but I certainly didn't feel with it on cross-country morning at an important event. I would feel physically sick before and after riding, and suffer from desperate headaches afterwards.

Nicky explained that all those symptoms occur when you suffer from too much nervousness. Everyone should have nerves to a certain extent, in order to perform well, but too many and the endorphins the brain produces trigger chemical reactions in the body which in turn produce these symptoms. This explanation alone helped me, because it showed there were physical reasons for what I was feeling, whereas previously I had thought I was a one-off. I know everyone says they felt sick, but I thought no one could feel as bad as me, so fearful.

I told Nicky that I used to walk courses with fellow competitors and mates and, if they were concerned about a certain fence, I would suddenly have their problems weighing on my mind, even if the fence hadn't previously been a worry for me. And if I was worried about a fence, I would go up to someone like Toddy and ask him what he thought – in eventing everyone is friendly and quick to help and share information, which is what is so great about the sport. But then, instead of just sticking to what Toddy thought, I'd have to go and find Ian or Lucinda or Mary and ask them too. Everyone would say something completely different so that at the end of it I didn't know whether I was coming or going. The fences that worried me would cause me a sleepless night. All the obstacles would grow out of all proportion overnight; the ditches would get deeper and wider as I lay sleepless. So, in my mind, I was making the course unjumpable before I'd started.

The other thing I told Nicky was that I was puzzled as to why my first course walk was always the best one. For my fellow competitors, the more often they walked it, the more jumpable the course became, whereas I'd be quite happy the first time. It was only afterwards that it got worse and worse. Nicky immediately pointed out that the first time you walk a course you're still three days from jumping it and your nerves haven't come into the equation; you've got a clear head. She made me realise that the first walk has to be the most important, so ever since I have tried to walk all the big tracks entirely on my own at first so that I'm not distracted by different views.

My second walk would be with Mark Phillips; he is a very good trainer, and after our brush over his comments about me in *Horse & Hound* he had been very kind and helpful and would give me cross-country advice. Since he began training the American team, though, my companion on the second walk has usually been our team manager, Yogi Breisner. The principle is that this second walk person must be someone whose opinion I respect; the difference now is that I don't then follow it up by going and asking loads of other people what to do.

For the final, third walk I concentrate on my own again.

Nicky taught me mental games for course-walking. She advised me that, if I find a fence I'm concerned about, instead of thinking of all the problems I've had at this type of fence before, I should think about the many times I've jumped it well. She taught me only to let a fence enter my head in a positive way; to think: 'I'm not going to let anything go wrong here because I've jumped it successfully fifteen times before.' Everything was geared to finding a positive slant.

All this advice gave me a new system to go by for course-walking. What's more, Nicky's reiteration of the phrase 'paralysis by analysis' made me realise that I mustn't let myself drift into thinking about the cross-country course when I was on my own. So I started playing a computer game of Snakes; nowadays it's Go Hamster Go, on my mobile phone.

Another problem that I had was being so panicky that I wouldn't be able to find things on cross-country morning, like gloves or my hairnet. They were, of course, always in the same place, but I'd be in such a state that I couldn't think straight. Nicky advised me that I must organise enough time for myself to get everything organised in a pile, and that I must give myself time to focus. So now I get everything ready together, and I don't let my mind drift on to the course. After I've got changed, I sit down and ride the course in my mind in a positive way, visualising jumping every fence very well. This seems to put my mind at rest. The process is getting easier, but I still find I have to be disciplined not to let my mind drift. This is hard, because your brain seems instinctively to want to play tricks on you.

Nicky asked me about my routine in the ten-minute box before cross-country at a major event. I said that on the biggest tracks I'd get on the horse and 'razz it up', tickling it with a stick or spurs before setting off. When she asked if I did this at a one-day event, I admitted that I didn't, so she pointed out that straight away I was giving the horse the message that something was completely different. Now on the big occasions I behave much more calmly when I get on the horse.

I also found myself telling Nicky that I had a tendency to over-ride the first few fences. Then I'd get a hang-up about thinking I mustn't interfere with the horse, so instead of trying to adjust the stride I'd just let the horse take the next fence on a flyer and, as a consequence, frighten myself. All the time there was an inconsistency in the way I rode.

Nicky said: 'If you ride a fence badly but you get to the other side all right, just bin those negative thoughts. Don't think about what happened or what went wrong at the previous fence – that's over and done with; instead think about keeping a rhythm. If you find your mind drifting as you're riding around, focus on something like how the horse feels underneath you.' The idea was that I must think about anything that would distract me from self-punishment and retrograde thought.

Through Lottery funding, we had other team talks. Another psychologist gave us an example of how terminology can affect you. He gave the example of some world-class skiers whose trainer had told them they mustn't do such and such going into a turn. They complained: 'This terminology isn't helping; try telling us what we should be doing, not what we shouldn't.' In other words, I *should* try to turn instruction into a positive, not a negative: to begin my instructions to myself with 'do' instead of 'don't'.

In another talk we were told about the importance of rehydration. I do drink a lot of water on a daily basis at home because it's easy and on tap. But in the lorry there isn't drinking water to hand and I now realise that I was getting dehydrated at events. Dehydration has an effect on your mental sharpness and reaction times. Now I'm much more aware of the need to drink water and carry far more bottles of it in the lorry.

Until now, I just hadn't been aware of any of this. All these little things have helped me approach my competing in a different way; and, curious as it may seem, having developed these systems, I never again woke up with the dreaded vibes.

I had three or four more sessions with Nicky that spring, and in May 1998 she came down to Badminton to help. For once, I was not so much terrified as excited. I wasn't plagued by that awful crippling fear and I felt much more relaxed. I knew that I had a system in my head – just like I have a basic system for training a horse or even cooking supper – and, finally, that it was a comforting system that would help me deal with my demons.

On the Friday night I slept better than I'd ever done on the eve of cross-country. The next morning, I sorted all my stuff into an organised pile and went through the course in my head in a positive way. Henry had done a good dressage test and so I set off across country feeling competitive. I was actually enjoying my ride – and then it all went tragically wrong.

About three fences from home, on a flat galloping stretch, I just felt Henry give way underneath me. He had broken down, gone irreparably lame. This is a horrendous feeling on a horse, like hitting a brick wall; it is probably like having a blow-out on two tyres in a car – except, of course, that a horse is not a machine. Henry had broken down in the middle of doing something he absolutely loved; the trouble was that he was such a bold jumper that he never saved himself.

I pulled up immediately and waited helplessly for the horse ambulance. I think many of the spectators were confused at my sudden departure. We were all absolutely shattered; it was awful for the Jewsons and for Nini, who looked after him.

Henry was taken to the veterinary hospital at Cambridge, where he was found to have two seriously ruptured front tendons. With hindsight, he should perhaps have been put down straight away. But Andy Bathe, who was the British team vet, was also Sarah Jewson's vet; he knew the horse well and between them they decided that they wanted to do everything they could to save him. Sarah adored Henry, and he had been such a little personality in the sport. Because he was small and skewbald, everyone loved him and his expressive way of going. The road to his recovery was terribly hard and he has never been ridden again; but, because he was half pony, it wasn't like retiring a Thoroughbred who wouldn't do well out at grass. He is still alive, acting as a companion to young horses, and is very much part of the Jewson family.

After Badminton, Nicky, who has herself competed in dressage, admitted to me that she had had no idea how much the sport involved mentally. She said that the whole experience had been an eye-opener for her: that she realised that however hard you worked to get things right, there were still a myriad elements that could go wrong. For me, Henry's breakdown was one of my worst eventing moments ever; it made me realise that losing a competition means nothing in comparison to losing a horse. I shed a lot of tears over the next few weeks.

Normally, after Badminton, I would have been really looking forward to my weekend at Punchestown. But the trauma over Henry, combined with a far worse human tragedy, completely overshadowed the weekend. A few weeks before Badminton, on Easter Monday, an Irish rider called David Foster had been killed at a one-day event. His horse had flipped over some rails into water and landed on him; by the time he arrived at hospital he was dead.

David was not only the most lovely person – a hugely popular character in the sport and Ireland's best-known rider – he was also a seriously good horseman. His death really shook a lot of the top riders, bringing home to them, perhaps for the first time, the risks of the sport. It also seriously unhinged many of the male riders' wives, because David left behind a wife, Sneezy, and three young children.

The first person in England Sneezy rang was David Green, who was a great friend. The news went around the close-knit English eventing community like wildfire and, because the funeral was two days later, everyone embarked on frantic arrangements to get to Ireland. People made a huge effort. Some drove the length and breadth of England to catch ferries, and when Andrew and Jayne Nicholson missed the boat at Holyhead, they chartered a tiny plane in order to get there in time. Tina and I flew over together; we had been in such a rush that we managed to arrive with not a bean between us, but the show jumper Edward Doyle, a good friend of William's, kindly picked us up from the airport and took us to lunch.

I think there were about a thousand people at the funeral; the entire international eventing community seemed to be there, and I have never seen so many people so broken up. It was very moving, and we all just felt desperate for Sneezy, who got through it with amazing dignity.

So Punchestown didn't feel right at all. I remembered that it was only the previous year that David and Becky Coffey had got everyone singing in the canteen. I was in such a state about Henry that I spent a lot of time on the phone checking he was still alive; there were complications with his treatment and I was frequently in tears. For once, partying was out of the question; I felt very anti-social and kept myself to myself in the lorry, only seeing my family. It was another case of picking myself up after a big knock and trying to keep myself channelled, and it was not a good time.

I was riding Rocky. He did a very good dressage test and we went well across country, until a combination fence where the distance was quite short for him, and he left a leg behind. I remember seeing a photo of the incident and I don't know how we stayed together. After that awkward moment, we had a stupid run-out at the ditch in the middle of a coffin two fences from home. But even then, because of our good dressage, we were, frustratingly, still in eleventh place; it was another case of 'if only'.

Tina not only had to put up with me being gloomy, she then had a bad fall and her leg got squashed against a fence. We later found out that it was fractured, but she was desperate to get a qualification for her other horse and so she still show jumped. And, then, of course, I had to drive all the way home.

There was more bad news to come when I got there. Each year the Lottery funding is reviewed in May. I was shell-shocked by the speed with which a letter arrived at home after that year's review telling me that my funding had been withdrawn. Every penny helps in eventing, and this was a serious blow. Also, the Olympics, that big elusive holy grail for all sportspeople, was only two years away, but now it seemed that I didn't have a horse in sight. Once again, I was out of the picture.

That summer a new competition was devised at Hickstead by Dougie Bunn and Paul Schockemohle: it was a Grand Prix in which eventers would compete against show jumpers, and because William and I were such good friends with Lizzie Bunn, of course we both received invitations to compete.

There was a lot of talk and excitement, not least because the show jumpers would have to ride a dressage test, which formed the first part of the contest. Then there was a jumping course which would incorporate some of Hickstead's famous feature fences, like the Derby Bank and Devil's Dyke, and would also contain knock-down 'cross-country' fences outside the arena in Dougie's back garden.

I decided to ride The Tourmaline Rose, who was a bold and accurate jumper, and I let William ride Rocky. If I'd known what Rocky was to achieve later, William certainly wouldn't have been allowed the ride!

The dressage was very amusing. William can do fast trot and slow trot, but he hasn't got a clue where the letters go around the arena or where he is meant to be going next. It was quite difficult to teach him and, in hindsight, the dressage test used at Hickstead was far too difficult for the show jumpers and was rather unfair. William's only other experience of riding a test was on a young novice horse of Bar Hammond's – and on that occasion he had got so confused that the judge had had to get out of her car and spend ten minutes explaining where he had gone wrong. But this time he had to learn the test – we weren't allowed to shout it out – and he actually did very well. I must say that he also looked pretty good in the kit – he borrowed Eddy Stibbe's topper and tails, which were in a rather sweaty state after a number of different-shaped men had been in and out of them.

The contest itself took place in an atmosphere of huge hilarity. Everyone entered into the spirit of the competition, and one of the funniest incidents was when the show jumper Piet Raymakers got away with riding two horses. He had two similar-looking chestnuts, one of which he reckoned was good at dressage, so he rode that one first and then switched to the better jumper. He was still last after the dressage.

The course, which was designed by Robert Lemieux, was fairly imposing for the eventers and there were a lot of accuracy questions. It amazes me how many event horses become shell-shocked by the Hickstead arena and won't go near some of the fences – in fact some of them got pretty wild. The class was tailor-made for Rosie, though, and we were the only ones to have a clear round so we won, even though we did have a run-out coming back through the water into the arena: fortunately run-outs didn't count, only knock-downs.

The BBC commentary on William's round was great. He knocked down so many fences that when he came to jump the Irish Bank, Stephen Hadley said: 'With any luck he'll do us a favour and knock this down too.' But, in a funny way, I think it was the turning point of Rocky's career.

By now, Rainbow Magic – Sam – was really my best hope of ever getting back into the big time because Tramp's soundness problems had become evident. Sam went well in the British Open at Gatcombe to finish fourth and then went on to be fifth at Blenheim. Meanwhile, I took Rocky to Burghley, his first four-star event, despite the fact that we hadn't technically achieved a clear round at a three-star yet. It was just his good dressage that had given him adequate results to qualify.

Although I had made progress mentally, and was doing my best to hang on to Nicky's instructions and think positively, Burghley was yet again a disaster and I pulled Rocky up on the cross-country. As I did so, I managed to salvage the mildly cheering thought that I could still take him to the three-star at Achselschwang in Germany because Tina was going. She hadn't got on to the team either, so we were both in the same boat. It would be a long journey, on which we could relax and chat, and we thought a trip to one of our favourite events would do us good. The idea was to make it a holiday to the

Munich Beer Festival, with the three-day event being a secondary interest. We had both pretty much had it with horses.

Here again Rocky did a very good dressage test – and then the same thing happened. He tried to make up too much ground in a combination fence, I couldn't shorten him in time and he stopped. All my rides on him had actually been good – it wasn't as if they were scratchy rides – but always one little thing would go wrong and it would be yet another wasted opportunity.

By now quite a lot of people – including Tina – were saying to me: 'Why on earth do you keep riding that great big goat of a horse? He's far too big for you.' Part of me was inclined to agree – but, for some reason, something kept me hanging in there.

6

Triumph and Tragedy

Although 1999 was a year of a great personal triumph and breakthrough for me, it was also, sadly, probably the worst period in the history of the sport.

The season was under a cloud from the start when it gradually leaked out to us all that Polly Phillipps's team horse Coral Cove had failed a dope test at the previous autumn's World Equestrian Games in Rome. This was hugely embarrassing; it meant Britain would probably be disqualified and, along with the bronze medal they had 'won', our all-important qualification as a nation for eventing at the Sydney Olympics in 2000 would be lost.

Henry had not been the only potential British team horse to go out of commission for that championships – none of the horses from the gold medal team at Burghley in 1997, those ridden by Mary King, William Fox-Pitt, Ian Stark and Chris Bartle, had been available either, due to a catalogue of injury. After continual setbacks, Giles was faced with a terrible struggle actually to get a team together. It was, therefore, considered a wonderful result when Nigel Taylor, Gary Parsonage, Karen Dixon and Polly won a team bronze medal behind the Kiwis and French and, at that stage, ahead of the Americans – and it was Polly's good performance that had clinched the medal.

The powers that be decided that Polly should appeal to the FEI (International Equestrian Federation, the governing body) against the test findings. In hindsight, this was perhaps a mistake, because of course it didn't work: a positive dope test is pretty irrevocable, and so it was announced in the spring that Britain had lost the medal and the Olympic qualification. The ensuing bitterness was awful. All this caused much lorry-park debate, in fact it became an all-consuming topic, even though – or perhaps in part because – no one knew what had really happened. And we never will. It became known as 'the Coral Cove affair' and, as the hearing had taken place just before Badminton, it overshadowed the event's fiftieth anniversary celebrations.

On a personal level, I was struggling too: I had no horse for the Sydney Olympics and, in fact, as far as I could see, no horse to ride at top level ever again.

Emma and I had long chats about whether we should try Rocky at Badminton; I was keen to have one final crack of the whip with him there, but I did realise that if this was a flop Emma should ask a man to take him over. It was frustrating because Rocky and I were still being placed on his three-star runs, but with a silly incident each time, and we knew that if only all the phases could come together at the same event he had a good chance of winning a major competition.

So I went to Badminton with quite an open mind as to what would happen next, still trying to help myself by using the mental systems that Nicky Heath had taught me. Nicky had instilled in me the need to work on my strengths more than my weaknesses because that was the only way I would grow in confidence. So we took the same approach with Rocky, making his training at home easier for him. William helped me a lot with Rocky's jumping, building courses based on different distances so that he had to learn to adjust his great big stride. We would pull all the ground-lines (poles in front of fences which act as a guide to take-off) further out to help him find the right take-off point and we left the distances longer, which he liked. This improved his technique because he was being asked to do something he found easier, and therefore he grew in confidence. As a result, Rocky's whole jumping technique started to change; he became more careful and softer to ride.

For myself, I had to work on just sitting still on him and not trying to fiddle with his stride. This went against my instincts, but I knew that if I tried to argue with him, he would shut down, lose his co-ordinated, balanced canter action and start to 'run'. This whole process was a big breakthrough in Rocky's progress and, subconsciously, I began to pin all my hopes on him.

As Rocky is syndicate-owned, whenever he ran I would be followed by a huge entourage of people who have become known as the Barmy Army – Emma and her husband Andrew Pitt, Emma's parents Di and David Lewthwaite, and all their friends and relations. Whenever Rocky was competing, the area around my lorry would turn into a car park. This is what was so special about Rocky: the fact that he brought a large family of people together. He meant the world to them and I like to think that, in return, they've had wonderful fun out of his participation in the sport. It was great for me to have so much support and to be able to give so many people pleasure when things went well. However, the downside was that the bad days made me feel I was letting even more people down than usual.

Another controversy in the sport this year was that the FEI was trying out a new scoring system intended to make things simpler and give more importance to cross-country performance. There were to be no fractions in the dressage scoring, a time fault for every second over the time across country and forty penalties for a stop. However, the bigger scores that resulted meant the field became strung out and people started feeling under pressure to go too fast to catch up. Also, because the show-jumping phase wasn't changed in line with the other elements, the end result was often a ludicrous gap on the final day – in fact at Badminton Ian Stark ended up with four fences in hand to win (fortunately he had only one down).

This, on top of the Coral Cove row, combined with the fact that the course designer Hugh Thomas had roped the Badminton cross-country course very tightly to try to slow us down and influence the optimum time that year, saw complaints at an unusually high level. There is always a certain amount of nervous wittering at major events and riders will usually find something to complain about, but this Badminton got off to an unusually bad start.

Rocky did a very good dressage test and at the end of the phase was lying second behind the Canadian rider Stuart Black on Market Venture. This meant I had it all to play for but, fortunately, with my new-found calmness, I didn't feel under too much pressure. Instead, I had the relaxed feeling that anything could happen for, despite the previous hiccups, Rocky was not a chicken across country. He is a brave horse and I was confident that he had the scope to jump the fences. My only worry was what might happen if he found himself in a situation where he had to dig himself out of trouble at a fence; Rocky is not the sort of horse you could describe as having a 'fifth leg'.

Cross-country day began dry but finished in a quagmire; it rained and rained. It was a classic example of a competition which splits into two. Many riders' results directly followed from the luck of the draw – Ian and Toddy, who finished first and second on their young horses, were right at the start of the day; they didn't even complete on their second horses. I was drawn in the middle, by which time the rain was tipping down, and with the already tight turns now slippery too, it was the worst possible type of cross-country course for the conditions.

But I felt confident because Rocky loved the mud from his hunting days with the Grafton. I was drenched by the ceaseless rain, but I had the most fantastic ride across country – until we came to the Lake, which required a bounce in, three strides to a jetty in the middle of the water, and a bounce back into the water again. The rain made the water deeper – after this Badminton, a new rule was created to reduce the maximum depth permitted in water – and though Rocky bounced in brilliantly, the depth of water affected his stride. He landed all wrong on the jetty and sprawled on top of the jump there rather than clearing it: so we earned a ruinous forty penalties.

He went on to finish the course brilliantly, but I was gutted because, again, we'd been unlucky. The new forty penalties for a stop appeared to put us way out of the reckoning. But only twenty-four horses completed the event – an unacceptable result by modern-day standards – and many of those running at the end of the day retired. So bad was the wreckage of cross-country day that our clear show-jumping round on Sunday miraculously brought Rocky and me up to sixth place.

There was considerable fall-out in the sport after Badminton. PERA (the Professional Event Riders Association) asked Hugh Thomas, who was at that time also chairman of the FEI Eventing Committee, to a meeting to discuss our dissatisfaction with the scoring and things became really quite aggressive. What with that and the continuing Coral Cove saga – complicated by the fact that Polly had been a worrying casualty at Badminton, suffering a frightening fall after a bad mistake at a bounce fence – the atmosphere in the sport was unsettled, to say the least.

But, for me, ironically, this was the start of a new, positive era. I was put on the longlist for the European Championships, and I was over the moon. Badminton was followed by a successful Punchestown. I took Sarah and Richard Jewson's General Salute ('Nobby'), from whom I had had an awful fall at Weston Park (when I was knocked unconscious under the water but fortunately the paramedics were at that fence to drag me out, and he won the two-star section there). Nobby was a lovely grey horse that I'd been riding for two years; he'd come out of racing and had been bought from Susie Wales, who was married to my Norfolk friend Wally's father. Nobby was a lovely type and a great jumper, and it was a real thrill for the Jewsons when he won his first three-day event.

I also rode Nick and Barbara Walkinshaw's home-bred Walk On Top ('Meter') in the three-star section. He had previously been ridden by Andrew Nicholson, who had sent him to me the year before, mainly because he had a problem with his dressage that he thought I could sort out. I was excited about Meter because I'd known the Walkinshaws for years – I'd once stabled with them for a one-day event at Highclere and they'd been so kind and hospitable. They are lovely people and I knew they would be great to have as owners.

By Punchestown I'd worked hard on Meter's dressage and he finished a creditable thirteenth. He was strong for me, though, and you could tell he'd been ridden by Andrew because he was so quickly away from his fences. The moment he landed he'd be gone, and I would be quite relieved when we got to the next fence when he would come back to me.

But what could have been a refreshingly happy weekend was completely destroyed when on Sunday morning we heard the tragic news that Peta Beckett had been killed the day before riding a novice horse at Savernake Forest. Peta had got a last-minute call-up to ride as an individual at the 1998 World Games and this year, at Badminton the previous weekend, had been thrilled to go clear at her first attempt. I didn't know her that well, but she was a popular and beautiful girl – she used to be a model – and we felt desperate for her husband Mervyn and their two little children. Everyone felt very sick for the rest of the weekend and Nigel Taylor organised for all the British riders at Punchestown to wear black armbands.

Peta's funeral took place the following Friday, after which many riders made their way up to Chatsworth, where horse trials were being run for the first time since the late 1980s. Chatsworth is perhaps the most beautiful setting of all the horse trials and it was a restorative weekend after so much sadness. I was second behind Ian Stark in the CIC on Rainbow Magic and despite the generally sombre mood I couldn't but recall my happy days there on Barnaby when I was only eighteen.

But the happier interlude at Chatsworth turned out to be the calm before the storm. At Bramham a fortnight later, the Coral Cove saga, which had been threatening to boil over for a few weeks, finally erupted. It all came to a head in an aggressive meeting with riders demanding to know from the British Eventing board whether Polly was going to receive a ban; many people felt she had got away lightly, given that Britain's medal and Olympic qualification had both been lost with Coral Cove's positive dope test. FEI rules state that in these circumstances the rider is the 'person responsible', but in this case she seemed to have been exonerated. People got very angry because no one seemed to be given any answers, and the atmosphere was heated, to say the least.

Polly herself finished third in the competition, which was won by Leslie Law on Shear H_2O, and at the final press conference, which I attended because I was in fourth place on Rainbow Magic ('Sam'), a load of riders, headed by Toddy, suddenly came in at the back of the room and demanded that Polly explain herself. Polly couldn't really say anything and it was all hideously embarrassing. I knew that some members of the press felt she was being unfairly hounded and that things had gone too far – and they probably had; but the situation was not helped by the apparent reluctance of anyone in authority to seize hold of the problem.

I found it difficult to know what to say to Polly, whom I'd known since we competed against each other in Pony Club competitions. In many ways it boiled down to two sides – hers and Andy Bathe's – and I knew them both well, as Andy was married to my friend Charlotte and, as a promising vet, had a lot to lose. By this stage we knew that the Phillippses had asked him to treat Coral Cove for a sore back and he had injected Coral Cove with a small amount of painkiller. The same substance later showed up as a prohibited substance in the horse's urine during a routine dope test. After Bramham, both Andy and Giles Rowsell offered their resignations. Michael Allen, the chairman of British Eventing, stepped down too, and suddenly the sport in which I had thought I was finally making headway seemed in a shambles. I had been hanging on to the prospect of finally making it into a senior British team, but as I drove home from Bramham on that Sunday night I remember thinking that now none of us knew what was going on. Suddenly there was no team vet, no chairman, no *chef d'équipe* and no guarantee that, as a nation, we would get an eventing team to Sydney.

Sam's form was excellent at this stage and, with his Bramham placing following on from Blenheim the previous autumn, the Lincolns were excited about his future. He was lovely to ride in the dressage – if I told people he'd been naughty, they'd say: 'What, do you mean he twitched a whisker?' Yet I did have underlying concerns about whether he would possess enough speed for four-star level.

At the end of the month, another event rider was killed. We were at Chantilly, in the grounds of a chateau, at a beautiful event which, sadly, no longer runs. I led the first two phases on Sam, but we blew our chances with a couple of stops across country. Roger and Denise Lincoln were bitterly disappointed and I felt I had let the side down badly. But it soon seemed pretty irrelevant in the light of what had happened back in England while I'd been away: a young Australian rider called Robert Slade had died after a fall at Wilton horse trials that afternoon. I didn't know Robert well, but for his many connections who were all out at Chantilly it was a horrible long journey home across the Channel.

William and I were both invited back to compete in the Eventers' Grand Prix at Hickstead that summer. This time I borrowed Henke, a Grade A show jumper of William's, and got placed. William, despite his best efforts to be competitive, had another disaster. He rode a black stallion of Johnny Johnston's called Utopian Opposition who reared up in the dressage, prompting William to ask the judge if he could start again!

The next excitement was due to be the final team trial at Thirlestane Castle. Though it takes about eight hours to get to Thirlestane, it is a super event, very sociable and well worth the long drive. But this year it was derailed in the most ghastly circumstances.

On cross-country day, I was in the stables getting ready when I heard there was a hold-up on the course. Then someone mentioned that it was because Polly had had a bad fall with Coral Cove. A peculiar atmosphere descended – by this stage we were beginning to get slightly used to ominous waits – and, as we all milled around aimlessly, we heard the completely shocking news that Polly had been killed when her horse hit a fence and landed on her. After everything that had gone on, it was simply unbelievable. I was quite numb.

I wrote a long letter to Polly's husband Vere, but the circumstances were difficult and none of us really knew how to react. Because there had been so much hostility over the situation with Andy and the dope test, few people in the eventing community were welcomed by Vere at the funeral, which took place on a boiling hot day on the Friday of Burghley, an event at which Polly should have been competing.

The final trial was rerouted to Henbury Hall in Cheshire, where Rocky and I finished second behind Rodney Powell on Flintstone. I was stabled locally overnight before we were due to trot up in front of the selectors. To my horror, Rocky got loose early in the morning and went galloping up and down a long drive beside a field full of horses, who were going mad with excitement. He has always had escape-artist tendencies at events – it once took forty minutes to catch him at Thirlestane – but this time I was beside myself. I was just about to get into that final six riders for the European Championships and my horse had decided to kill himself! There was a main road at the end of the drive and it was only thanks to the loose horses that Rocky stayed in the drive. Eventually, a car drove in and blocked off Rocky's exit, but by this stage he had been galloping for twenty-five minutes and the selectors had specifically instructed us not to have done anything with our horses before the trot-up. Yet again, I was on the brink of my whole world going pear-shaped.

But all went well with the selectors, and it was with great excitement that I found myself included in the six riders going to the championships at Luhmühlen in Germany. Tina had been depressed because she'd had a stop at Henbury on The Gangster and thought she'd blown it, but she was in there too, plus Ian, who would be the most experienced team member, on Jaybee, his Badminton winner; the others were Katie Parker, Rodney and Jeanette Brakewell, who had earned her first Union Jack as an individual in Rome the year before.

First, though, we had Burghley to get through. It was a disaster. Sam's cross-country round fell to pieces, and then Meter had to be withdrawn after the steeplechase: he had strained a tendon again and these injuries would end his career. This was not a great morale boost, but again it was soon to be dwarfed by events: unbelievably, on the day after Polly's funeral, a fourth rider, Simon Long, died. He had a fall and his horse came down on top of him at a new sunken road fence where Blyth Tait also fell and broke his leg. We all saw it on the closed-circuit TV and just knew what had happened before we were told. It was another terrible day, especially dreadful for Simon's friends and family, and ghastly for all riders.

That night there was meant to be a party to celebrate the twenty-first anniversary of the Horse Trials Support Group, an organisation which raises funds for international teams and turns up to support us at overseas championships. Of course, no one felt like partying and the dancing was cancelled, but we got through it. The Princess Royal made a fantastic speech, encouraging the sport to keep its collective head. Somehow she managed to strike the right tone: sombre, yet rallying and eminently sensible.

This series of freak accidents shocked us all. We are all well aware of the risks we take in our sport, but to me it's more than a sport, it's a way of life. People get killed in car accidents, but that doesn't stop us from driving. However, as a rider I do try to do everything in my power to eliminate as many risks as possible. After a report looking into what had happened, there were new safety measures brought into the sport.

During Blenheim, team training took place – but, with so much at stake in getting the Olympic qualification (we had to finish as a team in the top three to get to Sydney), no one was allowed to compete in case there was a repeat of the stream of mishaps which had dogged British riders the previous season.

We left for Luhmühlen on the Sunday night. I travelled with Tina and we had our normal quota of drama. I'd been driving, at a rate which was definitely over the speed limit; we swapped places and Tina continued at exactly the same pace. Five minutes later she was hauled over by the police for speeding. But, being blonde and attractive, she got off with a light cash fine.

I have never felt pressure and nervousness like I did in Luhmühlen. The pressure on the whole team, in fact, was enormous, because it would have been unheard-of not to have had a British eventing team in the Olympics – this was what everyone was working towards and without it, for many of us, the whole pinnacle of the sport would have been lost.

There was a lot of speculation as to who would be picked for the team of four and who would be the two individual competitors. I felt quite relaxed at this stage, as I was sure I would be an individual and I didn't feel under nearly as much pressure as the likes of Ian and Tina, who were experienced and therefore dead certs for the team.

By this stage, in the wake of the Coral Cove fiasco, we had a new regime of officials, and the expectation weighed just as heavily on them. Mandy Stibbe had come to our rescue and taken over as chairman of selectors, with Bridget Parker, Lucinda Green and Angela Tucker as her fellow selectors. Jenny Hall, who works for a Lambourn practice and was well known in the sport, was our new team vet, and Chris Bartle, who had been unaffected by the upheavals, was still our dressage trainer with, on this occasion, more of a team manager's role. Our *chef d'équipe* was ex-SAS man Mike Kingscote, whom we nicknamed '0900 Hours' – with him, meetings couldn't take place at nine o'clock, they had to be at 0900 hours!

I owe a huge amount to Mandy for the turnaround in my career. She is a fantastic person who had been in the sport for many years as a rider and had represented first Britain and then, after her marriage to the Dutch rider Eddy Stibbe, the Netherlands. It was brave of her to take on the role of chairman of selectors because in more ways than one she was in a difficult position: for one thing, she had been on the British Eventing board during the Coral Cove drama; for another, she was young – younger than Ian, who had far more team experience than her – to be in a position of such responsibility. Having only just retired from active participation in the sport, Mandy was still very much one of us – and yet she managed to stamp her authority right from the start. We all adored her and wanted to do well as much for her sake as anything else.

My own debt to Mandy is rooted in the fact that she believed in me, and, so far, not many people in authority had done that. She had no choice but to come up with the goods that weekend in Luhmühlen, and her neck was on the line; yet she felt that Rocky's form and my dressage ability meant that, if the luck was to go our way, I could be in the medals. A lot of people questioned her judgement in picking me for the team, and some of the bitching that went on – mercifully far away back at home – was unnecessarily unpleasant, but still Mandy gave me that break.

The next hurdle was deciding the order in which we should ride. It was Jeanette Brakewell's first team as well, but it was decided that as she is so sensible and her horse Over To You was so good across country, she should be pathfinder. Tina was put second, I was third, the position in which I've been ever since, and Ian, as easily the most experienced, was anchorman, in fourth. We were a totally united team because of the pressure we were under, but there was a good spirit, and there has been in all the teams since. When I found out I was on the team, I was awash with nerves; but I was lucky in that William had come out to Luhmühlen, I had Tina with me, and my parents and Becky was there as reassurance. I also had the Barmy Army to support me, plus the Bunn family and several of my other owners, including the McIntyres.

The opening ceremony was held in the nearby town. It was very hot and the three of us women were sweltering in our Marks & Spencer air-hostess-type suits with scarves. We were also late and had to run down a cobbled street in high-heeled shoes. We then marched into the square in order of country and little children held up our national flags. The kid next to us passed out on the cobbled stones and hit her head, which was a bit dramatic, but could have been worse if we had allowed Ken Clawson to her rescue.

In the dressage I went into the lead, thanks to help from Chris and also a last-minute visit by Ruth during Blenheim, and the team was also in front. We knew, though, that this was only the preliminary – it was the cross-country that was looming large in all our minds. The course was typical of its maker, the renowned German designer Wolfgang Feld, with very big and technical fences; but all his distances were built on the long side, which suited Rocky. The first four fences were nice and inviting, then there was a daunting water complex. The quick route was up a mound over a pimple with a big drop in, up a step on to dry land, over a viaduct wall, back into water, up another step and a narrow fence with three strides to a big trakehner. There were plenty of places for it all to go wrong so, with the Sydney qualification in mind, team orders were for us all to take the slow route. It sounds chicken, but we had to give ourselves every chance of four clear rounds.

Tina and I decided we needed a good night's sleep before cross-country, so William and Tina's fiancé Phil Cook had to stay in the lorry. I couldn't sleep so I played on my computer game and followed Nicky's instructions, not letting my mind drift on to the course. I'd done everything she told me to do, and I'd walked the course on my own, but I still felt horrible, so sick. This was, at last, the chance I'd been waiting for and I mustn't cock it up. I told myself that it was time for my luck and Rocky's luck to change, and I did everything in my mental power to put the ghosts behind me.

It was an early start on Saturday morning. Poor Jeanette set off across country virtually in the dark and we all trooped out apprehensively to watch her. It had been a long time – ten years – since I'd been in young riders and had been part of a team abroad, but I suddenly realised that I wasn't the only one suffering from nerves; it was equally awful for all my supporters and for the rest of the team.

The whole day was a great team effort, but it was Jeanette on that dawn run who showed us that it was going to be possible. She was so calm and did brilliantly. Tina went really well too, and then it was my turn.

By this stage, I just wanted to get on with it. As the first two riders had gone well, there was no way I was going to be the one to let the team down. I was determined to do my bit. I'd been doing my mental tricks and was forcing myself to thinking positive; Mum kept herself busy by supplying everyone with sandwiches all day and William was helping in the ten-minute box. Chris briefed me as to how the course was riding and wished me luck, and William said: 'Get the hell out there and bloody well show them.'

I was relieved to get through the first water, but when you're riding these big tracks, you can't really think 'Thank God I've got through that' because then the next fence is upon you; you can't afford to relax and think how well it's going because you've got to be so sharp and ready for anything to be thrown at you.

There was a huge brush arrowhead which had caused falls. It was enormous and ugly and poor Rodney had fallen there. You needed to channel your horse and come at it with pace and total commitment because it was such a big fence. It was, though, the kind of fence that really suited Rocky and he gave me a great feel over it. I was so relieved; but, again, I knew I couldn't relax.

Luhmühlen is a twisty course and Rocky wasn't the ideal horse for the section weaving through the trees. I had to concentrate, not only on the fences, but on balancing him for every turn; having a slip-up would have been so silly, and yet all the time I was pressing to get the optimum time.

I can't say I enjoyed the ride, because there was so much at stake, but as I jumped the last fence and emerged from the wood into the open field where the finish was, I saw Becky dancing around, waving and screaming like mad. As I came through the finish, I got very emotional – we all did, as everyone close to me knew what this would mean to me. It was very special that William could be there and I know he was immensely relieved that I had gone well. An enormous weight suddenly lifted off my shoulders; the job was done.

Ian went well too, which made the day complete, and Katie Parker had had a good clear at her first senior championships; so apart from Rodney, who was by then in hospital with bad bruising, we were all in high spirits.

That night I couldn't switch off. After a good ride, the adrenalin rush and thrill make it impossible for me to relax. I just ride the course over and over in my head. William was allowed to stay with me that night, but it was only a single bed and I ended up spending the night on the floor.

Next day the team were in front by a fairly comfortable margin – I have to admit that here the new scoring system did work in our favour – but I only had two fences in hand to win the individual gold over the Swedish rider, Linda Algotsson, who is very good at show jumping. William helped me warm up and I tried to keep my head and stay focused. I had to remember I was there to do a job and ride Rocky in the way William and I had worked on. This is difficult, because with Rocky the rhythm has to be slower than for most horses; you have to keep him soft, ride with little leg, keep him as relaxed as possible and not thrust him in deep to fences. If he lost that rhythm, he would probably have four or five fences down.

It had helped that I'd been in the lead before and lost – with Metro at Bramham and Cartoon at Blenheim – and, though I was nervous, it was nowhere near as bad as for the cross-country. Obviously I didn't want to throw my individual gold medal away, but by the time I jumped, last of all, I knew the team gold was secure and with it, therefore, the precious Sydney qualification.

Clearing that final fence was a special moment, not just for me, but for our partnership, because Rocky had finally proved why he was worth sticking with. At last everything had gone right. Britain had won gold; we'd be going to the Olympics; and Rocky and I were European Champions!

Having two gold medals around my neck suddenly made all those years of slog worthwhile and, as much as it was a reward for me, it was wonderful for everyone who had stood by me – Mum, Dad, Tim, William, Ruth, Becky, my owners, and now Mandy – it was definitely a huge relief for her and one in the eye to her critics.

Afterwards, all the British team supporters came back to our lorries, which were parked in a block, and the champagne corks were popped. We all made speeches, including me, and then William was asked to say something. I was rather apprehensive, as he'd had quite a bit of champagne by now. Memorably, he said: 'All I've got to say is that I've never s*****d a European champion before.' I nearly died of embarrassment!

The strange thing about this sport is that one minute you're drinking champagne in victory celebrations and the next you've got to be stone cold sober to go and do something really mundane, like pack the lorry. Tina and I could only have one glass each because we'd got a nine-hour drive to Calais ahead of us. There we were going to swap horses, reload the lorry and go on to Achselschwang, which was another twelve-hour drive. There's always another event in our sport; no time really to let your hair down.

But it was the most wonderful drive. A mission had been accomplished – the only good thing to happen in the sport all year. And it was on that long drive that I realised that my first Olympics was suddenly within reach.

7
Sydney Olympics

When Tina Gifford and I arrived at Achselschwang we were definitely in party mood, despite the endless overnight journey. The annual treat at Achselschwang is the coach trip organised by the Steinle family to the Munich Beer Festival, where the funfair rides are out of this world. I love them, though Tina always feels sick.

Tina and the girls, Nini and Rachel, always nicknamed me 'Frumpy Funnell' because I have a penchant for polo-neck jumpers. This time, with my being the new European Champion, the girls decided I should be dressed up; they put me in slinky trousers, a tight crop top, leather jacket and loads of make-up.

I was reluctant to take the leather jacket off and bare my stomach but, as we'd been drinking enormous glasses of beer and dancing on the tables, I did get quite hot. I made my way through the huge crowds to the ladies, where to my horror I found out I needed money to get in. I was just about to turn round and lose my place in the long queue when this bird standing behind me put her hand on my backside and said: 'Don't worry, I'll pay for you – my ex-girlfriend was English!' It wasn't long before the entire event knew that all I pulled that night was a German lesbian! Thereafter, I decided to stick to polo necks.

Achselschwang is an event that goes out of its way to entertain riders; they certainly don't hold back on the food and drink. What with the party atmosphere and my euphoria after Luhmühlen, it was hard to focus on the actual competition. I was riding General Salute in his first two-star competition, and it was unfortunate that the Jewsons couldn't be there because he finished fourth.

Sadly, Nobby didn't really do much after that. Where I went wrong with him is that I should have faced reality and admitted that he wasn't going to be a top-class horse, even though he had a good jump. He was lovely-looking, though, and we should have sold him that year – after that the opportunity was lost. It was a hard lesson in the importance of assessing exactly where a horse is going and being honest with the owner. If a horse isn't going to make top class, it's better to sell it at the point where it has achieved good results and will, perhaps, make a good junior horse or schoolmaster for a less experienced rider who wants to have some fun. Otherwise, the risk is that the moment will pass; with horses, you have to capitalise on the good times.

Tina was placed at Achselschwang too, so we had a happy drive back. I was really excited about coming home, because I hadn't been in England since winning the Europeans. When I got back William and I went down to The Parrot for a meal. The following night he suggested that we go there again, for a drink; I really didn't want to go a second night running, but in the end he persuaded me. As we drove up to the pub, I saw there were loads of cars there and thought it must be Rotary night – but when I walked in I found they'd put on a surprise party in my honour.

Emma Pitt had organised it with William, and the whole pub was decorated with flags and pictures from Luhmühlen. Ruth came down from Norfolk and everyone who had been part of my team – vets and farriers as well as all the owners – were there. It was a very special night and we filled half the pub. We're lucky with The Parrot; it's a proper local and in a very friendly village. They've always been kind and followed what William and I do, and I love going in there.

I rounded off the season by taking Jurassic Rising to Le Lion d'Angers, where he finished fifth. Le Lion always makes a good end to the season. France's top course-designer, Pierre Michelet, produces amazing courses which are beautifully crafted with wonderful fence dressings in the shapes of animals and, with a lovely drinks party in the chateau and lots of nice places to stay locally, it's a good event for owners.

That autumn I received my second invitation to *BBC Sports Personality of the Year* – I also went the year Barnaby won Gatcombe. I love being asked to this because when you're sharing a stage with the top runners and footballers it makes you feel that you are not just an event rider but a real sportsperson. In that respect, it's the nearest thing to going to an Olympics. There's always a good party afterwards – and, although everyone mixes well, we usually end up with the jockeys because Tina, whose father was the champion racehorse trainer Josh Gifford, knows them all.

All in all, 1999 had been a good season for me, but that autumn there was a difficult episode. Denise Lincoln had mentioned to me that she couldn't justify keeping all three horses – Rainbow Magic, Midnight Magic and Primmore's Pride – and therefore wanted to sell one. She asked my advice on which one should be sold, but being fond of all three made it an impossible decision.

Rainbow Magic (Sam) I adored – he was part of the furniture – and it definitely wasn't going to be Primmore's Pride because of the ability he was showing, while Midnight Magic (Repo) had showed even better form and had upgraded to advanced by the age of six. With a wonderful frame of mind for the job, he was a fantastic cross-country horse and I was keen to wait another year before doing a three-day with him.

This was the first time I had to face up to selling a horse when I desperately didn't want to. Of course, others had been sold before, but those sales had been the results of pragmatic joint decisions by myself and the owner that they weren't going to do the job. However, I completely understood that eventing is an expensive sport and maintaining three horses was a big drain on any owner.

I knew Stuart Black was coming over from Canada to try Repo and it didn't come as a shock when he said that he wanted him. But just before that an American rider, Kathy Wieschhoff, surprised me by ringing to say that she had tried Sam. Kathy asked for some information about him and I told her that he was the most lovely horse to have about, wonderful on the flat and a very good jumper. However, as I am not a person to hide the truth, I said I had reservations about his speed for four-star level. I then explained the situation to Kathy and said that if she did like the horse, it would be helpful if she could make up her mind reasonably quickly as only one of them was for sale.

I heard nothing more until the day Repo was being flown to Canada. Then Denise rang to say that she had some bad news. My heart sank: I thought something had happened on the plane. Actually, the news was that Kathy had phoned that morning to say she wanted Sam. She had made a good offer and, obviously, Denise couldn't turn down the money. So now both horses were going.

I'd like to be able to say that both sales worked out happily, but they didn't really. Sam had been so successful in England, being consistently placed, especially at advanced one-day events, but he didn't show that form again. Repo made a great start when he won his first two-star three-day event with Stuart, at Bromont. He was then flown back here as a seven-year-old to compete at Blenheim, where he also went well, and the next spring he went clear round his first four-star, at Kentucky. Part of me was delighted he was going so well, but he was still only eight and I was worried that it was too much too soon. I had taken him slowly because he was a big horse who would take time to grow into himself. So I was shocked to see him being run at Burghley in the autumn of 2001 – his second four-star as an eight-year-old. He fell at the end of the course. I was quite upset by this and I admit that I went to see him in the stable when no one else was around.

The next time he appeared at Burghley, in 2002, he had another fall, and this time I had tears streaming down my face as I watched him. Again I went to see him, quietly on my own in the stables, and I got really upset this time. His groom said that she couldn't believe how he was with me and how he seemed to remember me, and that finished me off.

A lot of people think that a horse is just an animal that requires feeding and looking after, but to me most of them are people; they know who you are, and they react to you, and this is why I had fallen for each of these two individual characters. Losing one would have been hard, but I was distraught at losing two. I could, of course, completely understand why Denise did it – you have to take advantage of the good offers when they come, because if you turn one down the horse might go lame the next day. As a rider, you can't expect an owner to turn down serious money just so you can keep the ride; but I didn't take it well when I lost two special friends. However, the commission Denise gave me went towards getting my shoddy, wobbly wooden stables replaced with an American-style barn, which my brother-in-law Nick Funnell built for us.

At the start of 2000 a new team system was put in place with the appointment of Yogi Breisner as performance manager. This was a new role created by Lottery funding and went beyond that of *chef d'équipe*: he would be responsible for the training, monitoring and development of all potential British team riders.

Yogi, who was appointed at the same time as another Swedish coach – football's Sven Goran Eriksson – was familiar to all of us. He had had a huge amount of success in the 1980s for Sweden on a horse called Ultimus and, having spent many years with the great Swedish trainer Lars Sederholm at his Waterstock base in Oxfordshire, was highly thought of as a coach and adviser, not only in eventing but also in racing, helping jockeys and horses alike to improve their jumping technique.

I had never met Yogi before, but was immediately impressed that he made the effort to drive all around the country to meet every one of the contenders for the Olympic team. Straight away you could tell that he was going to be working on our side. He was keen to get to know us all as individuals and find out how we thought and reacted at competitions.

In those ten minutes before you set off across country, it is crucial that the *chef*'s words are the right ones. Some people need firm encouragement; others need a kick up the arse. Some can take on board the reality of what is going on in the competition; others have to be shielded. Yogi had only eight months and a limited number of competitions at which to watch us all before Sydney. It was a tall order to take on that job in Olympic year and with a different personality it could have been a disaster.

On that first meeting Yogi and I sat down and discussed Rocky's plans. The selectors were happy to give Rocky a bye at Badminton in order to save him for Sydney; but part of me really wanted to take him there, because he was now at the age – twelve – where he had the physical maturity to have a competitive crack at it. However, what did hit me – and four years later I felt the same pressure before Athens – is the constant terrible fear that the horse will injure itself. You become neurotic, wanting to wrap them up in cotton wool. Any athlete's major goal is the Olympics, so I got horribly nervous at every preceding competition, not about Rocky's performance, but about the risk that he might do something that would put him out of contention for the Olympics. It was, therefore, a huge relief – and some compensation for missing Badminton – that he won his major spring outing, the CIC at Chatsworth, without incident.

That spring Primmore's Pride had his first three-day experience, at Punchestown, where he was fourth. He really showed his potential and it was exciting for Denise, Roger and myself that, despite the anguish that had surrounded selling the others, we had been left with a big-time horse. With most horses it is difficult to tell by two-star level whether they will go on, but 'Kiri' gave me a great feeling of power and scope.

I renewed my association with Susie Cranston when she sent me Cornerman, a horse she had bred by the racing sire Neltino out of a mare by Lord Gayle, who was also Henry's sire. Susie had asked me to take him on the previous year, but at that point I didn't have a stable for him. However, losing Sam and Repo freed up space, and when Susie heard about this from Sarah Jewson, she was on the phone straight away.

Cornerman – 'Charlie' – had been ridden by quite a few jockeys. After his first few events with Lucy Kemplay under Ruth's tutelage, he went to Ian Stark, then to Anne-Marie Evans, and from there to Nini's younger sister Piggy French. I found it difficult to say no to Susie, but I didn't want to take the horse away from a young rider. I know from my own experience that if they don't get the chances, they won't get on. As an established rider by now, I felt I had a responsibility to help rather than impede up-and-coming eventers – and anyway, nicking rides from anyone is a complete no-no. But after I chatted to Nini and her mother Kate, I realised that Pig was actually quite happy about the situation; so I agreed to take the horse. However, I warned Susie that if I didn't have a good gut feeling about Charlie, I wouldn't compete him. He wasn't easy on the flat; he found it difficult to engage and work straight, upright and in balance. He also had a tendency to trip and he'd had veterinary problems. But, as with all horses, I was excited by the challenge.

After our first run at Poplar Park I straightaway felt happy with him, though the dressage needed work and I knew it wouldn't come together overnight. I got him qualified for Bramham and set off with him and Jurassic Rising (Fiver): two lovely dark bay eight-year-old geldings going to their first three-star. Yet again, I lost my cross-country lead at Bramham in the show jumping: two fences down dropped me to fourth on Fiver and Charlie finished seventh. It was frustrating not to win, but overall I was pretty chuffed with both horses at their first attempt at this level.

I went straight on up to Burgie in Scotland, stopping en

route at Ian Stark's for dinner. Burgie feels like the other side of the world but it's well worth the drive. The Lochore family, who own and run it, always offer great hospitality and it's a super event. I took Viceroy and Burke's Boy, who finished second and fourth behind Bettina Overesch on Woodsides Ashby.

Viceroy, owned by Sue and Lizzie Bunn, had started his career with us, having come as a four-year-old for William to show jump. He was the first stallion I'd ridden and he has a wonderful affectionate temperament. Viceroy was bred by mistake when his sire, VIP, escaped from his stable while at Hickstead with the American Nations Cup team and jumped into the field with Sue's Thoroughbred mare. One year later, Viceroy was the surprise result. Because of the breeding, Sue decided to leave him entire. At first he lived with the Bunns, and was ridden around intermediate events with Sue's head girl Sharon; then, when she was ill and unable to ride him, Sue asked me to take him on. Because of our great friendship with the family, I was only too happy to accept because I knew some fun days were guaranteed. We've had many laughs over the fact that I said I'd take him on because there wouldn't be any owner pressure. Lizzie is perhaps more competitive and gives me more stick than any of my other connections!

Burke's Boy was an older horse owned by Janet and Ian McIntyre. We were taking a big gamble on him because of his age – he was a nine-year-old who had done a lot of hunting – but I was attracted to him mainly because of his breeding. He was by Edmund Burke, the same sire as Rocky. When I first tried him, he felt like Rocky as a young horse; he felt as though he had similar strengths, but also similar weaknesses. He was a classy-looking horse, but we were warned that he could bite and that we should be cautious around him in the stable.

So our results at Burgie were really pleasing, with both horses placed at their first three-day event – and the success was particularly nice for Ian McIntyre, who felt very at home in Scotland.

There was great excitement that summer when Hickstead announced that a Lotus Elite car was to be first prize in the Eventers' Grand Prix. This year too, for the first time, they decided to cut out the dressage phase, realising that it wasn't adding anything to the competition and put the show jumpers at an unfair disadvantage.

I had Rosie back on the road for this. It was one of those competitions that I just knew she could win. Everyone else thought so too, so it was amazing to be so heavily tipped and for it to come off. Usually, when you are supposed to be a dead cert it all goes pear-shaped. I always dread riding in front of the show jumpers, too, because they often say 'Typical event rider – can't show jump', and I worry about letting down not only William, but also my fellow eventers. It was very exciting driving the Lotus around the arena, but it was to be the only time I did. We couldn't justify keeping it – when there are bills to be paid you can't pay them with sports cars! So it had to be sold, and the money was split between Anne Burnet and myself.

William rode Comex but, unfortunately, his luck didn't improve in his third and last go at this competition; he had quite a nasty fall over the wide ditch and hedge as you come out of the main arena. Luckily, all the advice on the tight turns and lines that he had given *me* when we walked the course together paid off on Rosie.

Meanwhile the build-up for Sydney was gathering pace. All year my mind was completely channelled on this one goal; I now know that I was focused on myself and Rocky to a selfish degree. Many times in my career I have felt guilty that I don't give my parents and William more time because I'm too wrapped up in my personal dedication to my horses. That year I think I was particularly blinkered as to what was going on around me and what other people were feeling. If I hadn't been so wrapped up in myself, I might have noticed the danger signs in my relationship with William.

This was the first year we didn't have a final selection trial. After long discussions among the riders, selectors and Yogi, we made it clear that we felt that every horse is different and not all of them are suited to any particular event for a final run. So it was left to us as riders to be open and to discuss the best possible way of getting our horses to Sydney in good condition. This is where Yogi and Mandy really helped the team situation, because this approach put more responsibility on us. They put their trust in us, showing they believed that we'd achieved what we had because of our own preparation and doing what we felt had suited our individual horses best before a major championship. Some horses just need a skip around a small course, others – and their riders – need to be inspired by a proper test around a decent-sized track. Likewise, different horses prefer different going.

Team morale benefited from this new thinking: we were no longer arriving at a championship wishing we hadn't been made to run on hard ground, or to be competitive at a final trial. In any case, selectors should make their selection on the basis of a whole history of major international results and the way you and your horse cope with different situations, not on the basis of a single one-day event. Obviously the horse needs to be sound and going well but, at the same time, a good horse shouldn't be ruled out of a championship just because of a silly run-out at a one-day event. This new system definitely produced contented riders instead of whingeing riders.

Early in the year we'd been measured up for our Team GB kit, but the whole Olympic thing hadn't sunk in then; it seemed too far away and you don't like to pre-judge your chances. As the weeks ticked by, each day I felt that little bit closer to going to Sydney and a bit more excited; then the other half of me would have to say: 'Look you're not there yet, a lot can go wrong.' I knew that the more hopes I pinned on it, the greater the possibility of disappointment.

There was no big formal announcement or get-together for the team because most of us knew whether we were going or not. Team GB held a big press conference on the Friday of Gatcombe, with the dressage, show-jumping and paralympic riders, and we were driven around the main arena where the public gave us a good send-off.

A few people vying for the reserve spots still ran at Gatcombe, but most of us didn't run our Olympic horses there. This was a bit of an unpopular decision from the event's point of view, but I have to say it was a relief for us. Our horses went into quarantine at Eddy Stibbe's Waresley Park stud on the Sunday evening of Gatcombe and there was a trot-up on Monday morning.

It was announced to the press that the team order was Jeanette Brakewell, Leslie Law (for whom it was a first British team appearance), myself and Ian Stark with Jaybee. The individuals were the Badminton winners Mary and Star Appeal, Rodney Powell on Flintstone, and Karen Dixon on Too Smart. Tina was travelling reserve on The Gangster and it was decided that Ian's other horse Arakai would be flown out as a reserve for him. Chris Bartle and Katie Parker also came into quarantine with us, plus Karen's second horse The Honourable Bob.

The Olympic format had been changed at Atlanta so that there were now two separate competitions in the three-day event – team and individual. I think most people would agree that team gold is the most important thing – it's certainly how riders view it – so I felt incredibly honoured to be in the team. But there was a part of me that would have loved a shot at the individual medals because of the way Rocky had gone the previous year. So while I couldn't help feeling inside that I would have liked to have been an individual competitor, I also knew that getting into the team was a huge honour and achievement, so I kept quiet about this.

Waresley Park has unbelievable facilities and it was a real treat being there. Some of us stayed in Eddy's and Mandy's house, and others were in a house at the end of the drive. Eddy is a very kind host – he was going to Sydney himself, representing the Dutch Antilles – and we couldn't have had a better place to spend two weeks in quarantine, using the gym, tennis court and swimming pool. We were allowed home during that time, as all of us had other horses to ride and businesses to run.

One awful thing did really stress me during that quarantine period. My scruffy little terrier Fingers had a phantom pregnancy and I took her to the vet to discuss having her spayed, something I had put off because I wanted her to have puppies. The vet gave her an injection to bring her out of the phantom pregnancy but that night she was so poorly that I rushed her straight back to his surgery. He operated on her immediately, but when they opened her up it was discovered that she was full of cancer and she died while under anaesthetic. It was the same as when Orville died at Ruth's – I hurt so badly inside and I cried and cried. She was such a beloved dog and I took it very hard.

The next major dread I had was the thought of Rocky flying to the other side of the world. The scene from the film *International Velvet*, where the horse is put down on the plane, kept creeping into my brain. But there couldn't have been a more experienced team dealing with the flight: Peden's, a company renowned for horse transportation. Three planes left from Europe, each carrying fifty horses, including the British-based New Zealand and Australian horses, so many of the teams were in the same situation. It was a massive operation; loading alone took five hours.

This was the worst part of the build-up, being stuck in England and not knowing how the horses were dealing with the flight. But Jenny Hall and two grooms travelled with them and Yogi rang when they refuelled in Dubai to say that everything was OK. Even so, the anxiety at this period was almost overpowering: after all those years of work, the whole thing could still go wrong because the horse hadn't travelled well. At night the magnitude of it all started to build up in my head, and I had to work very hard at keeping myself straight mentally. I was at severe risk of sliding back into extreme nervousness and negativity. The thought of how big the Olympics would be, with millions of people worldwide watching – more than Badminton, more than anything in fact – plus the usual worry about letting the side down threatened to creep in. Half of me was hugely excited, positive and focused, but the other half kept thinking: 'What if I cock up, and let my owners, horse and family down?' It was like an irrepressible little demon that had to be repeatedly swatted away.

We flew out as a team, taking hand luggage only – literally knickers, socks and make-up – because we would be wearing official kit the rest of the time. For the flight we had to wear awful nylon sweatshirts which had a label on the back saying something really stupid like: 'Beware of friction burns when sliding on the floor'! All our riding clothes were in the trunks that went with the horses, and all of that stuff had to be absolutely spotless because Australia is strict about mud and the risk of spreading disease.

Arriving in Brisbane, we went first to collect our Olympic kit at the Gold Coast Camp, which was Team GB's HQ. The kitting-out room, a massive hall filled with kit for 316 athletes plus all their support groups, was nothing but organised chaos and, despite all the earlier measuring sessions, none of our smart official uniform fitted us properly. Then we flew on down to Sydney, all of us longing to see our horses. When I looked over Rocky's stable door I couldn't believe that he hadn't lost any weight. I had sent him out slightly overweight, and was prepared for him to have lost condition, but all the horses looked amazing. But perhaps in comparison to my driving the long flight had been no hassle!

We were in quarantine at the Olympic equestrian site, Horsley Park, to the west of the city towards the Blue Mountains. Every day we had to put on overalls and tracksuits to go into the complex, which was pretty hot; but the system worked well and the facilities were amazing.

We stayed in a hotel called Panthers, which had a casino attached. We rode in the mornings and the afternoons were our own, so we'd go into Sydney for shopping or play tennis. It was an incredible atmosphere and I am still amazed at how well everyone got on, considering how much time we had to spend together. Everyone was in great spirits, and the second week was even more fun when the show jumpers, John and Michael Whitaker, Geoff Billington and Carl Edwards, arrived.

The last night we let our hair down in Panthers was Tina's

thirtieth birthday party. I was in seventh heaven playing on the slot machines, but it was a bit embarrassing having to wear our tracksuits in a casino. Playing roulette, I asked Eddy Stibbe what his lucky number was. He said twenty-seven, and I said seven was mine: so I put all my chips down on the numbers 7, 17 and 27 – and 27 came up three times! Then my competitor's number was drawn as 27 and I was convinced this would be lucky.

From Panthers we moved to the Olympic village for a week. This was a real experience. We had a balcony which looked out over the main Olympic stadium and I heard the choir practising for the opening ceremony, which was amazing. The canteen, which seated six thousand athletes, had every single type of food you could imagine at all hours of the day. It was one of the things that brought home to us what an enormous organisation the Olympics is. The scale of it is unimaginable until you see it.

The night before the trot-up, Rosemary Barlow, who has done the most fantastic job over many years fund-raising for the teams and organising supporters' tents, kindly arranged a welcoming drinks party for the horses' owners and riders' families. It was the first chance I had had for what seemed a long time to catch up with Mum and Dad and the Lewthwaites. The party took place in the British Consul's overlooking the harbour. We saw the Olympic torch being run through the streets and you could see the flames and hear the terrific noise. The opera house and bridge lit up with fireworks and suddenly it hit us: 'We're really here!'

Most of us were dead keen to march behind the Union Jack at the opening ceremony – the Olympic first-timers, Tina, Leslie, Jeanette and myself, were particularly determined to be there, though it was optional. All the marching athletes – about fifteen thousand of us – had to wait in a gymnastics hall, so we never saw the colourful bit of the opening ceremony, but it was hilarious. Lots of teams were chanting their own national songs, but every time the Americans, who had more athletes than anyone else, piped up, everyone booed and sang even louder to drown them.

When we were finally asked to move and go in country order, the queuing went on for ever. But it was well worth it, because when I stepped into that Olympic stadium, I could hardly convince myself I was really there. I think all of us were overwhelmed with the pride we felt by being part of Team GB.

At the same time, I knew I had to be particularly careful not to get blown away by the whole Olympic experience, as other people had told me how fazing it can be. The whole experience was like a dream: but deep down, I knew I had to keep my head and stay focused, and not allow the strange circumstances to interfere with my normal competition preparation.

So it was a great relief to me when we moved into our team house. In a hotel there's nowhere to wind down and relax except your room and, ungrateful though it sounds, constant eating in a restaurant is wearying. Janie Straker, whose husband Matt was our *chef de mission*, was a fantastic cook and produced lovely home-made roasts. We all badly needed to be able to veg out on a sofa, be normal and get away from the high-profile unreality of the Olympic atmosphere, and to that end the house was brilliant.

One of the problems of quarantine had been the limited hacking opportunities. We were all worried about the dangers of overdoing the flatwork, but it was difficult because there wasn't much other space. The horses felt well, they knew they were at a competition and they started to get clever. Even Rocky, who is sensible, had started to whip round and be quite bright.

The great drama of our preparation occurred when Rodney was out exercising Flintstone. The horse reared up and spun around, lost his balance, slipped over on to Rodney's leg and broke it. Rod is a great character in the sport and we've had lots of laughs with him. He's a real team player and characteristically made light of what must have been a ghastly let-down, putting all his efforts into supporting the rest of us. We were shattered for him because he'd had rotten luck the year before at Luhmühlen and seemed to have been jinxed ever since. This incident shook up the whole team and did bring a bit of despair into the camp.

The other awful thing that happened was Tina not getting a run. While I felt awful for Rod, I was quietly excited for her because she was reserve and I thought this would be her chance. She'd had rotten luck missing the Atlanta Olympics and, like all of us, she was really hungry for a chance. The Gangster was working so well out in Sydney – he looked amazing – but then, to her disbelief, it was decided instead that Ian would run his second horse Arakai as an individual. This was embarrassing all round because most of us felt it to be a very cruel blow. I felt so sorry for her, but she handled the whole situation amazingly well and held her head up high, never publicly letting on about how she felt.

The other thing I found very hard was not having Mum and Dad around: passes were limited and the available accreditation obviously had to go to Emma and Di and William. This is the anomaly of the Olympics – it's your big dream, but the people closest to you can't be with you. Becky didn't come because she was nervous about flying, so it seemed very strange without her. Mum and Dad weren't allowed anywhere near the stable complex and I hardly saw them. They had stuck with me through all the bad times – now here I was at the Olympics and they were unable to be with me. But we did have a brilliant international supporters' tent for owners, family and close friends, run by Rosemary Barlow, and that became our meeting point.

The next excitement was the cross-country course walk. It was a classic Mike Etherington-Smith track. The best thing about Mike's courses – he is the designer at Blenheim, Chatsworth, Kentucky and Adelaide – is that he builds very good tracks that never punish good jumping horses. He never produces harsh landings or uncomfortable striding, and horses really enjoy the feeling of jumping his courses. The Sydney track was beautifully built with lovely Aboriginal touches. It was a fantastic galloping course and every fence was something great to look at. Quietly, I knew that while there were a few questions for Rocky, the course would suit him. Dimensionally it was very big, but there was nothing trappy; it was inviting and it made you want to get out there and have a go.

There were three fences that concerned me, the third being a tricky sunken road. But it was the waters that made us all think. The first water was a serious downhill bounce with a steep drop and a slight right-hand turn to a big corner in the water. It wasn't overly complicated, but there was plenty that could go wrong. My biggest dread, though, was the second water: a rail turning to a log drop-in and three strides to a bank, then over a log back into the water again. It looked like a replica of my nemesis at Badminton the year before. But thanks to my sessions with Nicky I found a way of handling my anxiety. One of my mental tricks is that I try to tell myself that things happen for a reason, and suddenly I found a reason for this complex: that's why I had a mishap at Badminton – because it was preparation for Sydney. And under no circumstances was I going to let the same thing happen again.

William arrived in time to see my dressage test. I was so relieved to see him because he is always down-to-earth and funny, and brings normality with him. There had been talk that Matt didn't want our other halves sharing our rooms; we all protested, pointing out that we were all married and therefore unlikely to be having rampant sex – and if we were, that's what worked for us! Well, when William got into bed with me that first night the whole thing shot across the bedroom because it was on wheels and all the floors were made of slippery marble. Next morning William said to Tina: 'It's a good job we'd shut the door or we'd have been down in the kitchen!'

I've never been so nervous watching dressage as when Jeanette and Leslie went in. As a team, we were so hungry to win gold; there was huge British expectation as there'd been no medal since the silver in 1988 at Seoul and no gold since Munich in 1972. But we all had personal bests in the dressage and Rocky, apart from a couple of small mistakes, did a lovely test that put us in second behind Andrew Hoy on Darien Powers. Rocky also got his first ever mark of ten, in the walk. Unfortunately, the Aussies produced their personal bests too, so we were just behind them going into the cross-country.

I did my final course walk with William and Leslie. We were very focused and trying to be serious until I asked if they thought it was safe for me to be walking barefoot. William replied: 'Well, you don't see many Aborigines about now!' We collapsed laughing and suddenly Leslie and I started to feel a bit more normal.

And, for the first time ever, the show jumpers, wearing their shorts, walked the cross-country course – they were shocked to find it was such a long way. This was the first Olympics in which the three equestrian disciplines pulled together as one, and it created a great atmosphere. This was partly because the show jumpers already knew me through William, and partly because the Lottery scheme had brought us together as part of Team GB.

We felt pretty sick on cross-country morning. When I woke up I realised that I must still do my normal system, even though I didn't have my own base, my lorry, as usual. So I found a corner in the stable canteen for a quiet coffee, and mentally rode the course fence by fence in a positive way. I was just about to jump the dreaded second water in my head when Matt walked up with the Princess Royal – and I couldn't exactly tell her to wait while I finished my imaginary round, so we chatted politely. I never got to jump through the second water mentally, which is probably why it went so badly!

Jeanette and Leslie both did a great job; the relief for them was clearly so wonderful that I was really envious of them as I waited for my round. The same thing went through my head as in Luhmühlen: the first two team members had gone brilliantly, they'd done the job they came to do, and now I knew I couldn't let the team down. Yogi and William told me to get out there and ride for my life, and that's what I did.

I had a fantastic ride – apart from the second water. On the approach, Rocky made up too much ground; we got a bit close to the log going in and he left a leg at it. He twisted over it, but I was so determined and, by now, so instinctive in my reactions that I managed to sit back, even though I was only holding one rein by this stage. An image of the Badminton debacle flashed through my head and I thought: 'I must get through this fence somehow.' I got the whip out – goodness knows where this 'third' hand came from, but I was just determined that I wasn't going to go wrong.

By this stage, though we were still behind the Australians, we were keeping pace with them. Their first three, Andrew Hoy, Phillip Dutton and Stuart Tinney, had gone clear too, so now it was down to the anchormen, Matt Ryan and Ian Stark. We really needed Scotty's score if we were going to get ahead because at that stage we were counting Jeanette's lower dressage score. But it wasn't meant to be. Jaybee fell at the corner in the first water – but, being a real team player, Ian got back on and finished the course in his usual Flying Scot manner, because if one of our horses had been lame, we would have needed his score to complete the event as a team.

When Matt went clear for Australia it meant that we were still behind the Aussies to begin the show jumping; but still we were quietly confident that gold was within our grasp, because the three of us were on good jumpers. As we had three sound horses, we didn't need to trot up Jaybee – which was just as well, because he wasn't sound.

The time was tight in the show jumping and Jeanette found herself with a depressing six time penalties. Between the three of us we didn't go very well: Leslie and I each had two fences down. The ground was dead and Rocky wasn't jumping well outside the arena; I just couldn't get him how I wanted. William was doing his best to help me and, as much as anything, I felt I had let him down. Frustratingly, the Australian horses went even worse than we did, but by now we just couldn't catch them even though we had fewer fences down than they did. It just wasn't quite enough to get the team gold, and we were pipped by a tiny margin to silver.

Initially we were gutted. We had really believed we could do it – but we'd missed out. So close, and yet so far.

But the medal ceremony was very special. Standing on the podium and waving to the British enclave, where masses of

Union Jacks were fluttering, it sank in that we'd flown these horses to the other side of the world, we hadn't let our country down – we hadn't actually let anyone down – and we were bringing home an Olympic medal. Many thousands of talented sportspeople will never get the chance even to try for an Olympic medal, let alone win one.

After the press conferences, where I think we were still a bit subdued – we got some stick back at home for being downbeat on the TV – because it seemed so shattering to miss the gold, we went back to the supporters' tent and joined up with Mum and Dad and William. Then the champagne flowed and we could let our hair down. The alcohol loosened my emotions at last and I had to go back to the stables for a quiet ten minutes on my own with Rocky. This is the time I get tearful after a big win, when I'm on my own with my horse and it sinks in just what they've done for me, and just how much the whole achievement is down to a partnership. At this moment, words couldn't describe how grateful I felt to this horse.

8
Back Down to Earth

On the night we won our silver medal in Sydney there were considerable celebrations, though of course the three individual riders, Mary King, Karen Dixon and Ian Stark, couldn't let their hair down in the same way as their competition was about to start. Leslie, Jeanette and I stayed out to watch them but, though all three put up brilliant cross-country performances and finished in the top ten, sadly none of them was in a competitive enough position after the dressage to be in with a chance of an individual medal.

David O'Connor led from the start and deservedly won the gold, and Andrew Hoy, whose week it definitely was, the silver; but I think those of us watching were perhaps most thrilled that Toddy got the bronze. His retirement immediately after Sydney was a sad day for the sport because it was the departure of both an amazing horseman and a good friend. It has been a big loss to eventing in Britain – much of the colour went out of the circuit when Toddy went back to New Zealand and we still miss him and Carolyn, especially the parties. At the same time, though, we appreciate it all the more when he comes back with his trainer's hat on to help the Kiwis at the major events.

The rest of the eventers went back to England at this point, but William and I wanted to stay out in Sydney and support the show jumpers. In between competitions we went with the Australian rider David Green to stay with some friends of his, the Gunns, who had a beautiful cattle station in the Hunter Valley. We had an amazing day with them, riding stock horses and rounding up cattle; it was absolutely brilliant and I loved it. I was worried about galloping over the rocks and stones on the hard ground but the horses didn't seem to mind – no wonder Australian horses are so tough and successful across country. In the evening we went 'roo-hunting', but I wouldn't let William shoot one. I have always been fascinated by wildlife abroad and can never get my head around the fact that they might be pests. When I think of kangaroos, I think of Skippy!

We were planning to stay with the Gunns for a couple of days, but then we had a phone call from Mum telling us that Dad had been taken ill: he'd been rushed into hospital just outside Sydney with pneumonia. They were supposed to have left Australia by now and Mum had to go back because the Eridge horse trials, which she runs, was about to take place. We sped back to Sydney – a four-hour drive – and split the next few days between watching the show jumpers, who didn't have a particularly uplifting competition, and visiting Dad.

Although I was obviously really worried about Dad, the one upside of staying on was that I was the only one of the eventing team who got to the closing ceremony. It was unbelievable and I wouldn't have missed it for the world; there was an amazing feelgood factor in knowing that I'd won a medal and been part of one of the most successful Olympics ever.

Fortunately, Dad was well enough to fly home with me and William on the athletes' plane, and we were immensely grateful to the British Olympic Association for arranging this.

British Airways upgraded all the medal winners and, as a silver medallist, I went up to business class – if you got gold, you were in first. I wanted Dad to take my seat, but he refused and stayed with William in the back of the plane. I felt rather selfish about this, but Dad was adamant that he didn't want to ruin my moment.

It was a real thrill arriving back to such a big buzz at Heathrow, and I realised that I would have missed this too if I'd come home early. All of us who had won medals were ushered into a press conference at the airport – and that's when it hit me all over again what a really big thing the Olympics is, how many people back at home had been watching it and what it means to your country to be able to bring home a medal.

Then, there were Mum and Becky Coffey, who had come to meet the three of us at the airport – and suddenly life had to go back to normal. The downside to the Olympics is the amount of time you have to be away and the consequent loss of earnings – in my case, not only teaching fees but, more importantly, livery income. I could only keep three horses in while I was away – Primmore's Pride, Cornerman and Viceroy, all three of whom were going to three-day events on my return; so obviously, this meant I had to pay a groom, who kept them ticking over with hacking out. It's even harder for the show jumpers, whose horses can go out and win serious money on a regular basis – they can lose a great deal by being out of the scene for a few weeks. But the power of the Olympics is such that you can't turn it down; every sportsperson's dream is to go and try to win a medal, and the subsequent financial rewards from sponsorships can be valuable. But if it doesn't come off, as it didn't for Britain's show jumpers that year, the whole venture can make a big dent in your income.

So it was business as usual, and we set off that week for Pau, which is right down in the French Pyrenees – a massively long journey. There was so much rain that we felt sure the competition would be cancelled, but conditions on the course held up well and the event got under way as planned. Viceroy had been drawn number one: it was the first time I'd had to go first at a three-day event, and I wasn't particularly keen on the idea, but he went very well. Cornerman gave me a good cross-country ride, too, but later that evening when I trotted him up he was very lame. We couldn't find anything wrong for ages; then much later we discovered a minute puncture through the front of his boot, which could have been made by a nail. It wasn't a serious injury, but it meant that he couldn't show jump on the last day, which was frustrating because he was lying fourth.

We organised for those two horses to go home on another truck and drove back up through France to Le Lion d'Angers with Primmore's Pride (Kiri). Again it poured and we thought the event would have to be cancelled, but the organisers just cut the steeplechase to one circuit and it all carried on in sloshing mud and pelting rain.

It was all rather wearying, being away from home for two weeks in continual rain, and by this stage I was longing for it to be over – but it turned into a very thrilling event because Kiri won. This was hugely exciting, both for me and for the Lincolns, because Le Lion is an important event for highlighting a horse's potential, and so far this horse hadn't put a foot wrong. Le Lion is called the World Championships for seven-year-olds – lots of top horses, such as Darien Powers, Welton Romance and King Solomon, have started their careers here. It is also a breeding showcase, so there was great French interest in Kiri's pedigree, which was a boost for British breeding in general and in particular for Roger and Joanna

Day, who bred him. It was his first really big event, and the fact that he was continuing to show his potential gave us all great cause for optimism.

The biggest lesson I learned from the Olympic year is that all my top horses – Rocky at the Olympics, Cornerman, Viceroy and Kiri – ran across country brilliantly, despite the fact that they'd had very few runs. Mark Todd had been following this principle for a while and had cut down the amount of outings he gave several of his top horses. It dawned on me now that he was right – you needn't run horses endlessly in one-day competitions to prepare them for a three-day event. I realised that by minimising their cross-country runs you can preserve their careers, and this is what I have been doing ever since.

The Olympic celebrations continued with a reception at Buckingham Palace for all the medallists; it was a huge honour to be in the same party as people like Steve Redgrave and Matthew Pinsent. I had already got to know the pentathletes and had great admiration for Steph Cook, who won the gold on top of having a full-time career as a doctor. After the party, the eventers went on to have a boozy night at my brother's restaurant, Ghillies. Then at the end of the year the medal winners were invited to *BBC Sports Personality of the Year*, and it felt wonderful to be part of Team GB, which got the team award. It was a thrilling way to end a very special year, which will always hold fond memories for me.

All of these celebrations, I now realise, were a welcome distraction from my looming problems at home. I always tend to feel flat at the end of the season, even though I'm pleased to have a rest from the continual driving and packing, and I miss the buzz that comes from aiming at a big competition. The Olympics had been such an overriding goal for so long that I felt even flatter than normal, but some of this had to do with the fact that I had become aware since returning that all was not well within our marriage.

I had been so focused on Sydney that I hadn't hoisted in the fact that William and I weren't communicating. Now there was no getting away from it, and I was becoming increasingly anxious. William and I have never been an argumentative couple, so there weren't rows – I just felt there was a distance between us.

We somehow got through Christmas and New Year, and I felt particularly upset because this time of year can highlight problems in a relationship. We were drifting apart and I couldn't think how to stop it. I tried to mention it to William but I didn't have much joy, partly because I couldn't bring myself to admit we were having problems and was afraid that if I did, I would precipitate something awful.

We lurched on unhappily through January. I went up to London to have dinner with my brother Tim, who was also miserable because his own ten-year relationship was ending. As I listened to him, I knew I was in the same boat.

In February William and I set off on our second 'Equestriana' tour of lecture-demos, organised by Kelvin Bywater and Kevin Millman. The previous year, our first, had been very successful, and this time our good friend Dane Rawlins, who runs the dressage at Hickstead, joined us. The idea was to demonstrate to an audience our methods of training, putting across what we believe in, and what works for us, but in an entertaining, light-hearted way. Normally, people say that William and I bounce off each other really well, but this time I'm not sure either of us really had our hearts in it; by this time, in private, our manner towards each other had become quite cold.

As it happened, for the worst of reasons we didn't have to complete the tour. Halfway through the news broke out about foot-and-mouth disease, and the enterprise had to be called off: our next venue was near Exeter, an area which was particularly badly affected. At this point I didn't realise that we were on the brink of a national disaster: like many people, all I knew of foot-and-mouth I had got from the James Herriot books, and I had no idea it would turn into such a terrible tragedy for the farming industry.

At the beginning of March, I finally admitted to myself that we had to get to the bottom of what was going on in our marriage and I made myself confront William. The upshot of a long and sad discussion was that we realised we had drifted apart. William eventually admitted that he wanted to have a break – and that in fact he had felt like this for a while but hadn't wanted to rock the boat during the Olympics. So he went and stayed with Duncan and Clare Inglis, just coming home to ride the horses during the day. Because of the foot-and-mouth, he would be away a lot anyway, competing in Europe.

Selfish as it may sound, the foot-and-mouth crisis was almost a relief to me, because all the spring horse trials were cancelled; I don't think I could have faced the competitions, feeling as low as I did. Being stuck at home gave me a lot of time to think. Suddenly my world had been turned upside down, and I had to face up to the fact that I might lose the person who meant most to me. Through my dedication to the sport and my entirely self-centred view of my career and the build-up to the Games, I had taken for granted the one thing that was most important to me. I couldn't believe I had been so blind, and I have punished myself about it ever since. Because we had always got on so well before, I just hadn't noticed the increasing coolness.

I found it torture when William came to the yard and rode; I had to hide myself away, and I think he found it hard too. At first he wouldn't even come into the house, and I felt bad about that as it was his own home. I think he was taken aback by how badly I took his departure.

Mum and Dad were brilliant and came over the first night William left; but that week Dad was diagnosed as having a patch on his lung. He was admitted to hospital in London for an operation, and for a while things looked serious. Our family seemed to be being hit from all sides and, of course, I realised that Mum had enough on her plate without me offloading my problems on to her; so I had to put my own difficulties behind me as far as they were concerned. One of the good things that came out of this whole mess is that it made Tim and I much closer.

Apart from visits to Dad in London and dinners with Tim afterwards, I turned into a hermit. The horses were just kept ticking over by my staff, as the gallops were closed and we couldn't hack on the hill, and for a month I just didn't even bother to ride. I didn't eat properly, I started drinking more in the evenings because it helped me sleep, and I hated myself. Television was a nightmare because every programme seemed to be about couples either being terribly happy or breaking up. My one comfort was my dog Toes. She seemed to know I was unhappy and she never left my side.

Looking back, I can see that it must have been grim for the staff. I had a new head girl, Zanie Tanswell – what a time for her to start! It was a sad day when Nini French left at the end of 2000; she'd originally come on a temporary basis just before I had the shingles and ended up staying for five years and coming with me to the Olympics. She did a fantastic job at turning the horses out, she rode beautifully and she was a good friend who had become part of my life. But her aim was always to compete herself and have a yard; this she has now done, and in 2004 she rode at her first Burghley in 2004; I enjoy following her progress and am so glad it has worked out well for her.

I thought I would struggle to replace Nini, but my prayers were answered when a friend, Johnny Johnston, who was supplying us with shavings at the time, happened to mention to Zanie that I was looking for a head girl. The fact that she stuck out this awful spring was pretty amazing, and she too was to become a great friend.

Both William's and my staff were supportive and loyal to us both throughout this tense and unhappy period; in fact it was probably easier for them when our problems were eventually out in the open, as I imagine the atmosphere beforehand can't have been great. It wasn't easy for William's staff while he wasn't living at home, but Steven Franks did a great job in riding the horses while William's head girl, Sarah Ingeleson, was away in Europe, and he knew he could always come to me for advice.

My close friends were very kind, Duncan and Clare especially. Even though it was awkward for them, they never took sides. Clare was fantastic because although William was telling them that he couldn't see us getting back together, she could see that he wasn't acting as though that was what he meant, and she told me not to give up hope. Roger and Bridget Stack, who are well known in the showing world and who live nearby, rallied round and endlessly invited me to supper, providing me with continuous company; they too were kind and optimistic, but also gave me sterner support: when I got really low, Roger gave me a real talking to and told me to pull myself together.

Some of my friends were cross on my behalf and, of course, everyone wants to give you advice in these circumstances, but I wasn't bitter or angry. I just desperately wanted William back and, after everything that had happened to me with the horses, I wasn't simply going to give up. I tried to hang on to my belief that everything happens for a reason, which is how I dealt with the knocks in my riding career, and I slowly started to believe that somehow things would work themselves out. I came to feel strongly that either William and I would get back together and be stronger for it, or else I would recover, get on with my life and eventually meet someone else.

Laying hold of this strand of hope enabled me to get my act together with the horses. In May it seemed that the event at Saumur in France would go ahead and that British horses would be allowed to run. I directed all my concentration into preparing Cornerman and Viceroy for it and, armed with my theory about not over-running horses, was not bothered by the fact that they hadn't had a prep run.

The only thing that was seriously bothering me was the prospect of facing everyone from the eventing world. Having been part of the circuit for so long, I knew exactly how I would have been a topic of conversation, even among my friends, because that's how life is. Supper with Roger and Bridget was the boundary of my social life at this stage; my social confidence was at an all-time low and I dreaded leaving home. Of course, everyone was very kind at Saumur, but I was still wobbly. One night I went out to dinner and didn't even get as far as the first course before I was in tears and had to flee back to the lorry, which had suddenly replaced the house as my haven. But at least I was competing, and that was going well. Both horses excelled themselves in the dressage to lie first and second. I threw myself into the riding and had two fantastic cross-country runs – and this was without even any cross-country schooling, an experience which translated into a major breakthrough in the way I prepared horses in the future.

Viceroy finished a creditable second at Saumur but unfortunately, while trying to make the time on Cornerman I must have clipped a roping post on the course. We came home with a decent lead to win, but when we pulled up, blood was pumping out of his back leg: he had sustained a horrible wound on the fleshy part below the stifle. Thankfully, Jenny Hall, the team vet, was there to deal with it, but it was so frustrating because this was the second trip Susie had made to France only to see her horse unable to complete because of an unlucky incident.

The first main event to take place in Britain after the foot-and-mouth crisis was Burgie, thanks to the determined efforts of the Lochore family. I won it on a horse called Teddy Twilight, who had been bought by the McIntyres from Donal Barnwell as a four-year-old. He was thought to be by Edmund Burke, but this seems unlikely because he was totally different in type from Rocky or Burke's Boy. Teddy had a massive personality and was a real little athlete. Many times I found myself sitting on the floor looking up at him because he was so sharp at whipping round when something caught his eye. He was a challenge all right; but I felt that he had that tiger instinct and *joie de vivre* that would take him up through the grades.

My other ride at Burgie was Walk On Star, who was doing his first three-day event, and came fourth. 'Magic' was bred by Barbara Walkinshaw out of her own eventing mare and I'd had him since he was a five-year-old. He's a kind horse with a wonderful brain for training, level-headed and unfazed by whatever comes up; he had a consistent intermediate career, never coming home without a rosette. Although he never really impressed me at home by the feeling he gave me, which seemed to lack scope and potential, the minute you get to a competition he ups his game.

The next major event this summer was Tina Gifford's wedding to Phil Cook. My situation was hard on Tina because she was understandably excited but didn't want to rub it in with me; and in return, although I was thrilled for her, I don't suppose I was filling her with confidence. Going to a wedding wasn't exactly top of my list of fun days out at this stage, and it had never occurred to me that I would have to go to my best friend's wedding without my husband, but I had arranged a safety net. I made a pact with William Fox-Pitt that we would accompany each other because it was the only way we could both cope. William and I have always been great friends and he was another person I leaned on heavily that year. He was in something of the same boat as me because his marriage to Wiggy was in trouble. We talked a lot that summer and even managed to make jokes about how we could get tongues wagging by being seen together. It was thanks to him that I got through the day, but, though I did feel a bit wobbly in church, it was a fantastic wedding. Tina looked lovely and was very much herself, very natural. Phil is a lucky man.

Hickstead was another difficult occasion. This was my first outing to a show-jumping competition since the split, and by comparison, the eventing world had become a safe haven. I'd conquered getting out to horse trials, because there I was surrounded by friends; here I would be among William's friends and I dreaded it.

Another Lotus car was on offer in the Grand Prix and Rosie jumped the most immaculate clear round – the only one in the history of the competition – to win it for me. It was a fantastic win, brilliant for Anne Burnet, for the horse and for

Hickstead; but the awful thing is that it meant nothing to me because I felt so flat. I knew I was performing quite well and I was entirely focused because I was putting everything into my riding, but the result simply passed me by.

Competitions had become a wonderful escape from my problems. Sitting on a horse gave my brain a rest from the endless chewing over of my situation because it meant I had to concentrate on riding, on jumping fences and walking courses, and on being part of the competition. I had obligations to the horses and to my owners that had to be fulfilled. People were kind about asking me out, but I hardly ever went. The night after my win at Hickstead I came home to an empty house and dived into a comforting bottle of wine. I'd won a car, and yet I was at rock bottom because I had no one to share it with.

The cancellation of Badminton because of the foot-and-mouth had been a real blow, and I was wondering if Rocky, who was thirteen by now, was ever going to get his chance there. His preparation run for the Europeans was at the Scottish Open Championships at Thirlestane. Ironically, in view of my reduced capacity to appreciate it, this was another great outing results-wise: all four horses jumped a double clear and Rocky won.

There was much debate as to whether Burghley could run, because if foot-and-mouth forced its cancellation too there would be serious implications for the sport's finances. A group of people agreed to underwrite it and Bill Henson, who has always been one of the most innovative directors, took the gamble and ran the event. The course wasn't the most glamorous it's ever been due to cutbacks, but as riders we were just grateful to have the competition.

Cornerman and Viceroy both went to Burghley, for their first four-star runs, and I was dying for Charlie's luck to change for Susie's sake. For the first time, I rode in new colours: the black and orange of Online Finance, who sponsored Blyth Tait and Paul O'Brien and agreed to support me at this competition. Apart from team competitions, this was the first time I had discarded my yellow and black.

Blyth is a wonderful personality and is one of the people I most look up to in the sport, not only for the amazing results he's had, but also for his unstinting generosity and wholehearted contribution to the sport. I owe him a lot because it was through him that I met Mark Bulson and got involved with the clothing company Toggi, which now sponsors me, and also Joe Giannamore, who ran Online Finance. Joe lives near me and I had been giving him lessons as he was just starting to compete in eventing. He has since become a very good friend.

Cornerman's fifth place at Burghley was a welcome result for Susie, who had endured many frustrating disappoint-ments, and also for me, because it had been five years since my last good Burghley, with Henry. Viceroy completed with just a little mishap at the end of the course when he was running out of steam. This was a good effort for him and I was delighted.

The next weekend was Blenheim, where Kiri oozed class and finished fourth, again giving me that wonderful feeling of power and scope. The winners were Kim Severson and Winsome Adante, who were to go on to win Kentucky three times and be team world champions.

Foot-and-mouth continued to wreak havoc, with Windsor's date postponed to September: but the delayed event produced a second three-day win this year for the McIntyres when Burke's Boy gave me my third Windsor victory. Then, suddenly, the Pau European Championships were upon us, and the pressure was on: not only was Britain favourite to win gold, but I was heavily tipped to defend my title and win another gold with Rocky, which would make him the first horse to win back-to-back European titles.

As Scotty had retired from the British team, he was replaced as anchorman by William Fox-Pitt riding Stunning. Tina got an individual slot on her new top horse Captain Christy but, yet again, Rod suffered an unbelievable piece of rotten luck when Flintstone incurred a minor injury; and yet again he put on a cheerful front and came out to support us all. Caroline Pratt, who was reserve, got a last-minute call-up to ride as an individual instead.

Pau is not etched on my memory in the same way as Luhmühlen. I suppose this is because results were not the priority in my life at this stage, and I can really only remember a few mechanics of the competition – the rest is a blur. I was particularly sad because it was my birthday that week and Lizzie Bunn arrived bearing a card from William.

Pierre Michelet is a clever course designer and, though I'd ridden the cross-country at Pau twice before, we were all surprised by how technical and difficult it was this year. There wasn't one particular bogey fence, but there were so many places that offered the possibility of a run-out. The worry was that it wasn't going to be a great course for Rocky; it wasn't his preferred type of big galloping track, but instead was full of tight turns which I could see causing us difficulty.

The competition got off to a good start when the team took the lead after the dressage and I was in second place behind Germany's Ingrid Klimke. Jeanette put up her usual brilliant trailblazing cross-country round, but Leslie had a frustratingly disappointing round on Shear H_2O, with stops in both waters. This put William and me under more pressure, but Rocky proved what a class horse he is when he handled the demanding twists and turns without any problems.

Poor William hated having to wait so long for his turn, but he has the right head for going last and he and Stunning zipped around brilliantly, so at the end of the cross-country we were still in the lead as a team. Ingrid had withdrawn when her horse went lame on the steeplechase, which left me in the lead individually.

However, the French were close enough behind us to make the final phase a real test of nerves, as they are good show jumpers and naturally the home crowd was willing us to have fences down. The time allowed in the show jumping concerned me because it was measured tightly and Rocky much prefers a slower rhythm. He was jumping well and I had a fence in hand to win, but we had to make a tight turn to the last combination. It was a treble with one stride to the middle element and two strides to the third; the distance was short anyway, and particularly so for Rocky. His back end gave way on the point of take-off and we crashed through the last element. I then had only five strides to get myself together for the last fence, which I couldn't afford to have down. I didn't care what we looked like – it was just a case of survival and it must have given everyone watching heart failure. But we did it.

So we had secured two gold medals again; and straight after the medal ceremony and press conference, there was a big celebration back at Rosemary Barlow's supporters' tent. It was a special win for the Pitt–Lewthwaite syndicate, who had been so patient, and for the big contingent of British supporters out in Pau, but the most important thing for me was that Dad was well enough to be there. The four of us had an emotional family reunion and I realised that this was more important than winning; we'd all been through a lot that year and, finally, something had gone right.

Competing had been a wonderful antidote to my personal problems and, despite everything, it had been a fantastic year for me in that respect because I hadn't had good results with just one horse, but with all of them. Yet still I was dreading getting back to home and reality.

On the positive side, I had come to the realisation that whether William came back or not, I could cope on my own and that things would work out. It was the first time I'd been single for twelve years, since before Adam, but by now I was coping much better and had been going up to London regularly to see Tim and meet up with old friends. There was an Olympic ball in London and I decided to go with Rodney Powell as my date. We've known each other for years so we shared a room with the biggest bed you've ever seen and mirrors everywhere. I had borrowed a dress from Zanie, which I thought was a bit too trendy and revealing for me, but Leslie Law, who was with us at the ball, said: 'No, Pippa, honestly, it's fine.' Just as he said that, a waiter walked past with a tray of tea, which went flying. Leslie said: 'See, even the waiter thinks you look good!'

The problem was the uncertainty: I didn't know whether we would get divorced or, if we did, what would happen about the yard – just talking about that made me feel ill because it was my home and I couldn't imagine being anywhere else. William and I had both been doing a lot of travelling and therefore hadn't seen much of each other, partly because we'd been avoiding the issue of our relationship. I knew that we had to have a discussion about the future and I was terrified that it would end up with the decision to divorce – because I still adored him.

So when William told me he wanted to come back to me, I was completely muddled. I had been steeling myself for the prospect of his never returning and, as you do in these circumstances, I'd tried to cheer myself up by making mental lists of all the things that annoyed me about him. Some of these things I'd blown out of proportion, turning them into great big pluses of his not being around. I also felt that I'd gone through the hardest part of the whole saga now and emerged intact, and I knew I couldn't go through such a physical and mental low again.

William was very understanding and realised that after seven months of hell I wasn't going to just say: 'Oh darling, please come home – it'll all be fine.' But I had also learned that it is possible to give up too easily with a marriage and I owe a lot to the example of my parents, who stuck it out through some difficult times. Agreeing that William and I should try again was the best decision I've ever made – certainly more important than any sporting decision.

I realised that I couldn't go through the rest of my life wondering if I should have given it another go. We'd been together for ten years and we'd had so many laughs and amassed so many memories that I didn't want to throw away. It wasn't so much that he was my husband as that he was my best friend; and that was the overriding factor that made me decide to give it another go.

9
Can It Get Any Better?

The Christmas of 2001 was a much happier time than that of twelve months earlier. I was worried about how William and I would put our troubles behind us – and I suppose one never completely forgets an episode like that – but I knew I had to look to the future. Our 'reunion' was, in fact, surprisingly easy. My gut instinct had been that everything happens for a reason and I knew we would now be closer because our problems had made us talk to each other properly and appreciate one another more.

We spent Christmas Day on our own, doing the horses together, and in the evening we went around to Roger and Bridget Stack. At that stage, when we had only just got back together, the news wasn't entirely public and we didn't want to make a big thing of it because we didn't know yet if it was going to work; so we avoided too much socialising over Christmas. Also, my family, who had gone through the mill over the split, were lukewarm about William's return, especially Dad and Tim, who were doubtful that I'd done the right thing. So, as we were still finding our feet again, we spent a quiet New Year in Norway with Geir (Jimmy) and Elizabeth Gullikson in their lovely chalet in the mountains near Kitsveldt, site of the Olympic downhill run.

The championships of 2002 was the World Equestrian Games at Jeréz in Spain, and both William and I were in contention for the British teams. But for me the main focus was Badminton. I was really looking forward to it. Rocky had missed the last two Badmintons, first because he was being saved for Sydney and then because of foot-and-mouth, and now I felt he was actually ready to win it. I knew that a horse with two European titles had to be capable of winning, and I was really excited at the prospect.

I also had four other competitive advanced horses of the calibre any rider would give their right arm for: Primmore's Pride, Cornerman, Walk On Star and Jurassic Rising, all of whom I knew were all capable of putting up good performances at their international spring events.

So I had much about which to be optimistic. However, with every January comes the nightmare of working out a programme to suit all the horses. It's like a massive jigsaw. First, I decide which three-day event I plan to do with each horse, and then I work backwards from those dates to decide which one-day events they should do to prepare. Every horse is different and needs a different prep run. All this, of course, has to be balanced against owner expectations and the places at which it suits them to have their horses run – and on top of *that*, you have to be aware that you might be balloted out of a particular event, which will throw the whole pattern out. The interests of the horse have to come first and, as a result, it's not always easy to keep everyone happy.

My main Badminton build-up competition is usually

Belton in Lincolnshire, which takes place in early April. It's one of my favourite events – the venue, at a stately home, is beautiful and, as everyone always goes there, it's a good chance to watch all the top horses and riders and an opportunity to make a good pre-Badminton assessment. This time I had four horses entered in the advanced sections there – Cornerman, Rocky, Primmore's Pride and Viceroy – and all four were in competitive positions prior to cross-country day.

Having done the first two phases on Saturday, I have often found horses to be quite fresh going across country on Sunday at Belton. My first ride this Sunday morning was Cornerman, and we got as far as the sixth fence, a big ditch in front of a post and rails. Our approach was fine, but on the point of take-off his hind foot clipped a front shoe, which delayed his take-off for a split-second, resulting in his hitting the fence hard. He sent me absolutely flying and I thought I'd been thrown clear, but as he scrabbled to stay on his feet he trod on my left ankle.

The minute it happened, I realised I was injured, and immediately absorbed all the implications for my build-up to Badminton. I wasn't sure if I'd broken my ankle, but I couldn't put weight on it. I was whipped off to Grantham Hospital in an ambulance, leaving behind some devastated owners whose horses I couldn't ride, and during the journey to hospital I was weighed down by a terrible dread that I was going to miss yet another Badminton with Rocky.

Luckily, I was wearing zip-up boots, as everyone does nowadays, so the boot didn't have to be cut off. Even so, when it was taken off, I was in agony. The swelling just ballooned and an X-ray showed that I'd chipped the bones in my ankle, so I was put in an open-fronted plaster to allow for the swelling. I was distraught.

I got back to Belton, looking pretty dramatic with my leg in plaster from the knee down; luckily, Sue Bunn was there and was able to drive my lorry home for me.

At this point my Badminton prospects must have looked dubious to everyone else; but I was absolutely determined, come what may, that I would be in there. Next day I went straight to the British Olympic Association medical centre in London and had the plaster taken off so that I could have physio on my ankle. The X-rays taken there revealed that the joint wasn't actually broken: I had ruptured ligaments, and the chips that had shown up must have been from an old injury. I'm sure a lot of riders are rattling round with similar old fractures that they've ignored. Most riders' first reaction is to get back on the horse; we're always very reluctant to have any injury looked at, in case we're told to have a lay off – I always try to rush away from ambulance men when they come towards me. Riders are a tough breed by necessity; we tend to put up with the aches and pains because giving in can mean a loss of income or missing an important competition – and no one ever wants to give in to that.

Through the BOA, I had treatment from its physio, Gillian Morgan, who was based at Bisham Abbey. William lent me his automatic car so, as the damaged foot was my left, I could still drive. Gillian then put me in touch with a local physio called John Fairley, whom I have been visiting ever since.

I couldn't ride at all, let alone walk on the ankle, and it was absolute agony. I had physio treatment every day, I made myself do weight-bearing exercises and I used the horses' magnetic boot. I also put their Ice-Tight clay on my leg, wrapping it in Clingfilm, and applied loads of ice – all things I'd do with a horse's injured leg! Zanie Tanswell and the girls kept the yard going and they did all the fitness work. I felt rather like a racehorse trainer at the gallops, sitting on the bonnet of the car watching the horses work.

Since the days when I had gone for help to Nicky Heath, I had got into the habit of not leaving a single stone unturned in my preparation for a major event. Now it had all gone belly-up because the horses hadn't had prep runs and I'd had a bad fall; but I knew I had to turn all this negative preparation into a positive. I told myself that if I did get to Badminton – and it looked doubtful at times – for once I wouldn't be tired. I wouldn't have had to drive the lorry for miles to compete four horses the weekend before. It would be like Sydney, when I was well rested. And it wouldn't matter that Rocky had missed his Belton run because he'd gone so well the year before.

Another problem was that Cornerman was also entered for Badminton. I did realise that I wasn't fit enough to ride two horses and, therefore, that Susie would have to be disappointed. Cornerman had been drawn first in the running order and I thought it was crazy to try to ride him as well, as I didn't know how my ankle would hold up and the strain might jeopardise my chances on Rocky.

I finally got on Rocky the Friday before Badminton and rode without stirrups so I didn't have to put any weight on my ankle. On the Sunday, I went up to Eddy Stibbe's for a cross-country school because I knew that I needed to prove that I was fit enough to ride. I had a school over a few fences, with the ankle well strapped up. This, plus my boot, gave the ankle a lot of support and, though my leg wasn't that effective, it was actually easier to ride than walk.

When I finally got to Badminton, I felt so thankful just to be there. At the same time, though, I did feel under pressure because we definitely started as favourites.

Rocky did a lovely dressage test for me. One of the dangers in the last week before Badminton is that one can overdo the flatwork. Rocky has always loved his flatwork, but he can get bored if you give him too much of it and so, in hindsight, it suited him mentally that I couldn't work him beforehand.

Rocky is the most amazing horse on whom to ride a test when there's a lot of atmosphere. The minute you go into a big arena with a lot of people watching – and we were near the end of the day on the Friday, when everyone watches and there is an air of expectation – you can feel him change gear immediately. He just rises to the occasion, you feel him grow under you and the movement just continues to improve. This in turn makes my spirits rise and I feel proud and exhilarated – he makes me want to show him off as best as I can. It's a real buzz riding a dressage test on Rocky – and it had been three years since we'd last done a major event on home soil, at Badminton in 1999, so it felt great to have done such a good test in front of a home crowd. At the end of the phase I had quite a strong lead over Andrew Hoy on Darien Powers and it was a great feeling – a brilliant start. We were on the way.

One fun aspect of that Badminton was the launch of my first book, *Training the Young Horse*, and I was touched to see the long queue of people waiting for me to sign their copies. This was a practical book which I had written with Kate Green, beautifully illustrated with pictures by the well-known eventing photographer Kit Houghton. It was a project which had occupied a lot of evenings the previous year and, though at times we had all found it a chore, it had also been a good distraction from my troubles. We'd have progressed a lot faster if everyone concerned hadn't had to listen to many of my wobbly moments but, with the aid of a few bottles of wine, working on this had in fact been one of the happier episodes of 2001 and I was thrilled with the end product.

The Badminton course had a new look, with the start and

finish in the main arena, and this made for a great atmosphere. I hobbled around once, but after that the director Hugh Thomas kindly gave me permission to drive around and just get out at each fence for a look. It was, in fact, a nice course – but suddenly I felt the old pressure building up again. However, I stuck by my trusted mental system that night and slept well. William had come down in time to see my test and we slept together in the lorry. After his absence during my big moments the previous year, it was now especially lovely to have his support.

I had a very good cross-country round, with not one single scary moment; it was a dream Badminton ride. Coming into Huntsman's Close I was bang on time and, as I was aware that there had been a couple of falls – for Jeanette Brakewell and Rod – and some other problems, I decided that I had a healthy enough lead to play safe here and so took the long route. This did, however, cost me some time faults and now I no longer had a show jump in hand over Andrew, who had ridden the most beautiful round.

Saturday night was a new experience for me at Badminton. I could not sleep. The cross-country had been such a good feeling that I wanted to jump it over and over again in my head and I couldn't switch off. Meanwhile, William, the two dogs and my brother Tim all seemed to be snoring and fidgeting noisily, and I had such a bad night that I got up at five o'clock. I always get up early on Sunday morning anyway to check the horse for the vet's inspection, but I think Zanie was surprised to see me quite so early. At 5.15 a.m., with no one else about, I took my horse for a walk to pick grass in front of Badminton House. It was lovely, just me and my horse: one of those rare moments. I relived the day before and wondered about the day ahead and whether I was going to fulfil my dream. I actually felt quite peaceful and resigned to what the next few hours held for me. No one could take away what my horse had achieved over the years, and all our wins went through my head that morning. I just revelled in spending time with Rocky, realising what he had done for me and what we'd come through together.

I felt quite emotional at the trot-up, watching Zanie take Rocky through the test because I was too lame. I think she felt very proud to be running up the leading horse, and I was pleased for her, because she had put in so much extra work this time because of my injury.

After the trot-up, the morning seemed very long. This is one of the most frustrating things about a three-day event: the whole weekend has been manic, you've had to leap out of bed early for the trot-up and then, if you're fortunate enough to be in contention, it's a long, long wait.

Having William around on these occasions does take the pressure off. He walked the show-jumping course with me, pointing out where I could save time, and boosted my confidence by helping me in the warm-up. The last thing he said to me was: 'Pretend you're at home – just shut out the whole Badminton thing, the crowds, the expectation. Ride with your head, keep focused and concentrate on riding.'

Although Rocky looks a good jumper because of his scope – and he is if you get him in the right rhythm – if you can't get him going right, as happened at Sydney and some one-day events when he was younger, it's horrifying how quickly the fences start falling. However, some pressure was taken off me when Andrew Hoy had an unfortunate round and dropped out of contention. I was briefly aware of this, and knew fleetingly that at least Badminton would be won by a British rider, as William Fox-Pitt had gone clear on Tamarillo – and that I had one fence in hand over him.

Rocky is one horse that you really do have to ride properly – you can't get away with a single mistake. Therefore, my mind was totally taken up with trying to keep him soft and in a rhythm. I was concentrating too hard to think about the pressure or the consequences of a mistake.

We had just one time fault. Had we had the last fence down, it would have been disastrous – I'd have finished on the same score as William Fox-Pitt, who would then have won because he was faster across country. But that didn't happen. We'd won.

Landing over the last fence was an amazing feeling. I was full of such mixed emotions that I didn't know how to react and it's always difficult to think of something sensible to say when you're interviewed on TV.

I'd known since 1999 that I was capable of winning Badminton on Rocky, but it seemed such a long time coming. I was emotional because William was there and suddenly everything seemed to have gone right; I was flooded with gratitude to Rocky; and I was so relieved to be able to reward all the people who had been so good to me. Mum and Dad were beside themselves, as were Tim and Becky Coffey and Zanie and, of course, Rocky's owners Emma and Andy Pitt and David and Di Lewthwaite.

I was swallowed up in a flurry of presentations, a press conference, photo-call, a brief champagne celebration back at the lorry – and then, suddenly, I was driving the lorry home in a totally normal way. There's so rarely time to wallow in a big win because you're always unpacking and packing up for the next event.

The following weekend we were back in the lorry for the long drive to Chatsworth, where Jurassic Rising finished second to Blyth Tait on Ready Teddy in a good prep run for

Saumur. There was a sad note, though. I had lent Burke's Boy to the New Zealander Bryce Newman to ride that spring, as he was one horse that I felt did need some proper work while I was laid up. Bryce had come over to try to get selected for the World Games; he's a talented rider and, as he needed some spare rides to occupy him that spring, I had been only too happy to lend him Burke's Boy, on whom he'd had good results. In comparison to the New Zealanders, we don't really know we're born in England. They have to risk everything to cross the world with a horse they have faith in and think is good enough to be selected for a championship; this means a huge personal and financial risk, and it didn't pay off for Bryce that year as both his horses went wrong. He then had the most horrendous fall off Burke's Boy – the horse head-butted a fence in the water and knocked himself out, to the horror of the watching crowd. He was taken to Newmarket to be examined and then back to the McIntyres for a break, but I was worried about him.

After Chatsworth there was another quick turnaround and it was off to Punchestown with Kiri and Cavalcade. The latter, owned by Jane and Andy Crofts, was a big horse by the jumping sire Cavalier. I had been eventing him since he was five – he was another horse on whom I won the Burghley Young Event Horse finals – and he was a bold, clean jumper, but also a big, strong horse to ride. I could contain him at the one-day events, but Punchestown was our first three-day and I soon realised that I couldn't hold him. There was a nasty moment halfway around when he ran away with me and I had to pull him up to a standstill. But I knew that the Crofts wanted him to get a qualification so he could progress in his career, and also that we had come a long way for me just to give up. So I hacked him home slowly, not letting him go, and he went clear; but towards the end of the course there was another terrifying moment.

The second last obstacle was a famous Punchestown fence called the Newgrange Mound, which involved jumping on and off a mound. I had Cavalcade anchored up to that point, but of course I had to slip the reins to go down the drop and when I went to shorten them, he was gone. I have never been so scared as I was approaching the last fence. I couldn't even turn him away from it because I had no energy left. Fortunately, we met it on the correct stride and survived.

As we finished, I was shrieking to everyone that I couldn't stop. The muscles in my arms had gone into spasm – they were just bulging and throbbing. I made up my mind at that very moment that Cavalcade wasn't the horse for me. He needed a man on board, and I was happy that the Crofts rerouted him to William Fox-Pitt.

After a massage on my arm muscles, I climbed aboard Kiri and, again, he filled me with excitement and that wonderful feeling of class. He tired towards the end of the cross-country, and we had a near-miss at the Newgrange Mound when he hit the rail on top, but it had been a good round and I was thrilled with our second place.

This month was just a constant re-packing of the suitcase. No sooner had we got back from Ireland than I had to turn around – in the same day – and set sail for Saumur with Jurassic Rising. But it seemed that nothing could go wrong for me this month; we won that and, two weeks later, I won Bramham on Walk On Star.

Suddenly my new panic was that I'd used up all my luck before the World Championships. When everything goes right, as it did for me that May, you think the sport is easy and the long hours just melt away; when it's going wrong, it's a drudge, everything feels exhausting and impossible. But I was seriously on a run now and it was an amazing feeling.

The most exciting aspect was that at last it looked a near-certainty that William and I would be in a championships together: the first ever eventing–show-jumping husband-and-wife team. William had been having a very good run on Denise Stamp's mare Amber Du Montois. Just as I was winning Bramham, he was on the winning Nations Cup team at Lisbon, which was easily one of Britain's best show-jumping results in a while and quite a cause for celebration. After Bramham, I flew out to Barcelona to support William, who was jumping there. It was a thrilling weekend because he won the Grand Prix, for which the first prize was a car. He then jumped another double clear for Britain at the Nations Cup in Lummen, Belgium, the next week and then, following Hickstead, he was selected for the team at the World Games. Everything was going brilliantly for both of us.

I set off for Gatcombe, where Kiri and I were second behind Andrew Nicholson on Mallard's Treat and so – Andrew being a New Zealander – won the national title. William, meanwhile, had flown to Dublin, from where he phoned to tell me the awful news that Amber had gone lame. We didn't know how serious it was then, and hoped it was just an infection, but it turned out to be worse than that. I just couldn't believe it. The previous year, when I hadn't been taking too much notice of what William was doing, he'd been in contention for the European Championships with Vechta, who had also gone lame. It just seemed so unfair; I have always longed for William to be on a team and yet every time the luck just goes against him at the last moment.

This quite deflated my own preparations, but I knew I had to crack on. Rocky had a good prep run at Thirlestane and finished third in the Scottish Open, and I had a good confidence-boost when Kiri was sixth at Burghley, his first four-star. He led the dressage and gave me a fantastic cross-country ride, albeit with a few time faults. He showed that the step up in class was no hindrance to him, and it just reinforced my confidence in him.

Meanwhile we had, of course, been having team training, but the build-up was nothing like the preparation for the Olympics when there had been a month's quarantine beforehand. I had been working Rocky in a special rug to help him acclimatise to the heat in Spain, and we'd been training with Yogi Breisner, Kenneth Clawson, the show jumping coach, and Tracie Robinson at Waresley. The team was the same as for Pau, except that William Fox-Pitt was riding Tamarillo this time, not Stunning. Tina was taking part as an individual with Captain Christy, and Polly Stockton was the new kid on the block with the former Mark Todd ride Eye Spy, with whom she'd been having some good results. The combination of Rocky's form plus William and Leslie having been second and third at Badminton and the consistency of Jeanette's performances over the years meant that we were easily the favourites, on paper, to win the gold medal. It was my first World Championships and, clearly, I had a live hope of being the individual champion, so I was very excited. In fact we were all fired up about Britain's prospects as a whole, and there was huge expectation.

Yet there was also something missing. The horses were ready to go out and win and the riders were well prepared, but there were little things that weren't right, and when a lot of minor things slot together it can make a difference, although I still can't put my finger on the real problem. There was somehow a lack of cohesiveness, a slight weirdness about the whole situation, and it certainly turned into the most strange competition.

A lot of it was because we were tired. Four of us, myself, Tina, Leslie and Jeanette, had driven up to the East Midlands Airport to see the horses off. We had to wait in the lorries until the horses took off and, in doing so, missed a night's sleep to drive home and pack. In hindsight this was crazy, but our main priority was our horses and we wanted to be the ones to see them off.

We flew out to Spain the next day to baking heat and some fairly lengthy administration. The horses had travelled well but the accreditation took an exhaustingly long time. We had a nice hotel to stay in, but there weren't enough cars for us all and the cross-country course was at least a twenty-minute drive from the main venue. It seemed that we were always hanging around waiting for someone and it was difficult to co-ordinate everyone. When you're used to being independent, this was tough. We couldn't just go back to the hotel and chill out and we didn't each get enough time to ourselves. This made us aware that we would need to plan a strategy for Athens more carefully.

I was third to go for the team which, unfortunately, meant that I followed Germany's Bettina Hoy on the grey Woodsides Ashby, who is like a pure dressage horse. Bettina was absolutely magical; she got a record mark of 20.8 and everyone went wild. It was a very hard act to follow, even for Rocky, but we still managed to be second, on 28. William Fox-Pitt had also done a very good test and our team was just fractionally in the lead over the USA.

This was rewarding for our trainer Tracie Robinson, who had spent a lot of time on us. She was formerly head girl at Talland School of Equitation and for the dressage rider Dr

Wilfrid Becholsheimer; she's taught Toddy and Carl Hester and is the most brilliant, enthusiastic teacher who can actually make dressage fun. Tracie would be hilarious to video – she gets so animated when teaching that she literally dances the movements, skipping half-passes and flying changes around the arena. She's an invaluable member of the team because she gets on so well with everyone and, having done her bit, she always mucks in on cross-country day. Tracie often ended up with the unglamorous jobs, like washing down on Phase C and being stuck miles away out on a limb which meant she didn't get to see us go across country.

The cross-country course at Jeréz, which was designed by Mike Tucker, was a good championship track. It was imaginative and impressive, with an appropriately Spanish flavour and wonderful fence-dressings. The course was manmade, and on virgin soil, but although it looked beautiful and green in the dry, dusty Spanish landscape, the going was actually hard and slippery.

The first water complex had everyone worried. My initial impression was that what happened there wasn't going to depend on skill, it was going to be down to luck. The complex involved going up a ramp which had a log perched ominously on the top, followed by a very steep slide like a ski-jump down to water. There were two strides in water to an island, a bounce over a house and then a bounce off again over another fence into water. It was difficult to know how to ride it; you just had no idea how the horses would come down the steep slope and at what speed they would meet the water. It looked a complete lottery, and it was an ugly fence. Leslie decided immediately that he was going to do the long route, but the rest of us were scheduled to risk the straight way.

Jeanette was her normal fantastic self as trailblazer and made the course look completely straightforward; she went clear on Over To You and was also one of the quickest. It was a great start. Leslie, however, had an unfortunate aberration when jumping a series of fences on turns; his horse banged itself, which distracted him, and he circled in between the wrong elements and got twenty penalties. He was terribly upset with himself.

Then it was my turn. As I galloped in between the first and second fences the ground felt like a motorway; you could just feel the hardness of the going and I hated doing this to my horse. Rocky didn't seem to mind, but he wasn't jumping as cleanly as he had done in the past and was a bit low over his fences – but I didn't have time to worry about that.

During the morning I'd seen quite a few riders go through the water in a variety of styles, some more successful than others. I was concerned because I knew the island part was the sort of fence where I needed to be spot-on because Rocky just doesn't have that fifth leg. The whole complex reminded me of the ghastly jetty incident at Badminton in 1999 and I knew a good stride up on to the bank was crucial if the whole thing was to come off.

I started off quite well. I didn't want to come too quickly down the bank and I managed to achieve the right control, which quite a few others hadn't, but in the first stride in water Rocky pitched and his nose went down under the water. I just couldn't pick him up in time. Somehow he got up on to the bank, but he never had a chance of picking himself up to jump the fence on top so, like Leslie, I too had twenty penalties.

It was a horrible feeling, but because I was in the team I had to keep going. It seemed the longest, most punishing course I've ever ridden, because as well as the ground being hard it was so twisty to ride. So many landings involved turning within two or three strides of touching down, so that you had to punish the horse by hauling them around just as they landed.

I was gutted. Rocky so deserved to do well at Jeréz which, I knew, would be his only chance of a World Championships. I have ridden, and reridden, that fence over and over again in my head, but I still don't think I would have done anything differently. Sometimes you make your own luck, and I don't think it was ever meant to be – we just didn't start right.

The team's fortunes were now going pear-shaped, but we still had William, who is usually a brilliantly cool anchorman. He had a great chance of individual gold and, his thinking being that you don't win gold medals by taking long routes, he also went the straight way at the water. Tamarillo slipped and got too fast, and they had a virtually identical stop to mine.

The whole debacle was reminiscent of what happened to the New Zealanders at the World Games in The Hague in 1994 – they were dead cert favourites to win then, yet three of them fell across country. Luck wasn't on their side that day, and it wasn't on ours on this occasion.

To make matters worse, neither Tina nor Polly had a great day either. Captain Christy hated the ground and Tina, out of sight after the dressage, just rode him around for a slow clear. Poor Polly was eliminated for five refusals; Eye Spy didn't want to know, and it must have been a pretty awful introduction to the senior team for her.

All of us felt shattered that Saturday night; we hadn't got a medal in sight, we felt so bad for Yogi, and we felt we'd let our country down as well as the huge number of supporters who had either come out to Spain or who were following the competition on the BBC at home. It was a dismal, soul-searching evening. All that was left for us to do was to try to hold our heads up high on Sunday, do the best possible job we could and try to salvage something.

But it's a funny old sport. Our team show-jumping performance turned out to be the best. What we lacked on Saturday, we made up for on Sunday with good jumping by all four of us. But this still wouldn't have got us a medal – until the highly placed riders, mainly the Australians and Americans, suddenly started to hit fences like it was going out of fashion. We just couldn't believe it.

If we'd known in advance that bronze was all we'd end up with, we'd have been horrified; but to go from the prospect of returning home empty-handed to winning team bronze and individual silver was suddenly terribly exciting and almost funny, and our supporters were so relieved that you'd have almost thought we'd won the gold.

We beat the disbelieving Australians to the team bronze by just 0.4 of a penalty, and suddenly Jeanette, who had done so much for the team over four years, was climbing higher and higher up the order; she ended up with the silver, her first individual medal. Without Jeanette we wouldn't have won a team medal, nor would we have qualified for the Athens Olympics. This was one championships from which we were all desperate to get home.

The Americans, for whom Kim Severson was definitely the heroine, won the team gold, and the ever-improving French won silver. Perhaps the most satisfactory result was Jean Teulere winning the individual title; he is an amazing horseman who had never previously won anything big enough to gain the recognition he deserved. It was great that a rider of that calibre won the title, and no one begrudged him his victory. In fact, France were the most successful nation at that Games, with medals in almost all disciplines, and they showed what a force they would be at the 2004 Olympics.

My year ended happily with first and fourth places at Pau. Cornerman made up for Susie's Badminton disappointment by winning; he was brilliant and I feel strongly that there is a big four-star win in him one day. Teddy Twilight was fourth in his first three-star; he was really starting to reward my efforts by showing me the talent that I believed he had and was a real challenge, a little person with a huge personality.

I finished the year second in the world rankings to William Fox-Pitt. Despite the disappointment of Jeréz, it had been by far my most successful year ever. My only worry now was how on earth I could better it.

10
Grand Slam

I hadn't thought that it would be possible to have a Christmas so bad as the one two years before when our marriage was faltering, but 2002 was, for a completely different reason, really horrible.

The previous spring I had been given a little black-and-tan terrier puppy called Fudge – known to all as 'Fudgey Funnell' – by Sarah Jewson's daughter Charlotte. I had wanted a friend for Toes, my constant companion and best friend during William's absence, who now shadowed me so persistently that I worried about leaving her on her own when I went out.

It happened on the morning of 17 December, the day before William was due to jump at Olympia. I was going up there with him and would be occupied running errands for the press office – by this stage I had rather grown out of the rosette girl role but still needed something to do while William was riding.

I let the dogs out first thing in the morning, as usual; the routine was that they'd rush out and do their business and then come back in for a biscuit. That morning I was on the telephone for about twenty minutes and by the time I finished talking, I realised that the dogs hadn't returned. Straightaway, panic set in and I immediately began looking for them.

My other dogs, Fingers and Spliff, used to go off hunting, as many terriers will, but these two never had. All day I looked for Toes and Fudge, and by the time it got dark I was beside myself. I had called the local police; then William and I drove around the lanes calling and calling for them. Eventually William went to bed, as he had a lot to do the next day, and he tried to reassure me that they'd probably be back by the morning, but I just couldn't let it go and instead spent the whole night outside shouting into the dark.

The next day William went up to London. He hated leaving me so distressed and I hated not supporting him, but there was no option. He had to get on with his job and there was no way I could leave home.

People were very kind. William went into the press office at Olympia and all the journalists wrote about my lost dogs in their newspaper reports. Mum understood how miserable I was and came over to help me look and make a poster; between us we distributed five hundred of them. The huntsman and terriermen from the local Surrey Union Hunt combed the woods and fields for miles with their terriers in case my dogs had gone to ground and got stuck,

LOST 17/12/02
2 Smooth haired Terriers FEMALES
Fudge: 11 month old Black and Tan
with sticking up ears.
Toes: 5 years old Plain Tan.

Desperate to find our best friends.
SUBSTANTIAL
Cash REWARD offered
Call: Pippa & William Funnell on

but they told me that it was unlikely that a ten-month-old puppy would go down a hole anyway. Lots of local people were very concerned and a nice woman from the next village spent hours out with her Labrador looking. The local radio stations and newspapers rallied around with appeals.

I rang dog wardens and kennels, visited Battersea Dogs Home and logged on to lost dog websites. The more research I did, the more dreadful stories I heard about the awful things that happen to dogs, and I realised that I was not alone – hundreds of people's dogs were disappearing without trace. It was the most terrible feeling of helplessness, and I was tortured with images of them being frightened.

I had never even so much as read my horoscope before, but one day I plucked up the nerve to consult a medium. A friend also put me on to a 'witch doctor' in Africa through the internet. I wouldn't say the experience convinced me, but it was odd that they both came to the same conclusion: that the dogs had been taken by a couple of lads and had gone east. I drove and drove and drove, asking at farms and villages and somehow getting the nerve up to go into travellers' sites where, despite my reservations, the people were kind and helpful.

Mum, Dad, Tim and William's mother Dawn came over at Christmas, but we couldn't bring ourselves to celebrate. The house felt so empty. Much as I adore my horses, dogs are even more special because they live in the house with you, they get excited about seeing you and, to me, they are friends. William loved them just as much as I did – the moment either of us was away, the other would let the dogs sleep on our bed.

The horses came back into work in January, but I couldn't focus on them or the forthcoming season and I hardly rode, leaving poor Zanie Tanswell to bear the brunt of the work. For the first two months of the year I was obsessed with trying any avenue that might lead to my dogs. To this day I still pine for them, and even now the sight of a little brown terrier will make me jam on the brakes in the car. I still call for them by mistake. It's the not knowing that is so awful. When you have a life with animals, you know there will be low moments when they are ill and die, but nothing comes even close to the feeling of wondering how they died or, if they are still alive, are they being treated cruelly.

William was just as upset as I was, but he has always been able to be more pragmatic; a show jumper's life has to be more commercial than an eventer's and, unlike the drama I tend to create out of every arrival and departure, he is used to horses coming and going. He realised that for everyone's sanity I needed to go away and in February took me skiing in Courchevel. The trip was arranged through Di Lewthwaite, who found us a chalet right in the middle of Courchevel by the ski school, which was handy as our companions were Pete and Tara Charles with their young son Harry, Duncan, Clare and their daughter Amy, and Lizzie Bunn with her daughters Ellie and Georgia, who is my goddaughter. It was a great week, but four children under the age of seven were exhausting. There was no chance of a lie-in and William and I couldn't believe how four small kids managed to sound like a herd of elephants at 6 a.m.

Amy had fallen off her pony two days beforehand and was complaining vaguely of a sore shoulder. At ski school she said it really hurt and, though she still didn't make much of a fuss, Duncan and Clare eventually took her to the doctor, who announced that she had cracked her collarbone. Clare, who is actually a fantastic mother, felt terribly guilty and we teased her for ages about what a cruel parent she was.

There were, of course, après-ski incidents. William had been given a bright orange Norwegian team ski jacket by Geir Gullikson and it so happened that some big races were taking place in Courchevel that week. We were in a bar knocking back the schnapps when the real Norwegian ski team walked in! They took the sight of William in one of their jackets in good part and we got chatting with them. I was just so relieved that they saw William in a bar and not skiing. He is brave and fast on skis – and has left me way behind, as I am a bit windy, always worrying about injury – but, having a real show jumper's walk, he is rather bow-legged!

Before the start of the season, two new puppies arrived with the show jumper Andrew Saywell. The Saywells had once had a puppy of Spliff's and so these two are related to our old dog. Zippy is brown and white, and Mouse is brown. The original idea was that one puppy was for Mum and Dad, and one was for me, but I couldn't split the two little sisters because they loved each other so much.

Back home, I got more of a grip on the forthcoming season. I knew I was well off for four-star rides, I had a yard full of horses in whom I had confidence, and I knew that all my horses were capable of winning if I rode them well and positively. As long as I just had the necessary element of luck on my side, without which even the best rider can't win, things could go really well.

The downside to having so many good rides is juggling with the schedule in order both to be fair to all the owners and to find time to give each horse a programme through which you can maximise their chance of success. It sounds ridiculous – and many riders would love this dilemma – but having three horses capable of doing a spring four-star event is difficult because we are allowed to ride only two, and I had Rocky, Cornerman and Kiri. All eventing owners want to go to Badminton – just as all racehorse owners dream of getting to the Cheltenham Gold Cup or the Derby – and if you have more than two potential rides there, someone has to be disappointed. I knew I would have to tell one set of owners that they would be going to the four-star at Kentucky in the USA instead of Badminton, and I dreaded this.

Eventually I managed to reach a logical conclusion. I was adamant that Rocky should defend his title and felt that, at the age of fifteen, he had done enough travelling – he'd flown to Australia and Spain and trailed down to the south of France; and he'd also proved that he could be brilliant at Badminton. My gut feeling was that Kiri was the one with the best chance of shining at Kentucky; Cornerman had been a little unsettled in the dressage at Burghley and an expensive trip to America might be wasted on him.

Predictably, Kiri's owner Denise Lincoln was extremely disappointed when I reluctantly broke the news of my decision, and I knew that she felt she was getting second-class treatment. But with Lottery funding available to help send a team of British horses across the Atlantic, it was a golden opportunity for me to have a first ride at Kentucky and I tried to cheer up Denise by pointing out that we actually had a realistic chance of winning.

This year I decided on a different Badminton preparation. Tina Cook and I had heard that the international one-day event at Fontainebleau in France at the end of March would make a good pre-Badminton run so, for a change, we loaded up the lorry with Rocky, Cornerman and Tina's horses Captain Christy and Archrival and set off for a weekend in France. We were the only Brits going and it seemed rather an adventure.

The course came a bit of a shock, because it was demanding for that stage of the spring, but it turned out to be a most useful pre-Badminton run. Rocky had a blip on top of a bank when I didn't get a good enough stride on to it and so he stopped. This served as a sharpener for both of us and reminded me of how on the ball you have to be at that type of fence with him. But it was a great event and did the job that we wanted; we weren't planning to win, just to have a good prep outing.

Kentucky seemed to come up quickly after that. I had to have all my three-day horses fit and ready by the middle of April because I would be away for over a week in the USA and in May the major events at home come thick and fast. Therefore, everything had to be planned with military precision before I left for the States. The gallops I use, at the Harwoods' racing stables in Pulborough, are a forty-minute drive away and I didn't want to burden the girls with all the trips there.

Zanie and I had a conflab and she told me she was happy to stay behind and oversee the Badminton horses. This was good of her because most head girls wouldn't want to miss out on a trip to Kentucky, but she knew she could be more useful at home. So I took a friend of hers, Cara Bexton, to Kentucky. Cara was an experienced eventing groom who had worked for Tanya Cleverley for many years and often gave me a hand if I was short-staffed, so she knew the form. She went out with Kiri, which was something else for me to fret about as he had never been on a plane before. They flew to New York, where they were in quarantine for a couple of days before setting off on the fifteen-hour drive to Kentucky, and Cara kept me informed at all stages throughout the journey.

It was a good gang of us going out to Kentucky – William Fox-Pitt, Polly Stockton, Leslie and Rod – and, to give us a real championship feel, we had Yogi, Kenneth, Tracie and the vet Jenny Hall looking after us. I love foreign events because everyone pulls together and helps each other a lot more. This was my first trip to America, and being surrounded by so many people that I knew well and liked made up for the absence of my normal back-up team of William, my parents and Becky. It was a strange feeling for me, going to a three-day event without any of them. The Lincolns, of course, came too, and I was pleased that Nick and Barbara Walkinshaw decided to come and support us.

Although the competition is technically of the same standard as Badminton and Burghley, Kentucky has a completely different feel from either of those very English events. It's in bluegrass country, the centre of American bloodstock breeding, and takes place in an impressive park with white railings everywhere. The facilities for riders are fantastic and there's so much space. Because we were in quarantine, we had a private British yard fronted by a nice grass area where we put up a gazebo. We were thus set for a very united and happy camp.

For me, the whole event had a feelgood atmosphere. The cross-country course was beautifully presented, produced by the Olympic designer Mike Etherington-Smith, and had a really inviting feel. Right from my first walk I just wanted to go out there and do it. It was very big – every single fence up to maximum height – but perhaps a little kinder than Badminton.

I was initially concerned about Kiri because I didn't think he was quite going to the standard I would have liked on the flat, but Tracie gave me a hand and I started to feel more confident. Her reassurance paid off and we took the lead in the dressage phase. Kiri has got a naturally long stride and a big jump, but he can be a little 'rude' and argue against my hand with an 'I know better' attitude. He was in this mood on the steeplechase phase and gave me one of the most horrendous rides ever; he was far too keen, fought me all the way and even quite frightened me. For the first time ever I felt angry with him and during Phase C, the second set of roads and tracks, I took the opportunity to school him and tell him firmly: 'You have *got* to listen to me.'

Then, in the ten-minute box, while waiting to go across country, I said to Yogi that I thought it would be better if I got on him earlier than usual so that I could get him paying attention to me. I knew I needed to get him where he would 'come back' to me the moment I asked, rather than two or three strides and a fight later. The system must have worked because I had one of the best rides I've ever had on Kiri. I was right up on the clock up to the eight-minute stage and then, somewhere between eight and nine minutes, I must have knocked my stopwatch because it switched off. As I no longer knew if I was on target, I decided to take the direct route at an influential complex near the end of the course. It had been causing problems and quite a few riders were beginning to take the long route – I had been dithering over it and, had I known I had time, I would have done the same, but I didn't dare risk it. As it was, I finished bang on the optimum time. This was an example of how much the luck was with me this year, though at that moment I didn't realise just how lucky it was.

It was a good day for the Brits. All five of us went clear and were lying in the top ten; it felt thoroughly satisfactory, with everyone pulling together. Nick and Barbara had been fantastic, spending all day washing down horses in the ten-minute box.

Then, yet again, Rod had a terrible stroke of bad luck in that his horse Colour Coded was not fit enough to show jump. It was terribly disappointing for him, because this was a new horse that had gone brilliantly across country and could have put him back into contention for the British team. But, as always, Rod never allowed his own problems to cloud a party atmosphere and he continued to support the rest of us.

The show jumping at Kentucky takes place in a sand arena and the track was technical and up-to-height with a tight optimum time, so I took particular care to work out time-saving routes. Polly jumped a brilliant clear round on Tangleman which brought her up to second place above William and Moon Man, who were unlucky to have a fence down.

I had the luxury of six penalties – more than the cost of a fence down – to win over Polly, and Kiri was jumping with his normal exuberance, not feeling for one moment as though he had exerted himself the day before. As I expected, we went clear – but, as we came through the finish line, I looked up at the electronic scoreboard and saw to my horror that I had notched up six time faults. For a dreadful few moments I didn't know how to react because I hadn't a clue whether I'd won or lost. In fact, I finished on exactly the same score as Polly and, as my cross-country time was quickest and nearest to the optimum, I won. If I'd taken that long route at that cross-country fence, I'd have lost – that's how close the margin between winning and losing is in eventing. Polly had put up just as good a performance overall, but it was I who had the luck.

As Kentucky is sponsored by Rolex, the big excitement was winning a Rolex watch, and a few moments later, when being interviewed on telly, I blurted out: 'I'm so pleased – now I can get rid of my cheap plastic Swatch watch!' Unfortunately, Tim was watching back at home on Eurosport and he had given me the watch for Christmas – so for a long time afterwards he wound me up, saying: 'That's the last Christmas present you're getting!'

I was overwhelmed with relief that the trip had been a

success for Denise and Roger and that they'd had proper compensation for missing Badminton. Kentucky is a great event for owners, with a fantastic post-event party and lots of goodies; and from the rider's point of view, the advantage of being away from home with just one horse is that you have much more time to spend with the owners. As soon as it was over, though, I'd had to get straight off the horse and into a car going to Cincinnati airport in order to get home in time to turn around for Badminton. It was pretty chaotic with all five of us trying to change in the car but, once on the plane, we got straight into the champagne. With four of us finishing in the top five – Leslie was fifth on Shear L'Eau – we had more than justified the Lottery money which had been spent on sending us out there, and it was a lovely triumphant feeling for the whole group.

As the flight progressed and we all quietened down and tried to sleep, I dwelt a bit more on my win. That was the moment it suddenly dawned on me that if only I'd gone a bit quicker across country on Kiri at Burghley last year, I would have won the Grand Slam. Back in 1998 Rolex had offered US$250,000 – an unimaginably vast amount of money in eventing – to the rider who could win three consecutive four-star events (Badminton, Burghley and Kentucky). With a Badminton win under my belt the previous year, it was ridiculous how close I'd come to winning all that money.

One of the most satisfying aspects of winning a four-star event is that while your victory may be only momentary as far as public recognition is concerned, your fellow riders will know exactly what it has entailed. We know that only a small minority of horses and riders even compete in a four-star, let alone win one, because, as I know only too well, so much can go wrong on the way with horses. Many of today's best riders have never won a major title and, sadly, some of them never will. That's how elusive real success is in our game. So I did, briefly, feel frustrated that I hadn't seized my moment at Burghley eight months before.

But there was no time to dwell on Kentucky. I landed on Monday morning, worked the horses that afternoon, repacked and travelled to Badminton on Tuesday. Early on Wednesday morning I rode Rocky out under the stables arch and into the park at Badminton. My absence at Kentucky had meant – just as it had the previous year when I was injured – that I could not overwork him and bore him. Again he seemed to grow underneath me and I had a lovely reassuring feeling that he was saying to me: 'I know why I'm here and what I've got to do.' Inevitably, I was one of the favourites to win and there was pressure to defend my title, but the win at Kentucky had really buoyed me up. It took the edge off the mental strain.

Cornerman, on the other hand, was feeling a bit bright and undisciplined. He had been drawn first of my two horses and I thought: 'Oh dear, I'm going to have to do a lot of work to get his mind right before the dressage.' He produced some stunning trot work in his test, but in the walk, never his best pace, he became distracted and then wasn't quite with me mentally in the canter work. This meant we lost marks in the last quarter of the test, but he still got a competitive mark because of his super trot.

It pelted with rain on Friday, and by the time I was due to do my test on Rocky conditions in the arena had deteriorated into a slippery, squelching mess. But this was the least of my worries because, out in the warm-up area, I was experiencing a moment of panic. Although Rocky's calmness is a plus, it means he can sometimes feel quite ordinary and flat, and I couldn't imagine that he was going to produce a winning test.

But, as we trotted through the entrance to the arena, he immediately changed and lifted his game, and minutes later we were in the lead, this time just ahead of Bettina Hoy on another grey, Ringwood Cockatoo.

I don't know whether it was the fact that I had won Badminton already, or the confidence boost of Kentucky, but I was much more relaxed than I've ever been there on cross-country morning. In fact I was so calm that it slightly concerned me – the usual gut-wrenching nerves seemed to be strangely absent.

Being drawn early, Cornerman got the best of the going and, although he was a bit green in a couple of places, especially when he slipped at the large bounce into the lake, he put up a creditable first Badminton performance.

Then the rain really fell. It had filtered through to me that there had been quite a bit of trouble on the course, especially at the Lake, and a Swedish rider, Anna Hasso, had a nasty frightening fall into the water and had to be airlifted to hospital with a broken hip. This meant I had a thirty-minute wait to start instead of ten minutes, which doesn't do much for the nerves.

Nevertheless, although a lot of riders had been concerned about the Lake, I had refused to let it bother me; I knew the distance there would suit my two horses, who were both long-striding. It was the same with the weather: I had to turn this to my advantage too. Instead of thinking: 'Oh God, it will be really slippery and horrible,' I tried instead to think about the successful runs I'd had on Rocky in wet, deep going. Because he has so much scope I didn't think he'd be fazed by the mud; and I also knew that his early career had been in the hunting field, where horses learn to deal with all sorts of going.

As the day progressed it became clear that there was a

problem unfolding at a new complex called the Carisma Puzzle. Here you had to make a turn on a downhill descent and jump a big, wide open ditch before bouncing straight over a brush fence and turn to another narrow brush. The problem was that horses were misjudging the ditch, perhaps because in the rain the edge of the bank was losing its definition. Eventually, with eleven horses left to go – of which Rocky was the last – it was decided to remove the fence from the course. I wasn't actually worried about this fence – Cornerman had already jumped it well and I knew that Rocky was well capable of clearing it too – but I could see why it was a sensible decision to take it out.

That day Rocky gave me perhaps the most memorable ride of my life; so much so that halfway around the course I had to remind myself not to be too complacent, as it surely shouldn't be feeling this easy. Rocky was just loving the mud, lolloping through it with his ears pricked, and all I had to do was try to stay focused and not enjoy it too much. It was one of those great rides which you don't forget, with a wonderful horse just foot perfect underneath you.

There was, inevitably, considerable fuss over the removal of the Carisma Puzzle from the competition. Bettina was particularly upset because her horse had made a mistake there and thereafter, believing her winning chance was gone, she had continued rather slowly. It was later decided that all riders who had faulted there and then completed should have those penalties deducted; everyone who had jumped the fence, as I had on Cornerman, had a few time penalties taken off. Bettina had subsequently accrued too many time penalties to be able to challenge for first place. In any sport there are, inevitably, hard luck stories as well as good luck stories, and I know that Bettina felt hard done by. As a consequence of this adjustment,

Cornerman went up to third place at this stage, behind the Finnish rider Pia Pantsu, who had gone brilliantly at her first Badminton.

William walked the show jumping course with me. It was a funny track, with great long stretches between fences but not many turns or related distances. William was anxious about me because he knew I'd nearly lost Kentucky with time faults. He instructed me to take a line inside the wall to the water, to save time, and he tried to drum it into me that I must maintain a good rhythm or I'd get behind again.

I don't think I rode Cornerman particularly well. He isn't the easiest horse to show jump, but while anyone can have one fence down, we had two. We still finished sixth and won the best young horse prize for Susie, but I was frustrated with myself and immediately thought: 'I must *not* ride like this on Rocky.' The word 'not' is bad for my mental state and was banned by Nicky Heath, whose insistence that all instructions must be positive was one of the big lessons that turned my career around.

I set out on Rocky in the rhythm in which I know he jumps well, but it was too slow for this course and there weren't enough turns to allow us to make up time. I think, also, that I was perhaps too confident of my big lead over Pia, who had jumped clear but was still over ten points behind me. Poor William, of course, was well aware that I was going much too slowly and when I had a fence down, part of the treble, he thought I'd blown it. I had six time faults – again – and, with that rail down, I finished just 0.4 of a penalty in front of Pia Pantsu – one of the tightest winning margins in the history of Badminton.

When you're in the lead, everyone expects you to win. If the scores are very close I thrive on that pressure because I feel that

I've got everything to go for, but losing a commanding lead – and I'd never had so much leeway before on Rocky – would have just made me feel stupid.

I gave my back-up team near heart failure. William was speechless. All he could say was: 'Well, I suppose a win's a win!' He knew, as I did, that it wasn't the greatest performance, but somehow that's how life goes. Again, that little bit of luck was with me to tip the balance.

This time I wasn't as emotional at winning, but when I got to the press tent someone said: 'You've got one of the all-time great horses here,' and that nearly set me off. What an amazing horse Rocky was to have achieved all this for me! To think that in 1998 I'd been so close to giving up the ride on him; five years down the line and he'd won two Europeans, two Badmintons and an Olympic medal. There aren't many horses with a better record.

I felt amazing. I was on a complete high – after two four-star wins in just two brilliant weeks – there's no way sport can get any better than that. No one in eventing has ever achieved two big wins in so short a space of time.

Twenty-four hours later, though, I was boarding a ferry for Compiègne in France, leaving a night earlier than planned in order to avoid a ferry strike. There was a big crowd of British-based riders, including myself and Tina, plus Antoinette (Ants) McKeown, a rider who had become a good friend during 2001 and who these days completed an unholy trio with Tina and myself in the lorry. Ken Clawson, Dan Jocelyn, Andrew Hoy and Rod were part of the convoy and, on Tuesday night, fourteen of us decided to go out to dinner.

Rod, who knew the owner of the restaurant, made it very clear that I would be footing the bill. Like an idiot, I agreed to pay for drinks, which was a big mistake. It was the first occasion in such a long time that I'd completely let my hair down – next day someone told me I was throwing glasses at the wall because 'I liked the noise' – and it was another three weeks before I noticed the horrific size of the bill. Everyone was, without exception, on top form and we consumed an unbelievable amount of alcohol.

Next day we all looked, and felt, very bad. Dag Albert and Rob Stevens had cycled to the restaurant and couldn't retrace their route – they didn't make it back on site until seven the next morning. Christy Lomax couldn't work out why she was covered with bruises until someone told her how many times she'd fallen over on the way home. Rod's head was covered in foundation cream – my handbag had been emptied and, for some inexplicable reason, we thought it was terribly funny to make him up. God knows what else happened; my memory of the evening is still blurred.

We all had to pull ourselves together hard for the start of the competition. I was riding Matter Of Fact, a horse I had been quietly bringing on since Sarah Jewson had bought him as a four-year-old. The event was a lovely introduction for young horses and Matty tried his little heart out to finish sixteenth in a big field.

The Walkinshaws' Walk On Star ('Magic') was scheduled for Saumur and so I took him to Chatsworth for a prep run, where he finished second in the international class behind William Fox-Pitt on the Apters' speedy one-day specialist Stunning. Much was made in the press of the 'rivalry' between William and me and the fact that he'd broken my winning run, but two weeks later Magic won at Saumur, his second three-star win. My first thought was: 'Oh God, this is actually getting too much.'

Anne Burnet's Jurassic Rising was disappointing at

Chatsworth, with a run-out, but I still felt he could put up a good performance at Bramham, where he had gone well two years before. He led after dressage and cross-country, and I seemed to be looking at yet another win, but we dropped to third with a rather poor show-jumping performance. By contrast, William had a brilliant one–two on Wallow and Ballincoola, scoring the first of *his* three three-day event wins that year – between us, we won every event at three-star level and above in Europe in 2003, bar Bialy Bor in Poland.

I was disappointed not to win Bramham once I'd been in the lead, but in a funny way I was also relieved. Another win would actually have been one too many: superstitiously, I didn't want to go into this crucial autumn season on the back of yet another victory. But it wasn't just superstition. I was aware that winning so often was having a negative effect on my show-jumping ability because every time I competed I seemed to be in a leading position which was causing me to ride defensively. The flip side of becoming accustomed to success is that every show-jumping pole in the final phase represents a potential life-change; each one is literally worth a significant amount of money and a major result.

I needed to get my head around riding lots of tracks and not worrying if I had fences down. I just wanted to go to some normal, smaller events and perform the show-jumping phase without that intensity. Fortunately, I had plenty of horses with which to practise. Dear old Viceroy was back in work after a year off with a leg injury sustained at Chatsworth in 2002; he won several one-day events on the trot that summer and confirmed what a fabulous fun horse he is. I also had youngsters to bring on, including the Jewsons' promising eight-year-old Best Of All. He also won two events running, so even on the domestic circuit I didn't seem to be able to get it wrong.

Then the Burghley preview press release entitled 'Pippa in line for Grand Slam' was released. Suddenly 'Can Pippa do it?' headlines were all over the place and it hit me like a sledgehammer that I was expected to achieve something that was surely totally impossible. Not since the Grand Slam concept was launched in 1998, and Blyth followed a Burghley win with a frustratingly close second place at Kentucky in the spring of 1999, had there been any real interest in the prize. There was certainly not the remotest conviction that any rider would have sufficient horsepower and luck to win three consecutive 'majors'. To put the task in context, it had been fourteen years since Ginny Elliot had even won Badminton and Burghley in the same year, let alone another four-star event as well. Now, suddenly, it seemed everyone had latched on to the idea that the unachievable was about to be achieved – by me.

The big question was: which two horses should I take to Burghley to try to clinch this Grand Slam, and which should I take to Punchestown in September to defend my European Championship title? Half of me desperately wanted to take Rocky to Punchestown. He was already the first horse to win two European titles back to back and I did want to give him that third go. But I also knew that to give myself the best chance of winning the Grand Slam I needed my strongest hand at Burghley, and that obviously included Rocky.

There had to be endless discussions with owners and both my husband William and Yogi, as performance manager for the national team, were in on the debate from the start. Realistically, we all accepted that in this scenario the Grand Slam had to take preference over the Europeans; I had a responsibility to the sport because here, for once, was a chance to get some really powerful publicity. Also, I not only owed it to everyone who works so hard for the sport to give it my best shot, I also owed it to William and myself and our future. Normally, a championships would always be a rider's top priority. We all long to represent our country and be on a team – it's the greatest honour there is. But the money on offer now represented mine and William's security; I was never going to have a chance to win that sort of money again. It translated into about £166,000, more than three times the first prize even at Badminton.

By July, it was decided that Cornerman would be my team ride at Punchestown and that Rocky and Kiri would give me a double-handed shot at Burghley. Magic would be kept ticking over as a reserve for all scenarios in case anything went wrong.

And, boy, did things start to go wrong.

It all started at Windsor racecourse, where Mike Tucker had organised a fund-raising Grand Prix for eventers as a fun warm-up for Hickstead, which I felt it would be ideal for The Tourmaline Rose. It was a baking hot day and, as ninety-five per cent of the fences were knock-down, most of us decided that we wouldn't bother wearing back protectors. Rosie jumped as well as ever, but she slipped on a turn between two narrow fences and met the second one completely wrong, catapulting me through the air. I landed heavily on my back and was in absolutely agony. I was frightened by the shooting pains down one leg and could hardly get up to hobble off the course. Over the commentary PA I heard Mike Tucker say: 'I hope this isn't the start of a reversal of fortune for Pippa . . .'

I didn't ride for a couple of days, but was too pigheaded – and panic-stricken about being made to stop riding – to be X-rayed. Instead I had several physio sessions and popped loads of Nurofen so that I could get back in the saddle. The discomfort, though, went on for weeks and made me both physically and mentally tired, which only added to my already jittery state of mind.

My top horses were entered for an advanced one-day event at Aston-le-Walls a week later and, though I was still on painkillers, I knew I had to get myself together to run there if I was to keep up the programme I had set for the horses. Rocky felt pretty blasé around the cross-country, obviously thinking it was beneath his dignity after Badminton, and he hit a narrow, upright fence. Yet again, I flew through the air, landing on exactly the same part of my back. I was terribly uncomfortable, but I knew I had to get through the afternoon's rides. Fortunately, I'd ridden Cornerman by this stage so I just went slowly on Kiri, but Jurassic Rising (Fiver) was one horse too many and I had to pull him up.

Next morning brought another disaster. Best Of All had previously suffered from a minor tendon injury and now, though he wasn't actually lame, I had a sickening suspicion that the problem had reappeared. When I feel a horse's leg, I usually know instinctively whether the heat in it signifies a harmless knock or infection, or whether the horse has 'done a leg' – in other words, injured its tendon. When it's the latter, it automatically makes me break out into sweaty panic. This was the ominous feeling that swept over me that morning, so I immediately insisted to Sarah Jewson that we got the leg scanned.

Best Of All travelled up to Andy Bathe at Newmarket. I anticipated that he would have to tell me that the horse wasn't destined for the top, but would still be able to compete, but I was wrong. The news was much worse than that, shockingly worse: Andy told me the scan indicated that Best Of All wouldn't stand up to life as an event horse of any kind.

There weren't many options open to us as to what to do with

him. I suggested that as he was such a big, powerful horse and a flashy and extravagant mover he could be used for dressage, but Andy said he didn't think he could stand up to being competed by a professional, and I knew that he wasn't an amateur ride. He wasn't safe to ride in traffic and he wouldn't be a great companion horse because he had a tendency to bully others in the field.

So there was no choice: Sarah decided to put him down. Sarah was shattered, as I was, but we both knew that we owed it to the horse not to see him fall into the wrong hands. I felt awful because I loved the horse and, because he was up in Newmarket, I hadn't been able to say goodbye properly. It was also hard on the girls, who loved him too.

This equine disaster was swiftly followed by another. My long-suffering owners the McIntyres had already had rotten luck with Teddy Twilight, who was out of action with a niggling windgall (a swelling on the fetlock joint) on which he'd had keyhole surgery that spring. Now it looked as if their Burke's Boy, who was back with me a year after his Chatsworth fall with Bryce, was not going to come right. I had worked hard to get him going, but he wasn't the same horse; I don't know if the problem was in his back, but he didn't seem to be able to link up physically and go in the correct way any more.

Although potentially a good eventer, Burke's Boy had problems too – one of them a tendency suddenly to bite with no reason or warning. He had given Ian McIntyre a vicious injury on the chest, and had also bitten two of the grooms, grabbing one by the hip and ripping through her jeans. Again, he was a professional's horse and there was no way he would suit a life as a happy hacker; so he joined Best Of All.

As I struggled to believe that I'd lost two horses from my yard, Denise Lincoln's two home-bred four-year-olds started coughing. I panicked and got the whole yard injected with an immune-boost, as I had horrible visions of a serious virus sweeping the yard, and sent the youngsters home.

Rocky has always had a tendency to react to pollen and, just to unsettle my nerves further, he started coughing too, so I decided to get him blood-tested. The weather was boiling in August – 35 degrees – so I couldn't do too much fast work and, on the day the vet was due, I took Rocky out for a hack first with Zanie. We were a mile down the road as we started to trot, I turned and met Zanie's eyes and, unbelievably, we realised simultaneously that he was lame, definitely unsound.

It was the last straw. I couldn't stand being on the yard a minute longer; every time I went out of my back door there was disaster. Moreover, if I was honest, my back still hurt too much to ride properly. I badly needed a change of scenery, so I decided to fly over to Dublin and watch William jumping on the Nations Cup team. Dublin is one of the best shows in the world and I thought a bit of Irish craic would sort me out. But on the first morning away I got a phone call saying that Rocky's blood test showed that he had contracted a virus which was usually only seen in foals and youngstock and can develop into pneumonia and lung infections. The prognosis was not good.

I was awash with doom and gloom. I felt tired, sore and negative; my whole yard was suddenly going to develop this virus and all the horses' whole careers would be threatened. Panic shot through me and I shouldn't think I was much fun to be with for poor William, who had concerns and pressures of his own.

Then, twenty-four hours and a sleepless night later, I had another phone call to say there had been a muddle in Newmarket and that Rocky's blood was absolutely fine! This was obviously a huge relief, but by now he had been jabbed full of drugs to ward off this mystery virus, so it wasn't necessarily going to be straightforward to get him back into full work.

The upside was that at least William had a good show at Dublin. The British show-jumping team, which was enjoying something of a revival on the Nations Cup circuit, was second in the Aga Khan Nations Cup, with William making the excellent contribution of a clear and four faults on Amber Du Montois. This should have put them on course to be on the British team at the European Championships at Donaueschingen in Germany later in the month, but, of course, nothing was to be that simple.

The selectors were much keener on William's other top horse, Mondriaan, a youngster who was ninth in his first major Grand Prix, at Dublin, and had already won the Falsterbo Derby and been second in the King's Cup that summer. He was later to be a good third in the Hickstead Derby. William was therefore expected to jump him in the Nations Cup in Dublin, but he had refused, feeling it was a year too early for the horse to come under that sort of pressure. As a result, his team chances went down the drain.

When I got back from Dublin, Rocky was re-examined and found to be one hundred per cent sound. His lameness was a mystery. But by now he had too many drugs inside him to compete at Thirlestane, so I left him at home and drove up to Scotland in a borrowed lorry as my old one had been sold. One week later the postman delivered me two speeding fines, the first points on my licence.

There was more bad news to come. While I was at Thirlestane, Barnaby, who was turned out in the field down the lane with William's old horse Comex, got caught up in wire and sustained a nasty wound. A raft of skin had peeled off his foreleg, like a sock that had slipped down, and the leg looked horrendous. He had been stitched and couldn't be moved, so now was confined to a stable up the road. I was desperate to get back and comfort him in his isolation.

Burghley loomed ever closer, and as it approached the media interest began to spiral. The main question was what horse I was riding there and, with the summer I was having, I was determined not to make any public announcement in case plans had to change. I just couldn't face explaining what was going wrong at home, even though all the equestrian journalists are very nice people I have got to know well over the years and, as sporting press go, they couldn't be more sympathetic. I felt bad dodging their phone calls, but it was like being under siege.

Rocky had been kept in work but I was worried that his fitness programme had now fallen behind. After another veterinary examination, which did not reveal any more signs of problems, I decided to give him another canter. Lo and behold, he pulled up lame again. This time the vet diagnosed a damaged tendon high up at the back of the knee, an unusual area for injury in an event horse. It was a serious blow, mainly because up to now Rocky had been such a sound horse. It seemed so unfair on him and I felt shattered. Emma Pitt and her family were terribly upset, as were Zanie and the girls. There was mourning all round and I organised for British Eventing to send out a press release so that everyone would know and in the vain hope of minimising phone calls. The British press got it while they were out in Donaueschingen, where our show-jumping team had a total disaster and failed to qualify for the Olympics. My journalist friends later told me that this bit of news was the final straw in a rubbish day for British equestrianism.

Still, all my options were covered as all four horses had been entered for Burghley and the Europeans, with a double entry for Magic. Now I rerouted Cornerman to join Kiri at Burghley and Magic to the European team, partly because I was still sure I wouldn't have to use the latter at Burghley and I knew that he really needed those extra two weeks' fitness work. I didn't make any of this public knowledge, though, so people still didn't know what I was planning.

It was a miserable time. I was down about Rocky and I hated having to confine Barnaby to a stable at the age of twenty-six. Every day we religiously redressed his horrible wound but the dressings kept slipping, the stitches wouldn't hold and it looked so ugly, with bits of flesh that looked as though they were dying.

As Magic had suddenly come into the equation, I had to take him for a run at Highclere, where he popped around easily, just playing with the course. Viceroy, too, was as cheerful as ever because he loves top-of-the-ground conditions. Fiver, however, definitely wasn't enjoying the hard going and I had many discussions with Anne about the merits of running him at Blenheim, which was what she wanted.

William was going abroad to compete, so I thought a good antidote to stress would be to stop working early and cook my husband a nice supper in the few hours we had left together before he was due to leave at about 11 p.m. And, unbelievably, at 8.30 p.m., there came a knock on the door. It was a girl from UK Sport, representing WADA (World Anti-Doping Association), waving a jar for a urine test. Obviously, you don't get any notice before one of these random dope tests – that would rather negate the point of them – and, unfortunately, I'd been to the loo five minutes before she arrived. I was also conscious that William's roll-up cigarettes were lying on the kitchen table – I was nervous that they looked like dope and was surreptitiously trying to sweep them under a newspaper.

So that was the end of the time I had visualised alone with my husband. A dope-tester has to follow you everywhere, to the fridge, the office, everywhere, to make sure you're not doing anything to affect the sample and it's pretty disconcerting. It's the hardest thing to pee into a jar with someone looking, even if you physically want to, and I had to keep downing water. It took me three hours, by which time William had to leave.

Next day I said to a friend – I was unburdening my problems every day by this stage – 'It's a bloody good job I hadn't resorted to taking anything.' And he jokingly replied: 'Well, it's not often they come two nights in a row so have what you like tonight!'

Then it was the week before Burghley and Kiri, thankfully, was on song. But all the dramas had made me so unconfident that I was nervous even pulling him out of the stable. If I could have, I would have just left him wrapped up inside. I was terrified he might get hurt and I drove everyone mad by being so neurotic. One day he spooked at some banners in the school and I was so worried he would knock himself that I made the girls take them down. That's how paranoid I had become.

On the Friday before Burghley started I took Kiri, Cornerman and Magic to the gallops. They felt a million dollars and well ready for the big task a week later. But when we got home and took Cornerman off the lorry, he was lame! Zanie and I chorused: 'Oh no, not another one.' Cornerman's symptoms were so uncannily like Rocky's that I could not bring myself to risk this valuable horse at a major three-day. I wasn't desperate enough for the Grand Slam money that I would have even considered risking one of the horses.

However, I hadn't yet ruled out taking him to the

Europeans, so the secretive juggling went on. Yet again I had to ring up an owner, this time Susie, to tell her that she would be missing another major event. This is one of the worst parts of my job, for, disappointed as I might be, I still have other rides; most owners have only one top horse and, therefore, only one chance. My owners are all knowledgeable enough about horses to take these knocks remarkably well, but it doesn't make the delivery of the news any easier. The only upside was that the Walkinshaws were now excited that Magic would get his opportunity, though they were of course sorry for me for being so stressed and felt bad for the other owners.

The same day that Charlie went lame, I had a discussion with my vet P. J. McMahon about Barnaby. PJ said that if he were me, he would have the horse put down. He told me that if the leg was to heal, Barns would either have to be confined to the stable for another two or three months or I could put some sort of fly protection on the leg and turn him out. I knew I owed this horse far more than to see him hobbling around a field.

As PJ was away I arranged for someone else from his practice to come around and organised for my brother-in-law David Funnell to sort out a cremation, as that is his business. By now I was a complete mess, crying my eyes out; William was away, so Mum and Becky came round to try to pick up the pieces. The vet and David were due to come at 5.30 p.m. and I arranged to spend what was left of the day on my own with Barnaby, who looked ridiculously well. I gave him a big tea with loads of carrots and brushed him and redressed his leg because I didn't want to see the wound. Forty-five minutes before the vet was due I decided to take him out for some grass – after all, I reasoned, he was going to be dead within an hour, so it couldn't hurt him. With that, Barns was off like a rocket, towing me out of the stable and into the field, marching away as sound as a bell. I thought: 'There's no way this horse wants to go yet.'

I looked at my watch and screamed down to Mum and Becks: 'I can't go through with this!' Then the vet and David arrived; they were both absolutely great and said that it was far better that I had decided now, even if it was the last minute, than that I should go through with the deed and regret it. So I led Barns and Comex back home and, on PJ's suggestion, caked Barnaby's leg in Dermajel and cut up a pair of jeans to put over it.

The sight of Barnaby out in the field and walking sound with half a pair of jeans on was the point at which my fortunes turned around, but at the time I was far too drained to register this. The phone rang ceaselessly with wall-to-wall press enquiries and I didn't know what to say to anyone because I didn't even know the answers myself any more. I had lost any hope of thinking positively – and in three days' time I was going to be riding for the Grand Slam.

On Sunday morning I rang Nicky Heath and told her: 'I'm struggling; you've got to come over and help me.' It was three years since I'd last seen Nicky, but she was great: she dropped everything to come round to me. Her first question was: 'Have you changed your system?' Then: 'Can you put your hand on your heart and say that it's because of what you've done that you've had these problems?' And I realised that I could answer: 'No, because my system is still the same.' So Nicky simply said: 'Well, don't beat yourself up. You can only control the controllables and, as it is for everyone, there will always be things that are outside your control. Don't blame yourself for all this.'

This was just enough to put me back on track.

The uncertainty over Cornerman meant that I was now down to one horse only for Burghley – Kiri. It was too nerve-racking. I wasn't brave enough to do a final gallop with him. All I wanted to do was get to Burghley, and when I arrived I was so grateful because at last I could concentrate on the job in hand. Exhausted, I kept myself to myself in the evenings, shut away in my lorry.

A lot of people rallied around to make my life much easier for those four days. Becky acted as a sort of liaison, smoothing the way, and Zanie was an absolute brick because, poor girl, she'd been as down as I was. There were, inevitably, a lot of press demands, but the Burghley press officer Candy Burnyeat, whom I'd known for years since her days working for Uncle Raymond, was another star. She was very protective of me and organised a press conference on the Thursday, which got the whole thing over and done with.

It can be difficult to find enough time to be with owners at places like Badminton and Burghley, where there are so many demands on your time, but here Mum comes into her own. She sets up her caravan, often next to Maureen Rawson, and feeds everyone. She is brilliant at looking after as many people as necessary and wining and dining everyone.

I also had other distractions, as I was involved with Jamie Hawksfield's Equestrian Vision company with which I had made a couple of videos, *Road to the Top* and *Training your New Horse*. I was delighted with both and was only happy to do my bit for publicity with a couple of roadshows for the public. I also had Magic to ride, as I had decided to do the dressage phase with him for experience, and I had a youngster, Laspen Rock Star, whom I'd bought with my Badminton prize money and then sold to Robert and Jo Tomkinson, to ride in the Burghley Young Event Horse final. (On the day we finished second in the final to Tina, which was a good result.)

Kiri had been drawn before Magic which at first felt a disadvantage, though it didn't really matter. He is good enough to get the right marks at whatever time he does his dressage test – it is generally accepted that the second day's marks tend to go higher – and I was thrilled with his performance. I felt it was an improvement on Kentucky but that, as a ten-year-old, there was still more to come in what was only his first season of major competition at the top level. A lot was riding on this relatively young horse.

As expected, by Friday night I was still right up there after the dressage, in second place behind Bettina riding Woodsides Ashby with Zara Phillips, who was attracting enormous publicity at her four-star debut, close behind in third place. The dreaded Grand Slam was, by now, very prominent in everyone's minds and discussions, and I seriously wondered if it was worth it.

Yogi was a star and walked the cross-country course with me. Then I sat down with him and William to watch a video of my previous year's round on Kiri, working out where we could take a tighter line and save time this year. Although the course was similar to 2002, this time we went into serious detail about where I could cut turns and make up seconds. After that I crashed into bed.

When I woke up on Saturday morning, I just didn't want to get out of bed and face the world. I would have done anything to have been anywhere else. I wondered why on earth I was putting myself – and everyone close to me – through this awful ordeal – for that's what it was: an ordeal. There was no way there was an iota of fun or pleasure in this particular competition and I don't know if I could mentally cope if I had to go through anything like it again.

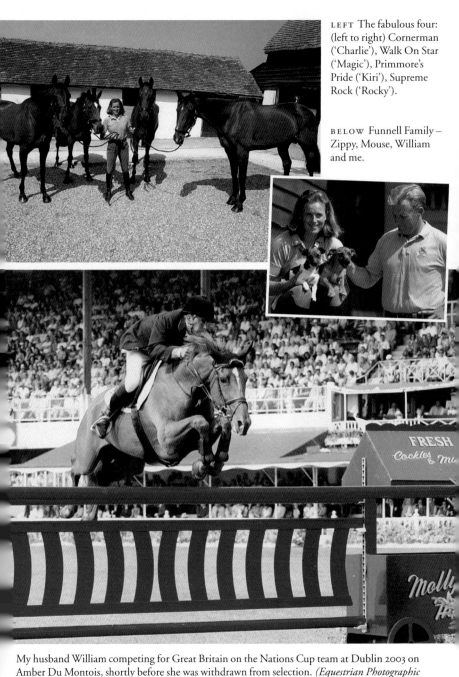

LEFT The fabulous four: (left to right) Cornerman ('Charlie'), Walk On Star ('Magic'), Primmore's Pride ('Kiri'), Supreme Rock ('Rocky').

BELOW Funnell Family – Zippy, Mouse, William and me.

My husband William competing for Great Britain on the Nations Cup team at Dublin 2003 on Amber Du Montois, shortly before she was withdrawn from selection. *(Equestrian Photographic Services)*

ON A TEAM AT LAST! THE EUROPEAN CHAMPIONSHIPS IN LUHMUHLEN 1999:

LEFT The gold medal team, Tina Gifford, me, Jeanette Brakewell and Ian Stark.

BELOW LEFT Very relieved after cross-country, with William and Ellie Brown.

ABOVE A quiet moment with Rocky after he gave me such a fantastic cross-country ride.

LEFT New European champion, with Rocky's excited owner Emma Pitt and Nini French, my head girl. (*J Morel/ PSV*)

RIGHT Rocky and I get to our first Olympics – schooling before dressage in Sydney.
BELOW The lap of honour with a silver medal round my neck.
BOTTOM My next Olympic horse in the making – Primmore's Pride winning Le Lion d'Angers at the end of 2000.
(Reportages Hippiques)

LEFT One of the happier days of 2001 – Tina Cook's wedding. *(Trevor Meeks)*

BELOW My ever supportive back-up friends: Yogi Breisner, Lizzie Bunn, Ken Clawson, Becky Coffey and David Green by the lorry in Saumur.

ABOVE I don't know what I'd have done without Becky in 2001.

RIGHT The Nolan family celebrating the end of a bad year – my second European title in Pau 2001.

BADMINTON 2002:
TOP Zanie Tanswell trots up Rocky for me.
(*Fiona Scott Maxwell*)
TOP RIGHT My first Badminton win is in sight.
(*Fiona Scott Maxwell*)
ABOVE Rocky's support team – the Barmy Army
at Badminton.
RIGHT A very good boy – Rocky the day after giving me
the first of two back-to-back Badminton victories.

GRAND SLAM MASTER:

RIGHT First leg –
Kentucky on Kiri.
(*Julia Shearwood*)
BELOW Two down, one to
go – Badminton on Rocky.
(*Steven Sparkes*)

RIGHT A cheque for
US$250,000 and a Rolex watch.
(*Fiona Scott Maxwell*)

BELOW The full set – with
Denise and Roger Lincoln at
Burghley. (*Fiona Scott Maxwell*)

ATHENS OLYMPICS:

ABOVE Setting sail
over the first water
complex.
(*Kit Houghton*)

RIGHT Kiri pulls out
all the stops to go into
second. (*Kit Houghton*)
FAR RIGHT The
all-important team
show-jumping phase
where Kiri jumps a
brilliant clear to clinch
a team medal.
(*Kit Houghton*)

RIGHT A proud moment
with fellow Olympian Sir
Steve Redgrave and the
Olympic torch.
(*Reuters/ Michael Stephens*)

RIGHT The next generation: Laspen Rock Star wins the five-year-old Burghley Young Event Horse final. (*Fiona Scott Maxwell*)

LEFT Leslie Law, Jeanette Brakewell, M King, me and William Fox-Pitt. Team G with our Olympic medals at Markopoul (*Kit Houghton*)

ABOVE The Olympic parade through London. (*Kit Houghton*)

RIGHT It wouldn't have been right if such a good horse as Kiri hadn't added Badminton, in 2005, to his list of successes. (*Kit Houghton*)

That cross-country day passed in a blur, but at least I could go early and get it over and done with. Kiri was truly classy, giving me everything. I finished just a couple of seconds over time, which meant I was in a joint lead on the same score as Zara, who had had a fantastic round and was the fastest of the day. Bettina, yet again, had suffered a piece of ridiculously bad luck with a stop at one of the easiest fences on the course.

I felt as relieved as if the competition was all over; in fact, after cross-country I felt that it *was* over. I was just hugely relieved that all that effort hadn't been in vain. The weight was off my shoulders and I thought: 'It doesn't matter what happens tomorrow; it's either meant to be or it's not.'

Nevertheless, Sunday seemed a long, long morning. A lot of people thought I had pretty much got it won because Zara's show-jumping record with Toytown was not great. I was pretty confident, in my head, that I would jump clear, but I was also convinced that Zara's fortunes had to change too. Because the winning margins at Kentucky and Badminton had been so close, with time the crucial factor, I was convinced – absolutely convinced – that this time I would finish on the same score as Zara and lose the whole shebang on a mere second's cross-country time.

The great bonus was that our show jumping had been brought forward for the benefit of the TV schedules and, to keep the spectators amused afterwards, there was to be a real show-jumping competition in the afternoon, in which William was riding. This meant that some of our show-jumping mates had turned up and this was a great antidote to my nerves, which by now were making me feel horribly sick. Geoff Billington came up to me and asked: 'Fancy a burger Pip?' at which I nearly threw up on the spot.

I watched Ants McKeown jump a super clear round and

then I turned away, as I thought that if I saw people knocking down fences I would start feeling negative again. Duncan and Clare had turned up with Amy, plus John and Lee Popely and their daughter Ella, and I went out to the collecting ring with them where we sat on some jumps piled up under a tree. We had a real laugh, just as if we were out to supper somewhere, and it took me right out of my awful here-and-now feeling. For a split second I thought: 'It doesn't matter what the result is; tomorrow I've still got to do the washing and, whatever happens, I've got my mates.'

But when I went to get on Kiri, I was tingling with nerves. The adrenalin was kicking in, but fortunately William was there to alleviate the situation with his usual relaxed humour. Andrew Nicholson, who was lying third on Lord Killinghurst, jokingly suggested I bribe him to have fences down. William turned round and told him that he shouldn't be worrying about me and Zara but about the people behind *him*. It's a funny thing that even though Andrew was definitely in a position to win himself, I was viewing the whole finale as a contest between myself and Zara.

Quite a few people, including Mark Phillips, had been teasing me about time penalties in the show jumping. But fortunately this particular worry was far from my mind because I had gained real confidence with the help William had given me. On the previous Tuesday he had made me jump every horse in the yard – the ones that were still sound! – one after another. This was brilliant, as I just jumped and jumped until I was naturally riding forward in a good rhythm and not interfering with the horses or riding defensively.

I am so self-critical that I never think anything I have done is perfect, but Kiri's show-jumping round that day was one of the best I have ever ridden at a three-day event. He was simply fantastic. A picture taken by the photographer Trevor Meeks of me smiling from ear to ear as we cleared the last fence, even though we hadn't even landed, was the cover on that month's *Eventing* magazine, and it summed up my feelings perfectly. Of course, I hadn't won then, but it was a great moment; I knew there was now nothing else I could do and that I'd done my best. I hadn't let William down, or the Lincolns, or anyone else.

It was a dream climax to a competition, with Zara last to go. Despite all my moaning about stress, I did register that, in her position as the Queen's granddaughter, she was actually under more scrutiny than me and that, at the age of twenty-two, she had put up the most brilliant performance under pressure. She fits in so well to the eventing scene, and puts up with all sorts of nuisances with such grace and humour.

Neither her father Mark nor I could bear to watch her and, weirdly, everyone else seemed to know that they had to clear a space around us. The pair of us stood together, isolated in the middle of the collecting ring. The silence was deadly. As long as the crowd was quiet, I knew Zara was jumping clear. And I thought: 'This is it. I've lost all that money by the tiniest of margins. I've come so near, and yet so far.'

Then I heard the crowd gasp and I knew I'd won. Mark was instantly generous, even though he must have felt a stab of bitter disappointment for his daughter. He became the first person to congratulate me on my Grand Slam, and I just burst into tears.

Then it was all a total haze; I was awash with emotion, unable to take anything in properly, but still I was dimly aware that this day was actually bigger than me – it was a momentous occasion for the sport of eventing.

When I eventually got myself together, my first thought was for the two horses who had done this for me, Kiri and Rocky.

Kiri was only ten, yet he'd won two four-stars in a year. What fantastic horses to earn me this place in the sport's history! No matter what happens to me from now on, I thought, I will always have this day.

11
A New Life

I was too tired that Sunday night after Burghley to enjoy my success to the full; the reality hadn't sunk in and, a year on, I'm still not sure whether I ever really took it in. When I said in the Burghley press conference that winning US$250,000 wasn't going to change the fact that I still had to wash up on Monday morning, I wasn't joking. I still had loads of boring jobs to do. It was a very long drive back to Forest Green from Lincolnshire, and I had just twenty-four hours to gallop three horses and get organised for two weeks away at Blenheim and the European Championships in Punchestown, Ireland.

It was pretty late when William and I got back, but we did go to The Parrot that night so that I could flash my new Rolex about. The girls came with us, Duncan and Clare drove over to meet us and Ian Sweet and his wife Dory were there too. Ian works for Eurosport and had just begun filming a *Mission to Athens* series – twelve months in the life of eight Olympic athletes from all over Europe, with me chosen as the British one.

Next day, loads of lovely flowers arrived. Meridian TV came up to film Kiri eating the amazing horse's cake, full of sugar and carrots, that the Burghley winner traditionally receives, while Denise and Roger looked on. But there was no time to enjoy all this because I had to turn around and go to Blenheim, where I was riding Viceroy (Leroy) and Jurassic Rising (Fiver). Blenheim is always a great event, friendly and well organised. It's a beautiful setting in the palace grounds, and with its usual nice Mike Etherington-Smith course it's always an enjoyable ride. But the preparation for *this* event had been a mini drama of its own as well. The event was so over-subscribed that, in accordance with the rules, we were told we could ride only one horse. I knew that it had to be Leroy and the Bunns' turn, which meant that Anne Burnet, Fiver's owner, would be disappointed. I hate having to put one horse over another but, just as Anne was becoming resigned to Fiver not getting a run, Yogi intervened. In accordance with another rule which states that the British selectors can request to see certain horses run at British events, I got to ride both my horses as the selectors were keen to keep the choice for Athens as broad as possible.

I also had a new groom at Blenheim, Charlie Benyon, who had only just started working for me at the beginning of August. Blenheim was her first three-day and she did a great job, especially as dealing with Leroy was quite a task. He is well-behaved for a stallion but the shiny, reflective plastic walls on the stabling caused problems as, when he saw himself, he thought it was a mare and got rather over-excited.

Both horses excelled themselves. Fiver was second after dressage behind a young French girl, Amelie Billard, who later came unstuck on the cross-country, and Leroy was right up there too. He skipped around the cross-country as if it was a Pony Club track and gave me a really enjoyable ride, while Fiver, whose three-day form has always been exceptional, went as well as he has ever gone.

I rode Fiver quite differently at Blenheim, an experiment that came off. He is a horse that tends to gallop on his forehand – in other words, he leans on the rider's hand, which is an exhausting feeling because you feel you've got to hold him up together. This time I let his head go in between fences and told him: 'You can find your own balance.' It seemed to work, which was a major breakthrough.

Saturday night saw one of the first indications of my new-found fame. I was taken aback at the amount of people who came to listen to me doing a chat show in the World of the Horse tent with Jamie Hawksfield. I talked informally about Burghley and the Grand Slam and it was suddenly relaxing to be free of any pressure, even though I was actually in the lead at Blenheim by this stage. I was touched by the huge queue of young fans. I love children and they are always keen for autographs, but their interest has increased hugely since the Grand Slam.

After a hot, dry August the ground at Blenheim was firm and I was surprised at how well both my horses trotted up next day, especially Fiver, as he has always been a horse that hates hard ground. It was the show jumping course-designer Maureen Summers's last event before she retired, and she had obviously decided to go out with a bang by building a decently big and technical course, which caused quite a few problems. I had a fence down on each horse but, amazingly, it was good enough to win on Fiver and be third on Leroy. Phillip Dutton, the Australian rider, was second and, sweetly, in the press conference he said: 'Finishing second to Pippa is as good as winning.' It had been another unbelievably successful weekend.

Zanie and Walk On Star (Magic) had arrived that Sunday morning, as the team was departing for Punchestown that night, and William came up to help with the show jumping. When we went back to the lorry after the prize-giving reception, William said: 'Where's my bag?' It had gone, and so had mine, which I'd hidden under some pillows. We'd been burgled.

I was absolutely stuffed; I had lost aeroplane tickets to get back from Ireland, all my credit cards and euros, my passport and my mobile phone, plus the bag, which was a rather nice one that William had brought me back from Dubai. Luckily, I'd hidden my Rolex – it's my most valuable possession and I'm always nervous about it but still rather keen to wear it. Six months later the bag was found abandoned in a hedge by one of the Blenheim gamekeepers with everything intact except the money and phone, but that wasn't much help when I had half an hour to set off for Ireland.

Team plans had been changing all the time since Burghley. Tina Cook was selected as an individual but she had a fall from Archrival at Burghley, and so the doctors said she would have to be signed off for two weeks with concussion. At that point, Mary King, who had been disappointed not to be selected, was about to go across country on King Solomon, so she had to be abruptly stopped, which was probably frustrating for her as she was in a useful position, and rerouted to the squad.

Meanwhile, Tina was distraught at missing out on the trip to Punchestown. She was determined that she was OK to ride at Blenheim and had managed to get a second medical opinion. She was subsequently passed fit, though it was now too late – and would have been unfair – to take Mary off the squad by this stage. But then, when we trotted up the team horses in front of Jenny Hall on Sunday morning at Blenheim, poor Polly Stockton, who was the other individual, found to her horror that Tangleman wasn't quite sound as he had bruised a foot. So after all that flap, Tina would get to the championships after all.

Selfishly, I was chuffed to be travelling with Tina in the end; we really are joined at the hip and it's not the same when we don't go together. We do occasionally worry that people might think there's more to our friendship than meets the eye – but I can guarantee there isn't!

Leslie Law and Jeanette Brakewell travelled together, while William Fox-Pitt and Mary shared a lorry. Within half an hour of setting off we had a distress phone call from William saying that King Solomon had somehow got his leg under the lorry partition and wedged under the pedal of William's quad bike. It is unbelievable what horses will do to themselves, always at the least convenient moment. William and Mary had to call the fire brigade and it sounded terrifying but, amazingly, Solly got away with just a few scratches.

The fact that I was riding Magic at the European Championships made it much less pressurised than it would have been had I taken Rocky to defend his title. Half of me would, of course, loved to have had Rocky in Punchestown, especially as Ireland is his birthplace. I felt that Magic could definitely put up a worthy performance for the team and even finish in the top ten, but I was under no illusions that I was going to win the individual gold again. I was also concerned because the run was so unexpected for Magic that I wasn't sure he had done enough in preparation. Though he's a bold horse, he was relatively young for a championship and all he'd done since winning Saumur in May was a quiet run around a small intermediate course at Highclere.

I was feeling lousy by the time I arrived in Punchestown; everything was catching up with me and I felt run-down and on the verge of a filthy cold. Therefore, after two weeks in a lorry, it was bliss to be staying in the smart City West hotel complex just up the dual-carriageway from Naas to Dublin. Usually we stay on site at Punchestown and everyone whoops it up in the racecourse bars every night, but I was so tired that a lovely big bed and en-suite room to myself was wonderful luxury.

The joke of the week was for people to come up to me and say: 'Lend me a tenner.' Of course, after the Blenheim robbery I didn't have any money! I borrowed cash from Tina and Yogi and, while I'm unusual for an event rider in that I'm not one to be glued to my mobile – mine is more likely to be switched off – when I couldn't use one I really missed it.

The team was first after dressage, but at Punchestown it's the cross-country that counts. Tommy Brennan, who is the course-designer there and a real character, is known for building tracks that are up to height in every way. After Frank Weldon retired from designing Badminton in the late 1980s, Tommy probably took over from him as the world's chief creator of the rider-frightener fence. The course looked awesome and there was water everywhere, which made me comment that Tommy must have been a duck in a former life. The final water complex looked ominously like another 'lottery' fence, rather in the same mould as the one that had been Britain's nemesis in Jeréz twelve months ago.

For the first time since 1999 our team order was changed. Leslie and Jeanette swapped roles as it was decided that Leslie tends to get his best results when he goes early on. He did a brilliant job as our pathfinder but, because I'd never watched him before – as number three, I would usually be busy doing roads and tracks during Leslie's cross-country round – I hadn't realised how desperately nervous his owner Jeremy Lawton gets. We were all up in the grandstand building at

Punchestown, watching Leslie on the close-circuit TV, and Jeremy got in such an unbelievable state that just watching him started to make me nervous.

Leslie finished clear and inside the time on Shear L'Eau and, as it turned out, he was the only one to do this all day. He set the team up brilliantly and my only concern at this stage was that I seemed to be feeling far too mentally relaxed. I was still riding on the back of my relief at winning the Grand Slam and wasn't feeling any pressure; ironically for once, it was my *lack* of nerves that worried me as I set off on the roads and tracks.

As I was trotting around, I could hear the commentary for Jeanette's cross-country round. She seemed to be going as perfectly as usual and then, suddenly, it was announced that she'd had a fall while taking the direct route at the last water. Over To You was the sort of horse who was clever enough to cope with this complex, where you approached through a tunnel before dropping into the water and taking three strides to an island with a bounce to a narrow fence and another bounce off. The drop into water made the distance unpredictable and there were a lot of problems here before later riders realised it was safer to take a longer route. Over To You missed when jumping up on to the bank and tipped over in a horrible dramatic horse fall, which meant Jeanette was compulsorily eliminated.

This meant that William and I now had to complete – and go clear – otherwise our gold medal would be lost. This was the first time anything had gone wrong for Jeanette in five years on the team and I suddenly realised how heavily we had relied on her before. My cheerful state disappeared with a 'whoosh' as the pressure and nerves came over me in a wave. I felt very sick and thought: 'Oh no, here come the nerves again.'

But Magic felt great on the steeplechase and, when I got to

the ten-minute box, Yogi gave team orders that William and I were to play safe at the water. I knew this would cost me some time and affect my individual placing, but it was a sensible and obvious plan which removed some of the chance element out of my round. That day marked Magic's transition from boy to man; he was really firing and just saying: 'Let me at it.' He was hungry to do the job and felt every bit a top-class horse in the way he ran across country.

The team medal was now dependent on how William went on Moon Man, but there is no one more professional in these circumstances, and, despite a nasty moment when Moon Man tripped in one of the water complexes, William never moved in the saddle. His clear round meant that we were still in the lead, but the French team, who were second, had gone brilliantly across country on relatively young horses. Even Nicolas Touzaint, who was the dressage leader, had gone straight through the final water, which was amazingly brave when you considered what he had to lose, and their number four, Jean Teulere, showed just why he is a world champion when he did the same on Hobby du Mee, a lovely little horse who was only eight at the time. Although we were in the lead, the French had still showed everyone what could be done and we were aware that they were becoming ever more of a threat in international eventing.

Mary had also gone very well, which more than justified the decision to include her in the squad, but Tina, who had put up a personal best in the dressage, had an uncharacteristically unfortunate cross-country round on Captain Christy, a horse who had never before faulted across country. It's pretty unusual for a whole squad to be feeling up at the end of cross-country day, and this was no exception, with both Jeanette and Tina feeling pretty low.

We all went with our owners to the 'black and white' ball held in City West that night in honour of Tommy Brennan where poor Jeanette had to put up with seeing her dramatic fall replayed over and over again on a big screen. Everyone was pretty exhausted though, and as soon as dinner was over most riders headed for bed, though apparently the party went on well into the dawn.

Next morning we had the nervous experience of praying that the three team horses left would get past the vets' inspection, especially as Moon Man was sore after his trip in the water, but fortunately it was more to do with stiffness than anything else and, once he'd been hacked out, he looked a lot freer in his movement.

Leslie was lying in bronze medal position at this stage, I was fourth and, with William and Mary in the top ten as well, Ken and Yogi had their work cut out to help all of us, as we were running in quick succession. We didn't have much in hand over the French either, so there was no room for complacency and any calmness I might have felt completely evaporated as the tension built.

Magic jumped a clear round, which was lovely because it put us up to the individual bronze medal position. Unfortunately, this was at Leslie's expense, because he had a rail down. But this was still good enough to secure the team's gold medal. We were all disappointed for Leslie because his performance over the weekend had warranted a medal and he was the only one of the squad never to have won an individual medal before. But, at the same time, I felt Magic's performance deserved a medal too.

That's the wonderful thing about horses. Some people might have thought I would be disappointed to lose my title, but results are relevant only to the horse you're riding. It meant as much to me to win a bronze on Magic as it would have done to have won a gold on Rocky. Magic had exceeded all expectations and his very presence at Punchestown had provided a wonderfully lucky break for Nick and Barbara Walkinshaw, who had the thrilling experience of seeing their home-bred horse win a team gold medal for Great Britain. I felt as though all my horses had decided among themselves that they were going to be winners in 2003; none of them wanted to be outdone.

With my plane tickets having been stolen, a lot of people went through a major headache to sort out my flight back to Birmingham. The plan was for me to join William at the Horse of the Year Show where a special award was planned for me at the evening performance that night. This meant, sadly, that I missed any team celebrations – I got straight off Magic after the medal ceremony and shared a car for the airport with Mike Tucker, who was on his way to commentate at HOYS. It felt pretty chaotic – the only identification I had on me was the front cover of the previous week's *Horse & Hound*!

It was fun at HOYS that night because Mike was able to announce to the audience there that Britain had just won the European Championships. My award was a new title, Equestrian of the Year, which was presented to me by the actress Susan George. And I was so pleased that I could finally watch my husband jump. He'd had a good weekend, winning a big class and finishing as leading rider, but we had been amused during Punchestown when a newspaper report got muddled between the pair of us and referred to William as 'she'.

I was so relieved that there was only one more three-day event before the season ended. I took Sarah Jewson's Matter Of Fact to Le Lion d'Angers; he tried really hard and finished fourth, which was a good result, but all I could think of was how glad I was that the 2003 eventing season was over. There was no time to draw breath though. I had a yard full of young horses to break and William was hectic too. No one could believe that we weren't going to have a holiday, but there was no hope of that.

The floodgates had opened with invitations and requests for interviews. I received an award at the Animal Health Trust's annual awards dinner and was voted BBC South Sports Personality of the Year, mainly, I think, as a result of my father's hard work canvassing at his local!

I went up to London to give an interview for Radio Five Live and another for *Woman's Hour* and when I came out of the studio I got caught up in the England rugby team's open-top bus drive through London after winning the World Cup; it was wonderful to feel the power of sport in lifting national spirits.

Rolex took a table at the *Sunday Times* Sportswoman of the Year lunch and invited me. I knew I was shortlisted for the award, which had been won the year before by Ellen MacArthur, someone I admire hugely, but I had no idea that I had got it this time. Any award is special, but with eventing being only a minority sport I was really touched that people outside the equestrian industry were recognising the achievement of the Grand Slam.

Then it was the Sports Writers Association dinner, where William and I were on the same table as the rugby player Richard Hill. The dinner was dominated by World Cup excitement, but I received the Pat Besford award for the Outstanding Sporting Achievement of the Year. I was overwhelmed when I saw the names on the trophy, among them Lester Piggott, Peter Shilton, Steve Redgrave, Gary

Lineker, Bobby Robson and Matthew Pinsent.

I still find these big sporting occasions extraordinary and don't feel worthy of being in such a line-up. Everyone knows everyone within the eventing world and, with the best will in the world, I know it will always be only a small pond. Therefore to get the chance to meet stars from other sports is fascinating.

I had always promised to hold a party if I won the Grand Slam, so my brother Tim kindly closed his Ghillies restaurant on the Thames in Putney for my celebrations. It was a great opportunity to thank all my connections – owners, breeders, vets, press and sponsors – but also Yogi, Mandy Stibbe, Lucinda Green, who had taken over from Mandy as chief selector, my team-mates and lots of William's and my close friends. Mike Tucker made a very kind speech, in which he referred to 'the Pippa factor' and how it was my relationship with my horses that gave me the edge. And then I had to make a speech in which, of course, I got terribly choked.

The part that finished me off was thanking Zanie Tanswell, because I knew she was going to leave me. She had dreaded telling me (and had been putting it off until after Burghley), but she had the opportunity to move in with her boyfriend (now fiancé), Chris King. He now had a yard of his own and, though neither of us wanted our arrangement to end – Zanie was particularly upset at the thought of missing a trip to the Athens Olympics – it was obviously a great chance for her.

It was a wonderful night; the bubbly flowed and everyone was on flying form. William and I went clubbing with some of our close mates and William's owners, Mark and Julie Slade. After all that, we ended up starving hungry at a drive-through McDonald's at 3 a.m.

My hectic schedule got even worse when it was the weekend

of the new Belfast International Show, where William was jumping and I had been asked to present a prize. Unfortunately, this coincided with William Fox-Pitt's wedding to Alice Plunkett, a talented and successful racing TV presenter. I was so thankful and happy that my William and I had resolved our problems, and it was similarly wonderful that William (Fox-Pitt) had sorted himself out by getting together with Alice. We've all known Alice for years – she is one of the nicest, kindest, funniest people and I was so chuffed when she got engaged to William that summer. Being one of my closest friends, I was sad to miss their wedding. But at the same time I was needed in Belfast and I wanted to support my husband.

I had another drama, though, on the strength of this trip. My bag was searched at the airport and I managed to leave my purse behind there. Next day, while doing the food shopping, I realised I had no purse so, for the second time in two months, I had another week with no money and spent a frantic time cancelling cards.

For many, one of the annual sporting highlights is the *BBC Sports Personality of the Year*. There had been masses of reminders everywhere, including weekly in *Horse & Hound*, to vote for me and I was rather cringeing that people had to be reminded! Because it was the fiftieth anniversary of the show, places in the audience were more limited than usual. Normally you see a few eventing chums and the jockeys there, but this time the only people I really knew were Mike Tucker, Harvey Smith and Derek Ricketts, who is the show jumping performance manager.

Halfway through the evening my relaxed enjoyment evaporated when a little microphone was pinned to my shirt. It had never occurred to me that I'd make it to the last five and be interviewed on TV, and I broke out into a cold sweat. I was wearing a tight-fitting gold shirt and I was terribly conscious that I must be showing unattractive sweat patches. It's one thing being interviewed on TV when you've just got off the horse; then you're so full of adrenalin that you don't think about being nervous – you only have to talk about your performance and the whole thing is spontaneous. But now I was suddenly surrounded by incredibly famous people and I thought: 'Oh no, I've got sweaty armpits and I'd like to die.'

The lovely Gary Lineker interviewed me, but I wouldn't say he's the world's expert on eventing and I think he was wondering what on earth to ask me. Thankfully the interview, which was a bit of a blur and probably not my greatest moment, was over as quickly as it had started and, when I saw it later, I realised that I wasn't as sweaty as I had feared! My first reaction when I heard my name called out was that of a kid in trouble at school but, even in my nervousness, I was aware of the fantastic honour of being part of the same occasion that honoured the rugby World Cup team and Jonny Wilkinson, who was the overall winner.

Ten days later the Olympia International Show Jumping Show made a great change of scenery because, after the disaster of my missing dogs the previous Christmas, I had finally got my 'job' in the press office working for Candy Burnyeat, also the Burghley press officer. It was all very relaxing and now the boot was on the other foot, because I had to make cups of tea, do the photocopying of results and run to fetch riders for interviews. But I think I may have been more of a hindrance than a help – at one stage Candy put a sign on my back saying: 'No one's asked me a question for five minutes.' She also put up a new label on the door saying: 'Pippa's Press Office'.

I did a bit of commentating for Eurosport and, with William, did some work with the former tennis player Andrew

Castle, who was working for TV. My parents came up for the annual British Equestrian Writers Association lunch and I was touched when Alan Smith, the *Daily Telegraph*'s long-time equestrian reporter, presented me with my third BEWA trophy, which goes to the personality the writers vote for each year.

Riders owe a lot to the equestrian writers for the healthy way they portray our sport. I have known most of them for many years now and admire their enthusiasm; they travel miles every weekend and are often dependent on British success to get their sports editors interested. Because they're all so genuine in what they write, riders feel comfortable and relaxed; we know we're not going to be misquoted or have things we say taken out of context, which can happen with journalists who have little understanding about the horse world. It's fashionable to complain about the press, but the reality is that in comparison with sports such as football or cricket, we know that in eventing we are lucky with our treatment.

But despite everyone's kindness, I was struggling with the sudden flood of demands on my time. I'd had four approaches from book publishers alone, not to mention masses of requests for interviews, speeches and charity work. In an interview for *Horse & Hound*, I was described as 'a cheerful but harassed hamster, whose legs couldn't quite keep up with its wheel'. It was so true; I knew I was overdoing the interviews and photo-shoots because I was saying exactly the same thing every time, but people were so clever they put me in a position where I found it impossible to say no. I had no idea how much I should be charging for anything, and I desperately needed someone I liked and trusted to take the pressure off me, but without upsetting people who had been loyal to me.

The rower Matthew Pinsent, who is a friend of the

Walkinshaws, was really kind and gave me advice on how to deal with the aftermath of the Grand Slam. He explained to me that I should get a PA in to help with the flood of letters. As a result of that conversation, I thought the perfect person to help me would be Becky Coffey. She was already coming in once or twice a month to do bills, run through the diary and do my competition entries, so it made sense for her to help me wade through the paperwork. The extra work created by all the publicity wasn't fair on Jenny Kleboe, who has been with William and me for a long time and who does our accounts and answers the telephone two mornings a week. Becky and Jenny both helped me enormously with the huge backlog of paperwork, because if there's one thing I have a phobia about, it's picking up a pen and writing!

In many ways, the best thing to come out of the *Sports Personality of the Year* evening was a chance conversation with Sally Gunnell and Colin Jackson about agents. Sally promised to contact an agent called Jonathan Marks from MTC for me, and the next day he rang me up. We arranged to meet at Olympia and, straight away, I felt very comfortable with him.

Jonathan represents a lot of people in athletics, including Colin, and came well recommended. One of the things that I liked was the fact that he made it clear that he wasn't going to rush in and take control over my existing sponsors. A lot of agents will try to push for extra deals with existing sponsors, which can be disastrous. Over the years, my sponsors have become friends, especially Phil and Julie Middleton from Equine America, and Mark Bulson and Roy Aspinall from Toggi, with whom I have been dealing directly for over five years. There's also Jo Bower from Creature Comforts, who supplies us with shavings, Alan Chadwick from Virbac, who supplies the worming product Equimax, Jamie Hawksfield from Equestrian Vision, Devacoux, who supply all my tack, and Horseware Ireland, who give me rugs, and Tim and Ben Page from Allen and Page Horsefeeds. As a result of the Grand Slam, I also gained an agreement with Rolex, who support a variety of sportsmen. It's important that I maintain personal contact with all of these people, otherwise why should they want to continue to sponsor me? I don't see what there is in it for a sponsor if they don't get personal contact with the rider they're supporting.

The agreement between Jonathan and myself was a new situation for both of us; I hadn't gone down that line before, and was nervous of it, and he hadn't been mad enough to get involved with an event rider before. I didn't take on an agent in order to get lots more money but I had to face up to the fact that the Grand Slam really had changed my life, and Jonathan has made it so much easier.

The Grand Slam suddenly meant there was enough work to do in my office to provide someone with a full-time job. I couldn't possibly do it all because if I couldn't spend enough time in the saddle I wouldn't have been doing my job properly. Coping with this extra dimension to life was a new problem and the pressures began to get me down. The most important thing in my life is my marriage and, no matter what demands I have from horses or the outside world, I know that has to come first. But finding time for William, who had been so supportive during the unbearably tense time before Burghley, was easier said than done.

I couldn't wait for Christmas 2003, when I could sit in a chair, do nothing and drive nowhere. But, as they say, there's no rest for the wicked. In the joy of achieving something so big, I never imagined the responsibilities it would bring.

12
Olympic Year Again

The year in which an Olympics is due to take place seems to have a particular psychological effect on me; it's as if an invisible pressure trips in on 1 January and then permanently lurks like an ever-present shadow. Of course, pressure only exists as far as you allow it to; but amid the excitement and the sense of a big goal coming nearer, it is an additional mental strain, and this time I felt it especially as there didn't seem to have been any break from the stress of Grand Slam year.

The Olympics is such a big deal – literally the culmination of a lifetime's work. People would ask when the preparation began with Primmore's Pride (Kiri), and my reply would be: 'Nine years ago – when he was only two!' As a team, we were aware that we could leave no stone unturned in our preparation, and I knew that this would be a year of massive attention to detail. If we didn't have the luck with us in Athens, none of us would want to be saying: 'We should have done this,' or 'That went wrong because we didn't cover it in the preparation.'

The year itself got off to a rather hungover start after a New Year's Eve party at our friends Duncan and Clare's, but at least I only had two horses to do, Barnaby and Rocky, which was something of a result. Also, I had the relief of knowing that my new head girl, Zanie's replacement, was arriving on 2 January. Hannah Bailey came to me with a great recommendation from the Swedish rider Dag Albert, for whom she had worked for six years. I was so relieved when she agreed to take the job because I really didn't know how I was going to replace Zanie; a competent and trustworthy team on the ground is crucial, and Zanie and I had been such friends, but I knew instantly that Hannah and I were going to get on.

Soon the stables were filling up again as the other horses returned from their winter holiday, and among them was a new face – Chamrock, an eight-year-old previously ridden by Fiona Cardrick and owned and bred by Sarah Johnson. I also collected three horses from my Norfolk owners: Blue Horizon, a 'too-slow' racehorse bought from Ken Clawson by the McIntyres, plus their Teddy Twilight, back in work after eight months off, and the Jewsons' promising Matter Of Opinion – 'Mop' – who was Matter Of Fact's brother. Kiri would come in later, as his two four-star wins of 2003 meant that there was no need for him to do Badminton this time. His goal was Athens in mid-August, so he could start work after my return from a trip to the Dubai Show with William, who had been invited to compete there.

This was the nearest we were going to get to a holiday this winter, but it was still a worthwhile break because William was only competing in the evenings, which left the daytime free for fishing and sunbathing with his owners, Mark and Julie Slade of Refco, plus their young son Callum. And the week ended brilliantly when William won the Dubai Classic Grand Prix on their horse Tibor. The only blot on the horizon was that Ian Sweet from the *Mission to Athens* programme had come out with us to Dubai, with his camera. I knew when I agreed to do the programme that there would be times when it would be too much, and being followed on holiday was one of them. I hate even trying on clothes in a communal changing room, so being filmed in a bikini definitely felt one step too far.

I returned to a flood of PR engagements and interview requests. There were three fashion shoots with other riders – presumably to show that eventers can scrub up reasonably well when helped by expensive clothes and a load of make-up – for the *Sunday Times* (when I got to wear the most fantastic £6,000 pale blue silk dress), the *Observer* and the *Daily Mail*. The last and, unfortunately, probably the least successful shoot was with none other than Lord Lichfield. The problem was that we were made to wear red dresses; I look awful in red and, standing next to Zara Phillips with her beautiful skin and features, I felt Frumpy Funnell had returned with a vengeance.

In the interviews, some of the newspaper journalists were really nice to talk to, but after a while I felt that I was saying the same thing over and over again and, with fourteen horses in work, it was a struggle to keep travelling to London to meet all these commitments and still get through all the riding. Fortunately I had a brilliant agent in Jonathan Marks, with whom I had a brainstorming session to work out how to handle all the requests and when I could legitimately say no.

One of the best assignments was BBC's *A Question of Sport*. I took Lizzie Bunn and Clare Inglis along for a girly night out and, as I was on the last of the three programmes to be filmed that night, by the time the recording began I'd had a couple of glasses of wine on an empty stomach and was feeling pretty relaxed. My team-mates were Ally McCoist and Chris Eubank, and I managed to answer all my questions correctly. However, embarrassingly, in the Beat the Buzzer round, when a question came up to which I knew the answer, in my haste I hit the light instead of the big buzzer button. I looked extremely dumb – and of course the incident was not edited out! Still, it was a fun night.

Another great occasion was the 'Women of Achievement' lunch with the Queen at Buckingham Palace. I felt hugely honoured to be taking part, alongside people who had done far more worthwhile things than I had. The highlight was being approached by the wonderful comedian Jennifer Saunders. I nearly fell over when she came up to me and said: 'It's Pippa, isn't it?' It turned out that her daughter rides and so she follows the sport.

There was also a terrifying day teaching at the British Eventing Trainers' Seminar, where the audience included not only serious trainers like Jennie Loriston-Clarke and Judy Bradwell, who have judged me at three-day level, but also Ruth McMullen, who basically taught me most of what I know! I don't usually suffer from nerves about speaking but this was daunting, though I did enjoy it once I got stuck in.

With all this gadding about, I was relieved and pleased when team training started at Waresley Park, even though it meant missing William's birthday. It was great to get stuck into riding and see my mates, and useful to be observed by the trainers Yogi Breisner, Ken Clawson and Tracie Robinson. But disaster struck when Teddy Twilight went lame after just ten days in work. I was horribly depressed about this, because it meant his operation hadn't worked. Teddy is such a special little horse and I longed for him to come right for the McIntyres, who are super owners. Sadly, this setback suggested that Teddy's eventing days were over. However, he has now got a great new home show jumping without the demands of galloping and going across country.

The Olympic countdown gathered momentum with a compulsory Team GB day for all Elite (Lottery-funded) equestrians, including the show jumpers and dressage riders. We had long discussions about how we would cope with the expected heat in Athens and work on our fitness. The doctor gave us a health check, and I suddenly realised that in addition to riding umpteen horses I was also going to have to run or get on my cycling machine every day.

And there was still a lot of running around to do. William and I went to the British Equestrian Trade Association fair at the NEC in Birmingham for two days to see our sponsors; I had to take part in the launch of a new range of Toggi breeches I'd been involved in designing, and William was busy with the Royston products, including his personal range of rugs. Then we were off on the Funnell Factor tour, which would involve a lot of driving and late nights, with evenings at Merrist Wood, Exeter, Addington and Osbaldeston. This was a lecture-demo tour by William and me, intended to be instructive but also a light-hearted evening's entertainment. It had been really well organised by Jamie Hawksfield of Equestrian Vision and every night was a sell-out. To begin with I was nervous, but once we got going it all seemed to come naturally. We took the mickey out of each other's sports – William imitated me being soppy with the horses and I did his bandy-legged show jumper's walk and grunt. As well as putting over some serious training points, I hoped that people could feel the good vibes between us and how we have a good laugh every day at home.

In the middle of the tour came Mum's annual dance at Tunbridge Wells in aid of Eridge Horse Trials, and a week after that the ERA (Event Riders Association) Ball at Cheltenham Racecourse. As number one in the world rankings I had to go to collect an award and William suggested we stayed over –

but, no, like an idiot I had to insist that we drive home. So it was three hours' driving and then just three hours' sleep, because I'd given Hannah the day off to recover from the ball and felt I had to help the other staff.

No wonder I was exhausted before the season even started. The opening event, the first weekend in March, was Stileman's – and, significantly, this was the first time in my competing life that I didn't jump out of bed thinking: 'Yippee!' I couldn't rustle up the energy to be excited. But there was no time to ponder on this, because the second weekend of the season was completely manic. I was competing at Tweseldown in Hampshire on the Saturday and, in the opposite direction, at Poplar Park in Suffolk on the Sunday. Walk On Star (Magic) was third at Tweseldown and I was keen to get away in good time to get ready for the next day's trip. But, oh no: the UK Sport doping squad arrived and asked me to do a test. I'd only just been to the loo and peeing on command in front of someone isn't the easiest. It was well after dark by the time I finally achieved it and I was now way behind on my plans.

After the 2003 season, when it seemed I couldn't do anything wrong, suddenly I was struggling to win even a few points. At Aldon one-day event I got more faults than I'd amassed in the whole of the previous year, all at the same fence but on different horses, and another weekend I drove 400 miles to have a run-out on Viceroy at Burnham Market. Tina and I returned to Fontainebleau, but that wasn't spectacularly successful either: I made a complete mess of the show jumping and, while Cornerman was thirteenth, I didn't dare run Walk On Star across country because the ground was patchy and I could feel an ominous heat in his front leg, in the area surrounding an old splint and close to his suspensory ligament.

Another thing that was getting me down was a nagging

toothache – and I am absolutely terrified of the dentist. In the middle of April Gill Watson, team trainer to the junior squad, brought thirty riders down to the yard for the day and, surviving on Nurofen, I took them round, talking to them about fitness and how sports psychology has helped me. I get a great kick out of helping young riders because I was so inspired by others in the past and it was an engrossing day, but by the time 6.30 p.m. came I hadn't even had a cup of coffee and the tooth was a nightmare. Three days later, on an emergency visit to the dentist, it turned out that I had an abscess, and once the dentist had relieved the pressure I felt much better – apart from the delightful prospect of deep root canal treatment after Badminton. That night I felt pretty weird, probably because the pus released had got into my system. I felt freezing cold and couldn't even warm up from the hottest bath I could bear. William was away and it was a horrible night.

The Badminton picture finally fell into place. The plan had always been to take Cornerman, but I had my doubts about Magic and got the vets Jenny Hall and P. J. McMahon over to look at him. Even though he was sound, there was still heat and slight swelling in his front leg; I couldn't risk running him. Having notched up a three-star win and a European medal the previous year he still had good enough form to be considered a back-up horse to Kiri at Athens, but it was nonetheless gutting for his owners Nick and Barbara Walkinshaw, who had dreamed of having their home-bred horse running at Badminton. As always, though, one person's misfortune is another's lucky break: Sue and Lizzie Bunn had been dying for me to take Viceroy (Leroy) to Badminton, and this was the perfect opportunity.

I felt quite differently about this Badminton. Because I had won it twice, and also because I was not riding either of my four-star winners – Kiri was being kept for Athens and Rocky was still on the 'rehab' list – I wasn't tipped to win and felt under much less pressure. However, I was still looking forward to being competitive with Cornerman, and in the dressage phase he did his best ever test to lie in joint second place with the favourites, William Fox-Pitt on Tamarillo, behind Andrew Nicholson on Lord Killinghurst.

On cross-country day the weather was desperate, with pouring rain producing a quagmire, and the organisers were brave to keep the event going. I have always had reservations about Leroy's speed and stamina but, bless him, he kept battling through the mud and rain, only to hit the gate into Huntsman's Close near the end of the course. I was catapulted through the air and landed among Leroy's front feet; he was unable to avoid trampling on me and one of his shoe studs dug into my arm, causing a puncture wound.

My immediate thought was to get back and prepare to ride Cornerman but, because safety standards are now, quite correctly, much stricter, the medical team at Badminton insisted that my arm be X-rayed at Frenchay Hospital in Bristol. They commandeered a helicopter, which felt embarrassingly over the top; on the other hand, I have always wanted to ride in one! The X-rays were clear, but I had to endure the traumatic experience of a tetanus jab (I am terrified of injections). William and Mum came to fetch me by car; they both said the right things, bolstering me by telling me that it was no point riding Cornerman unless I was going to give it a proper crack. I was actually hungry to give it a go; we were, after all, lying second and Cornerman is a good cross-country horse.

He was foot-perfect and full of running, despite the wet conditions; he felt like Rocky, purring along so easily in that confidence-giving way. When we got to Huntsman's Close I was careful to set him up and balance him before the gate – but, unbelievably, there was an action replay! Cornerman even left the same leg behind as Leroy, and I had exactly the same sort of fall.

It was an extraordinary sequence of unlucky events, but I was quite philosophical, if slightly frustrated. It had never entered my head that I would win Badminton 2004, and I had always felt that it might be William Fox-Pitt's year. Tamarillo had been injured the previous season, and it felt like his turn now; so, instead of being disappointed, I was thrilled for William, who so deserved it. I wasn't deflated at all. No one can have an unending stream of luck with horses, and this was nothing like the bad old years, when horses were refusing to go for me. Leroy and Cornerman had been enjoying themselves across country and going well, so I wasn't at all unhappy.

Interestingly, though, a lot of people later commented that there were camera flashlights going off in the dark of the woods. I don't want to make excuses but I'd like to think there was a reason for those two falls. I could accept it more easily if I had messed up on the approach and presented the horses incorrectly, but having watched the video with several highly respected people, I realised that it was simply a freak coincidence.

After a dreadful trip to the dentist – William drove me because I had to be sedated to get through the treatment – I needed to turn my attention to my Olympic horse. Kiri had already been fifth on his first outing of the season, at Belton, and the plan was to run him in the World Cup qualifier at Chatsworth, two weeks after Badminton. The main issue was cross-country bitting, in order to give me that crucial last ounce of control. I had a useful experimental session with Yogi at Waresley, though we didn't reach a conclusion.

I'd planned to run Walk On Star at Chatsworth too, but his leg had come up again. Even though he was sound, it was plainly crazy to jeopardise his future by working him. If you ignore minor problems they can turn into major career-ending issues, and he was far too nice and talented a horse to risk that. So we decided to give him a year off. Injury and lameness in my horses is the one setback which causes me to lose confidence more than anything. This year was not going according to plan! At the start of 2004 I had been listed for Athens with six horses. Now it was down to four. Anne Burnet was gutted when a scan at the Animal Health Trust revealed that Jurassic Rising, my Blenheim winner, wasn't right either. This time the previous year I'd been at every three-day event going – and winning them. Twelve months on and I seemed to be going nowhere. Ridiculously, my next three-day event would be Athens!

So by Chatsworth, a fortnight after Badminton, I was tired and depressed. I seemed to have lost my touch; nothing was going right. It was such a stark contrast with 2003. But, hooray! Kiri and I won the World Cup qualifier. Such a relief. Kiri performed one of his best dressage tests and we had a big lead over the rest of the field going into the cross-country. The terrain at Chatsworth, on the side of a hill, isn't the easiest for a long-striding horse, but after my session with Yogi I'd decided to try a new Cornish snaffle bit and it seemed to be working. Kiri was still headstrong near the end of the course, though, and there were a couple of fences we could have jumped much better – and, being a perfectionist, of course I dwelt on these too much instead of the many other fences where he was fantastic. Our show-jumping round, though, was as good as at Burghley the year before and we held on to our lead, beating Andrew Nicholson on Fenicio.

The only gloomy spot in an otherwise nice weekend was that I had retired Matter Of Fact across country. His owner Sarah Jewson was very upset and I realised, with some trepidation, that we would have to have a discussion about his future plans, as I was beginning to wonder if he was the right horse for me.

After Chatsworth it was an odd feeling not to be among those going off to compete in Saumur: I was torn between being frustrated at having nothing to ride there and enjoying the chance to spend a little precious time at home. William's spring was going as badly as mine: his top horse Mondriaan, with whom he had a realistic chance of getting to the Olympics, had gone wrong and I was distraught for him. He has worked so hard for so long, is so talented and really deserves a break, but every time I think he has got there, the relevant horse has a setback.

At least I got my Olympic call-up: Yogi phoned to say that I had been selected with Kiri, with Cornerman and Rocky as back-up horses. Of course I was expecting to be picked, with Kiri having won Kentucky and Burghley and done so well at Chatsworth this season, but it was still a relief and a thrill to get the actual call. As expected, William (Fox-Pitt) and Leslie were also in, and Jeanette Brakewell's good Badminton on Over To You clinched her place, which was good news, because we knew from previous experience that she can be crucial to team success.

We four were established as a team by this stage, but there was some speculation as to who the fifth member would be. (The Olympic format had changed – again – to teams of five competing for both team and individual medals, as opposed to the two separate competitions in Sydney.) We were delighted when it was announced that it would be Sarah Cutteridge. We had already nicknamed her 'Cool Cutty' for her extra-ordinarily sensible attitude at competitions, and we knew she would be an asset, strong enough mentally to be unaffected by the whole Olympic razzmatazz.

My only sadness was that I knew I would miss Tina. It would be the first championships at which I'd ridden without my best buddy being there and I felt gutted for her. She'd had such a disappointing time at the European Championships in 2003, then went well at Badminton on Captain Christy only to have a slip on the flat in the middle of a combination near the end of the course. I felt desperately sorry for her because I know the Olympics means more to her than anything and it's the third time the chance has eluded such a talented, world-class rider.

It was around this time that I got a call from a strangely embarrassed Simon Clegg, the British Olympic Association's *chef de mission*. He informed me that I would have to be registered at the Olympics as Philippa Funnell. Unbelievably, Pippa means 'blow-job' in Greek! Needless to say, this was a joke which ran and ran among my friends.

I was soon brought down to earth amid all the feverish Olympic excitement when Barnaby developed colic. A locum vet gave him a painkiller, but it became obvious that he wasn't improving. I was adamant that I didn't want to put Barnaby through surgery at the age of twenty-seven; it wasn't fair. He was clearly uncomfortable and I got in a desperate state because I didn't know whether to have him put him down immediately or to wait a bit longer. Colic is a funny thing, and horses can get themselves right again, but Barnaby had been sedated, so he wasn't presenting a true picture. One minute he was OK, the next he was obviously in serious pain, and he hadn't drunk anything. I was split down the middle: I didn't want him suffering, but I did want to give him the chance to get better.

The vet was so sympathetic and when she went off to grab a sandwich I sat with Barnaby in the field. It was a terrible afternoon; William was away and I became a complete mess, crying and constantly changing my mind about what to do. By the time the vet got back the sedation had worn off and I realised that Barnaby was in quite a bad way. I couldn't let him go through the night like that, and so I made the decision to have him put down. It felt like the end of an era; we'd been together for twenty-two years – over half my life – and I felt so privileged to have been involved with such a super horse. I still feel there's a huge void without him; when, six months later, Mum gave me a painting of him for Christmas, it triggered off a huge fit of weeping.

I was completely crushed by Barnaby's death, but I had to pull myself together and head off to Windsor with Ensign (Titch). This was a great excitement, as it was the first time Mum and I have owned a runner at a three-day event. Ensign performed a promising dressage test to put him up among the leaders, but then had an annoying run-out across country, which was more to do with lack of steering than with the fence itself. The one consolation was that there is less pressure when I'm riding for Mum – we just have a laugh about it – and at least for the first time this year I'd completed a three-day event! I was also pleased with the promising feel Ensign gave me. He's an ex-racehorse who had been sent to me by Ben Case, with whom I had worked at Ruth McMullen's all those years ago. We took him on as an investment, and at first he was hard work: a racehorse has to be retrained, which is harder than starting from scratch with a youngster.

I also took Matter Of Fact to take part in a new competition organised by Mike Tucker, an international team challenge. I was in the British team with William (Fox-Pitt), Zara and Cutty, and we got a lot of publicity, mainly because of the Olympic build-up coupled with Zara's presence. The idea had been to make it a fun event, but people seemed to take it remarkably seriously! We finished second to the Australasians. Again, Matty gave me the sort of round that made me question his ability to reach the top of the sport, and it was decided that he should go to Emilie Chandler, a talented up-and-coming rider who was pleased to gain an extra ride. Sarah Jewson would have been happy for me to keep him as a fun horse at two-star level but, much as I liked the horse, I have got to the stage where I have to be realistic and I don't want a horse for the sake of it. Time is too tight and I want to be working on horses that have got the potential to go to the top.

Meanwhile, back at home William was having more problems. He had been complaining about a niggling pain in his groin and had made the problem worse competing at the Surrey County Show. This was a worry because he had a good ride coming up at the Hickstead Derby meeting on Buddy Bunn, a horse bred and owned by Douglas Bunn – a really exciting prospect, because William had already been third in the Eindhoven Derby and third in the Grand Prix at Windsor on the horse. They kicked off Hickstead with a good win in a big class and were favourites for the Derby. It seemed like William's best chance for years in this special competition, which every rider longs to win, and he'd done everything possible to prepare, including taking Buddy Bunn cross-country schooling. But when he jumped in the Derby trial I could tell that he was in serious pain, and that night he had to face up to relinquishing the ride because, despite all the physiotherapy he'd been having, he couldn't do the horse justice. He suggested that John Whitaker take over on Buddy Bunn, and I so admired him for it. John is a world-class horseman and, after William had given him some help with the horse, he jumped an impeccable double clear to win. It was a fairytale result for Douglas, to have his own horse win the competition he devised, and I was delighted for John – but the victory was bitter-sweet for me. I was just devastated for William.

By now the Olympics were only two months away and I was worried that I wasn't more pumped up. All my mates were away competing at Bramham; it was the first time I'd missed it for ages, and I was feeling low, wondering why it was all going wrong this season for me and William. Was anything going to go right for either of us this year?

13
Athens

We had a quiet two weeks in the middle of June because William couldn't ride and I had nothing on. Most normal people would have taken the opportunity to go on holiday but I wanted to work on Kiri, Rocky and Charlie – and the young show jumpers William breeds in partnership with Donal Barnwell. Their programme had started in 1994, so the first crop were starting to get interesting – one, Billy Orange, was on a Dutch Nations Cup team that summer – and I was looking forward to getting more involved in the production of these youngsters.

Kiri's work level had been upped and I was galloping him regularly, three times a fortnight, in the special fleece rugs we had been given. They went right over the horse's body and up its neck to the ears, the idea being to make them sweat and help acclimatise them to the 90-degree heat expected in Athens.

Then at the end of the month there was a team training session at Waresley Park. It was such a joy to have Rocky back in action here and he was on great form; it was his first outing since his injury the previous August and he was as pleased as if I'd taken him to a party. The team vibes were positive, and suddenly the enthusiasm that I'd been lacking started to kick back in.

Jenny Hall, our team vet, who had been monitoring the horses all year, took blood tests and scoped them, using a tube to look into their lungs and take a sample of fluid to be tested for viral or bacterial infection. If you can catch these problems early enough they can be dealt with in time, before they get to the stage where they detract from performance.

As well as preparing for the heat of Athens, we'd also need to be used to jumping under spotlights, as by the time the second, individual, round of show jumping commenced it would be dark. Lights were hired to put up around Eddy Stibbe's outdoor school, but the horses were more surprised at having to get up in the dark than they were by the spotlights. And the weather was hardly Greek: it poured with rain that night. It was a useful exercise, because I found that my eye was naturally drawn to the light and it took a bit of concentration to keep looking at the fence, but the horses did jump well and it was good to know that we had practised. The big lesson I learned was not to eat beforehand – we had just eaten a huge Chinese meal and I felt pretty sick!

On 26 June I had the experience of a lifetime. For two months I had been keeping secret an invitation to be one of the Olympic torch-bearers carrying the flame on its journey through London. At first I didn't grasp the magnitude of the occasion. This was the first time ever the flame had crossed all five continents, and the way the day in London had been organised made me proud to be British. Somewhat dauntingly, I had been chosen to be the penultimate torch-bearer, lighting Sir Steve Redgrave's torch outside Buckingham Palace. The Household Cavalry kindly lent me a big, safe horse to ride down Birdcage Walk to the main gates of the palace, as this definitely wouldn't have been an occasion to suit any of my own horses; they'd have been overcome by the sheer volume of people lining the route. They'd even got the horse accustomed to a wheelchair, because the person to light my torch was Ade Adipitan, the Paralympic basketball player. They had done a sterling job, even though they'd had to improvise in training with someone sitting in a wheelbarrow.

Another milestone on the road to Athens was a trip to Earl's Court for Hannah and me to get kitted out with our Team GB outfits. By now, I had really perked up. I felt much more enthusiastic about life, not only excited about the approaching Olympics, but also because the work I'd put in on the younger horses was paying off, with some good results coming on Blue Horizon, Chamrock, Mop and Ensign. Thankfully, my *joie de vivre* and love of the sport seemed to have returned and I prayed they would stay with me up to the Games.

The last week before we flew out was taken up with galloping Kiri, having a last-minute lesson with Ruth and collecting my fabulous new Oakley Supreme lorry, bought with my Grand Slam money. William had an operation on his groin; he was pretty uncomfortable but cheered by lots of visitors, including Lizzie Bunn's daughter Georgia and Amy Inglis, who came dressed in nurses' uniforms.

By now I was just longing to get to Athens and to get the job done. It was all so near, and I got into a state of paranoia, dreading a silly accident with one of the horses or having a fall myself; you feel in limbo because you're so near and yet there's still plenty of time for something to wrong. The last two events before the Olympics, Aston-le-Walls and Lulworth, were nerve-racking but, amazingly, I finished up in one piece. Kiri felt fantastic, and William was able to hobble out and watch me jumping him. Our preparation had, I knew, gone according to plan; now the waiting was over and I'd just have to give it my best shot.

Then, at last, we were in Athens. We were one of the first Team GB squads to arrive at the Olympic village and it was thrilling to get there. It's an unbelievable place, in which you have this fantastic feeling of privilege to be mixing with the world's top athletes. The canteen seated over five thousand, with an enormous selection of food, from McDonald's to traditional Greek meals. I was already looking forward to a diet of taramasalata and pitta bread with the odd cheeseburger thrown in. The apartments in Athens were more spacious than those in Sydney, and the British Olympic Association had done a great job of adding extras, like TVs, comfortable chairs, fridges, even irons and ironing boards. I was worried about sharing a room because I do like to have my own space and sometimes be completely alone, but I soon felt relaxed sharing with Cutty, who was fitting in brilliantly with the team.

We were longing to see the horses, who were a 45-minute bus ride away at the equestrian centre at Markopoulo. The facilities were out of this world, which was a huge relief. The British horses had a block to themselves, with plenty of room for our kit and two air-conditioned rooms with showers and loos. Both Kiri and Hannah seemed in great form, and there was generally an atmosphere of high spirits in the camp. That night we had supper at Porto Rafti, an old fishing port ten minutes away from the equestrian site. It was a really enjoyable, relaxed evening with my team-mates and all the grooms and officials. It was great to catch up with Simon Brooks-Ward, who was acting as consulting adviser and joined us with his assistant Penny Henderson.

The first week in Greece was about everyone getting themselves and their horses settled into a new environment and adjusting to the temperatures, which were much higher than we were used to – in the mid-30s – and uncomfortable at times, though not humid. We knew we had to be careful not to get too intense too early with the horses' training, so their work was varied from dressage to a fair bit of hacking with a few faster canters. I was relieved to have done plenty of fast work at home as there were no facilities for galloping.

We got into a good routine of either running or working out in the gym in the Olympic village. I think we were all fitter than we had ever been, and I was pleased that I'd spent so many hours over the past three months either running or on my exercise bike, thick jackets and all. Afterwards, we would sit on the grass in the middle of the athletics training ground, transfixed by the perfection and variety of the track and field athletes, from the six-foot-six high jumpers to tiny long-distance runners and the powerful 100 metres sprinters. This is what makes the Olympic experience.

It was all going so well there had to be a setback. It came when Cutty was working The Wexford Lady and suddenly, for no apparent reason, the mare went lame. It was a real bolt out of the blue, because 'Letty' had always been a very sound horse: just one of those freak things that can happen so easily with horses – and always at the wrong moment. My instinctive response was to want to back off Kiri's work, but I had to resist it; I knew I must stick to my original plan.

The mood changed in a flash that night. We were devastated for Cutty, who immediately lost her accreditation and was transported out to a reserve camp, with no access to us. All her years of work and that elusive chance of fulfilling the Olympic dream had been taken from her in a split second of rotten luck – but the mental strength she showed in handling the disappointment proved that Cutty will definitely have her day.

More positively, Mary King and King Solomon, our travelling reserves, arrived to join us and this gave us a real boost, because we all had complete faith in this partnership; Mary is exactly the sort of person you want on a team, because you know she will produce the goods. She was the most experienced of all of us – this was her fourth Olympics – and she was desperate to win her first medal. With 'Solly' being so consistent, we knew that she wouldn't hamper our team chances in any way.

Leslie and I were asked to be two of the six British athletes at the official British Olympic Association press conference. I have been lucky enough to get to many eventing press conferences, but this was quite the most daunting one that Leslie and I have ever attended, simply because of the sheer number of representatives from the mainstream media, none of whom understood the peculiar complexities of our sport. I was disconcerted to realise just how much the press had talked up our chances as a team and mine as an individual. Extra media hype can often be the kiss of death; but still, it was no more pressure than I'd been under in the Grand Slam build-up, and I felt I could handle it.

We also went to the British Embassy in the centre of Athens to attend a reception for the whole of Team GB. I found it a really inspiring evening, being surrounded by past and present stars of British sport, and it gave me such a buzz to feel that we were all out in Athens fighting for the same thing: to produce our personal bests and win medals. My best moment was meeting Dame Mary Peters, who had won gold at Munich in the heptathlon.

It was decided that we wouldn't attend the opening ceremony. The BOA had advised against this for athletes competing within forty-eight hours, because it involves long hours of standing around. I was sad about this, because the opening ceremony in Sydney had mesmerised me more than anything else, and it is definitely one of the highlights of competing at an Olympics. But we were here to do a job and couldn't start the competition tired.

Once the first horse inspection was over, I had a chance to catch up with Mum, Dad, Tim and Kiri's owners Roger and Denise Lincoln at a party Rosemary Barlow had arranged. Not for long, though: we only stayed an hour and a half as we wanted to practise jumping under floodlights in the main stadium. For the first time Kiri felt lit up and excited, so I worked him for a further hour to get him focusing on me, rather than the other distractions.

When I first walked the cross-country, my worst fears came true. I knew instantly that it would not suit Kiri. In the new, shortened, format of the contest, with no roads and tracks or steeplechase phase and a shorter cross-country element (forty-five jumping efforts in nine minutes forty-six seconds, as opposed to twelve and a half or thirteen minutes), there is less galloping space and less time to set a horse up and get it balanced to jump a fence. Kiri is a big, long-striding, traditional three-day-event horse, and I knew at once that he would struggle to get the optimum cross-country time on this course. I'd have to waste time balancing him and shortening his stride. The terrain wasn't going to favour me either, as the last half was all downhill with tight turns and fences coming thick and fast, making it even more difficult for me to balance Kiri while maintaining a fast enough pace.

We all felt that this course, designed by the Italian Albino Garbari in an admittedly limited area – really just a strip of green among all the dust and rocks of this mountainous area west of Athens – was unrecognisable as a four-star in comparison to the big tracks at Badminton, Burghley and Kentucky that our horses had jumped en route to the Olympics. It was beautifully presented and built, but asked few technical questions. Not many of the fences were at maximum dimensions and the ditches were covered by high guard rails. This meant there was nothing imposing enough to make a horse like Kiri back off the fences, and nothing technical enough to make any riders choose long routes and gain time penalties. All in all, therefore, we saw that the cross-country probably would not be the most influential phase of the competition, which was sad for an Olympics. Despite all this, I managed to remain positive, reminding myself that I had spent a lot of time with Yogi working on controlling Kiri's exuberance and that this situation should be covered by what we had learned.

The first day of dressage got off to a solid start when – despite the unseasonal high winds which suddenly arrived, causing the flags around the arena to make an amazing rattling noise and hats to blow off – Jeanette (Brakewell) did a personal best test on Over To You and Mary got a good mark on King Solomon. Bettina Hoy, who excels in this phase, set a target that looked hard to beat, putting her eight penalties ahead of the rest of the field and giving Germany a commanding lead at this early stage. Next day, however, things got even better for us when Leslie and Shear L'Eau also achieved their personal best. Dressage has never been Leslie's favourite phase but the hard work he had put in, with help from Tracie, paid serious dividends, and a mistake-free test left him with a competitive score of 43.2.

As my test grew nearer I became more and more nervous and, for the first time, I was physically sick beforehand. I think the problem was my own and everyone else's high expectations. I had worked Kiri early in the morning and it was a bad dress rehearsal. I knew if he produced a repeat performance – inattentive and unfocused – we would not be near the top of the leaderboard. It is such a fine line getting the balance right: I didn't want to overdo the work, but at the same time I knew that if I didn't do enough I risked Kiri blowing up in the electric atmosphere. Every horse is an individual, and they vary so much from day to day. Again and again I have learned that you cannot necessarily stick to a set plan; you have to have a plan A, of course, but also be flexible and make sure you've prepared plan B or C as well.

When I finally got on Kiri an hour before my test it was an enormous relief: within five minutes I knew he was in a much better frame of mind. Thank God. Tracie had been excellent throughout, spotting every tiny detail, and when I rode into the stadium I felt confident and very clear in my head what I had to do.

It was a great test. The trot work in particular was the best Kiri had ever done. At one point I was awarded three tens and the crowd gasped so loudly that for a split second I thought I had gone wrong and looked up at the scoreboard. Kiri may have felt my hesitation, because he then got just a little bit tighter. My heart sank slightly as I knew that in order to help me through the serpentine loops – the movement he finds the most difficult – he had to be relaxed. So, though greatly improved on the previous year, I lost that last bit of straightness in the final loop on both reins and as a result didn't get the clear flying changes I wanted. I was marked down on those movements. But what we lost on the changes we made up on his halts – another aspect on which I've dropped marks in the past. Ruth and I had worked hard on these back home, Tracie had carried that help forward in Athens, and again the work paid off: all the halts were dead square, and we lost no marks at all. I was completely thrilled to achieve a mark of 31.4, though at the same time disappointed that my two changes had not been better. But with William's fantastic test, which scored 38.6, we Brits were in the lead.

By the end of the day, when the adrenalin was wearing off, I was feeling pretty rough with a bad stomach. But then, with perfect timing, my William arrived. It was wonderful to have him there; things always take on an air of greater normality when he is around, although I was sad that we couldn't be together all the time. (Husbands of competitors aren't allowed to stay in the Olympic village and so he was holed up nearby with my parents.) He had had a nightmare with accreditation but Will Connell, Team GB's *chef de mission*, managed to sort it out for the cross-country and show-jumping days.

Next morning the sickness came back with a vengeance, just in time for cross-country day. I got up at 5.45 a.m. to walk the course for the final time and give Kiri a good canter. He felt fantastic; but I was still worried, because it was soon apparent that our prediction about the course being straightforward was right: most of the early riders were coming home clear and fast.

Jeanette made a personal decision to take the long route at a combination fence near the end of the course where there was a step up to a Grecian urn, which served as a narrow fence. She felt the direct route would not suit Over To You and, though she performed her usual brilliant path-finding job, it did cost four time penalties. So, after that, Yogi told us all to take the straight route at this combination and to go for the optimum time because it was clear that if we accrued cross-country time penalties it would leave the way open for other teams to catch up and overtake us. Mary produced a great clear within the time, Leslie finished only just outside it and, later, William produced one of the class rounds of the day on Tamarillo. But before that it was my turn, for what turned into one of the most dispiriting rides of my life.

For the first three fences I felt I had Kiri in a great rhythm and was able to sit quietly. It felt good and as if we were going quickly enough. Then he hit fence four, which slightly unnerved me, but I had no time to dwell on it because I knew I just had to keep my foot down. By the time we got to the water at the tenth I was becoming increasingly aware that the obstacles were just not big enough to make him back off and respect them. At the water, Kiri ran in close to the first fence, which meant an untidy jump, but we managed to soldier our way through the rest of the elements safely. All the time I was conscious of the clock ticking as the fences were coming up thick and fast. By the five-minute stage I knew I was a couple of seconds down, so I had to keep my foot on the accelerator.

But the worst part of the course from Kiri's point of view, the downhill, twisty bit, was still to come. At some fences, like an open ditch, I had to take chances I wouldn't normally take, so desperate was I to save every second possible. Up to the seven-and-a-half-minute stage I was not too far off target. But from here on the bends got tighter and the nature of the fences meant I had to waste time balancing him, particularly on the downhill approaches, because for reasons of safety as well as for the team I knew I couldn't risk a fall.

I finished with 11.2 time penalties, making our round probably one of the slower ones of the whole day. I was desperately disappointed, but at least we finished in one piece. Within minutes of dismounting I had to rush to a press conference to explain to a large group of journalists, many from Britain's national papers, why I had incurred so many time penalties. It was hard to put this across, because what a rider feels and what the viewers see are often two very different things. Someone even queried why I had been selected on this horse, which I found upsetting. Even with my time penalties I was on the second-best score for the team – William was now the best – and there was still the show-jumping to come. Despite what had happened, I had no doubt that I was riding one of the best horses in the world. How could the British selectors not have selected a class horse of his calibre who had won two of the toughest three-day events of all in 2003?

After leading the dressage it was deflating to be in bronze-medal position, but we were still only two fences behind the French, who by now had taken over the lead with three fast performances. We may have been down, but we definitely weren't out, and gold still felt within reach. All the same, I was pretty low that evening, feeling that I had let my team-mates down, even though I knew they all understood the situation I was in. It is so lucky that we get on so well as a team and are quick to pick each other up. It's an amazing feeling to have that kind of support.

But then disaster struck. Suddenly, it was announced that Tamarillo had chipped a bone on his stifle (this is one of the most common injuries with event horses, particularly when jumping drops or into water, when horses can easily scuff their back legs on a fence) and would have to be withdrawn from the competition immediately. This was completely devastating for William, who adores that horse and who had been working for many years to win an Olympic medal. Not only had he achieved our best team score, but he also had the strongest chance of winning an individual medal for himself: he seemed our best hope at that stage. Already dispirited, we sank into complete misery, and our supporters were equally despondent. The British team was now in fourth place and might go home empty-handed after all the expectations, all the hype and all the pressure. Yet none of us had under-performed and none of our horses had let us down.

We knew we just had to keep strong, and when I woke up next morning, on the final day of the competition, I was feeling focused, confident and as though I had managed to put the previous day behind me. I felt sure we would win something. My husband William helped me work Kiri, who seemed to have come right back on to my wavelength. I felt very much as though we were working together again and hoped the show-jumping track would be technical and up to height, because this was a phase at which we could excel.

The show-jumping stadium was superb, a grass arena with excellent going against a backdrop of rocky hills. The atmosphere was incredible: this was nail-biting stuff for competitors and spectators alike, with the scores of the top four teams all so close. The whole result could end up being decided on an odd rail, and I just prayed it wouldn't be us who missed out on a medal. Right from the first round it was clear that the time was tight. The course was not overly big, but there were enough questions and a lot of fences with light rails set in shallow cups which wouldn't take much of a rub to make them fall. The tension was made worse for me by the fact that, with William and Tamarillo out, I would be the last to jump for the team.

I sat in the grandstand with William (Fox-Pitt) and Leslie to watch while my William was out in the practice ring overseeing the warm-up with Ken and Yogi. Jeanette had one fence down and Mary two, and Leslie and I began to feel our potential medal sliding away again because the Americans, lying third overnight, had two clear rounds, while the Germans also had a clear and were catching up the French.

Leslie left the grandstand to warm up while I made another dash for the loo, something that was getting to be a habit this week. Then I needed to find a place to be alone, to go through the course fence by fence in my head until it was time to get on the horse. By now I didn't want to know what anyone else was doing; all I knew was that Kiri and I had to jump a clear round for our country, our team and all our supporters. It just had to be done.

I definitely felt twitchy, and couldn't fend off a few last-minute panics: have I got the wrong bit on? Has my saddle slipped back? I worried that Kiri felt too bright and that I should have given him more work. I was so uptight that I asked Hannah to call William, who was helping Leslie. He came over and reassured me that everything was fine. Just having him there made me relax and feel more confident. I was thrilled when I heard that Leslie had jumped clear, but I didn't want to hear about the other competitors.

When I finally entered that ring, Kiri seemed to grow underneath me; he must have felt the atmosphere just as I did, but oddly enough, by this stage I felt quite calm. I had a job to do and I wasn't going to be distracted, and Kiri and I duly produced a much-needed clear round for the British team.

The competition was reaching its climax now. The USA's Kim Severson, next to jump, rode fantastically well, but had the very last fence down. She was devastated because it cost the Americans bronze – and handed it to us. Now we knew we would go home with a medal. It may have been the wrong colour, but it was still a medal, and the whole British camp was elated.

I was so caught up in the excitement and relief that we wouldn't go home empty-handed and so busy talking to the press that I didn't see Bettina Hoy's round – I just heard she had gone clear, and that the final Frenchman, Nicolas Touzaint, had had one down, which meant France was pipped to team gold by Germany. This was an extraordinary result – as well as a great credit to their trainer, Chris Bartle – because the Germans had not qualified as a team like most of us, at the European or World Championships; they had managed to qualify because they had enough individual riders in the world rankings to have five riders at the Games. As William Fox-Pitt pointed out during a press conference, this competition had been more of a glorified combined training contest (dressage and show jumping), with a gallop in between, than a true four-star event. I am not saying we would have necessarily won if the cross-country been a real test, but the results would certainly have been different.

And there was still the individual round of show jumping to go in the evening. Nicolas Touzaint was in the lead from Bettina and Kim, while I and Leslie were now fourth and fifth, which was quite an improvement on our previous situation.

We were milling around, busy congratulating ourselves on our bronze medal, when we realised that the team results hadn't been officially announced. Bettina and the German camp were looking terribly strained, and news suddenly filtered back that Bettina had circled through the start after the bell had gone, an error which should have incurred fourteen penalties. This would obviously change the results completely, and an inquiry was taking place. Not having seen Bettina's round, I couldn't give any opinion on what had happened, but there were endless phone calls with people watching on TV at home and among the spectators at Athens, and it was clear that a number of people had noticed her mistake. It would be awful to see the German team lose gold in this way, but rules are there for a reason. Why have them if they're not going to be observed?

We had to wait an hour before the course was open to walk for the individual jumping, so we decided to go up to the supporters' tent. I wandered up quietly with William, and he reminded me to stay composed and focused as I still had more work to do. We had a great reception in the tent because we knew we would definitely be going home with a team medal, although everyone was slightly confused as to whether it would be bronze or silver. I made my way straight over to Denise and Roger Lincoln to congratulate them on how brilliantly Kiri had jumped – and then I saw my parents and brother. In all my own tension, I'd forgotten how much they must have been suffering. But even then I didn't stay long because the tent was crowded and I didn't want to be distracted from what lay ahead, so soon William and I returned to the stadium. There was talk among the French that we shouldn't walk the course until the Bettina saga was sorted, but within minutes it was announced that she had indeed been given the fourteen penalties, which meant France had won gold, we had silver, the Americans had bronze and the Germans were demoted to fourth. It also meant that I would be in individual bronze medal position at this stage.

I walked the course three times, once with William and then a further twice on my own. It was a lot bigger than the team course, which would suit Kiri. On watching the first riders to go I noticed that the fence causing most problems was a horrible cream-coloured plank which seemed to merge into the side of the arena and was difficult for horses to focus on; it was also flimsy and fell at the slightest touch. What was more, whether because of the floodlights, or because tired horses were being pulled out at night to jump, many more poles than usual were being hit.

I was torn between excitement and nerves. Kiri was such a

fantastic jumper I knew he could go clear and I could therefore rise higher, but would it be enough to realise my dream of gold? After an unpromising start, the ultimate prize was suddenly tantalisingly close.

I saw that Bettina had not got back on her horse to jump (she had temporarily been demoted to eighth) and realised that the situation had changed back again. The appeal jury had over-ruled the ground jury, on the grounds that it was a failure of equipment and officials (because the timing clock had been reset during Bettina's round) and so we'd all gone back down a peg. It was confusing and unsettling, but I knew I had to concentrate on my own performance and not worry about the details of my place.

William warmed me up in the same way as in the previous round. We didn't jump too many practice fences, and I just tried to sit still and do as little as possible to enable Kiri to work it out for himself. I sat so quietly at one fence that he hit the back rail of an oxer, which made him go even higher next time, and so I was confident he wouldn't want to hit a fence when he got into the arena.

From the loud cheering I realised that Leslie had jumped another clear round, but there was no time to think about that because it was my turn. William had told me to canter up to the corner to have a look at the planks because this was the significant bogey fence. Perhaps it was the intense atmosphere or the bright lights, but Kiri felt a little less relaxed than he had previously. I tried to concentrate and ride this round like I had the last, and he cleared the fences with his normal extravagance. Then we approached the planks. Perhaps Kiri got a little tight and, if anything, went a bit too high with his body and just clipped the plank with his hoof. I heard it fall and knew instantly that my Olympic dream was over. I knew I had to keep my head for the rest of the round, but inside I was shattered. Still, we didn't make any more mistakes and I knew I could hold my head up and be proud of my fantastic horse.

Kim had another unlucky fence down and so her Olympic dream, like mine, was over. Bettina must have needed huge mental strength to continue after the controversy that was raging around her and, like Kim and me, she also had a fence down. But then, sadly, Nicolas, the last to jump on his fabulous grey horse, had a devastating round, accumulating nineteen faults. I don't know whether his horse was tired or the occasion got to them, but what a horrendous way to lose the gold medal, falling to tenth place.

So Bettina won her gold in Athens, and got her moment on the podium. Leslie had silver and Kim bronze. I was thrilled for Leslie because it was his first individual medal at a championships. It was his turn under the spotlight, and he had excelled in all phases. But perhaps it could have been gold for him, and bronze for myself, if Bettina's appeal had failed . . .

By this stage, even before the medal ceremony, the American, British and French *chefs de mission* had a team of lawyers working on reversing the situation, taking the case to the Court of Arbitration for Sport. For sure, no one wanted the competition to end in this way; but rules are rules, and Bettina, like others, had benefited in the past when technicalities had helped decide results at major competitions. By now, though, the matter had gone beyond equestrianism. It was a no-win situation, and the evening ended in a confused and bitter atmosphere. All I could register in my exhaustion was that it was all too late for me; so near and yet so far.

It was the middle of the night when we left Markopoulo for the last time, having had to wait for Leslie and Kiri to be dope-tested and then for the press conference. This took ages because of the controversy. Visiting sports reporters from the national papers were astonished by what had happened and the French team – who, for a short time, had thought they were gold medallists – were openly furious. There was considerable acrimony between French and German journalists, and everyone wanted to know how we, the British team, felt about the evening's proceedings and whether we were contented with the bronze. I was feeling absolutely washed out by then and was glad I wasn't the focus of the questions. It was awkward, but William managed to say, diplomatically, that after everything that had happened to us we were just thrilled to get a team medal at all and were enjoying the moment.

After all that there were only a few hours of the night left – and then, suddenly, my Olympics were over. I flew home, and two days later was competing at a one-day event at Brockenhurst. It was back to normal, and I felt as though I'd hardly been away.

I knew that the judgement on the medals might go our way at the Court of Arbitration, but I honestly didn't give much thought to the possibility that our team medal might be upgraded to silver and that I would get an individual bronze medal and Leslie the gold. As far I was concerned, the whole thing was over. When Yogi phoned me during the weekend to tell me that the hearing had found against Bettina, and that she and the Germans had been demoted, I didn't feel at all surprised. The result was, of course, wonderful and deserved from Leslie's point of view, but my own feeling was that it had been an unfortunate and extraordinary chain of events which meant we had definitely missed the moment. I was more pleased for the team and for Yogi at getting the silver than I was about my own promotion.

Whatever the final outcome, our performances remain the same; we know we did the best we could. I think as a team we deserved the silver and, though we put up good performances, we missed out on that crucial element of luck necessary for gold. If William and Tamarillo had been able to jump on the last day, I think we'd have won team gold. My overwhelming emotion now was huge relief that it was all over, that the waiting and the pressure were all behind us, and that I could look forward to enjoying the sport again. I had a couple of good preparation runs before the autumn three-days and this year I was really looking forward to Burghley, because I would be going in completely different circumstances from the previous year when I was in a state about the Grand Slam.

The Burghley weekend started happily enough. I really felt that I had finally mastered the dressage phase with Cornerman; by the end of Friday we were in the lead, and I was in party mood for the launch event that Katie White and Susan Lamb had organised, with the Horse Trials Support Group, for my book. Lots of my owners were able to come, and it was also a celebration of the British team's success at the Olympics. All the same, I was a little unnerved when I saw that the course designer Wolfgang Feld had included three gates on his cross-country course, and our Badminton fall at a gate lurked in the back of my mind.

There had been a funny, tense atmosphere all week at Burghley. Most riders were unhappy with the combined length of the cross-country and steeplechase, considering that the ground was so gluey after a record amount of rainfall in August. The cross-country was exceptionally long, thirteen minutes, on top of a four-and-a-half-minute steeplechase. Taking into account the big jumping efforts demanded, it was felt that this was too much of an endurance test. I know many riders who formally put their concerns forward to officials; however, no concessions were ordered, even though our rider rep, Eric Smiley, a well-respected senior competitor, repeatedly attempted to negotiate.

I am not particularly militant at the best of times, and I was tied up with my book launch, but one reason I didn't get involved in the debate was because I felt the distances and fences were still within the rules of eventing. We as riders should know these rules and be prepared to get our horses ready to perform within them. To see so many horses either finishing tired or not coming home at all, as happened that day at Burghley, is not acceptable; but on the other hand we can't get away from the fact that the winner, Andrew Hoy, had two horses that went round the course easily, not looking at all tired and finishing with very good times.

In my view it wasn't just the ground that made horses tired; the weather was humid and hot and – a factor that some people haven't considered – the first five minutes of the course contained some seriously big jumping efforts which came up thick and fast. Horses were arriving at the first water complex more tired than they normally are at that stage. The ground conditions were actually good in the early part of the course; it was later on that it got sticky. What I think was taking the toll was the series of big fences one after another, built in such a way that you had either to close the horse up to fit in an extra stride or open him out to make him take off further out and achieve a bigger jump – a constant readjustment that contributed further to tiring the horses.

However, these issues were driven out of my mind by an awful gut feeling that something was wrong with Cornerman. When I pulled up after the chase he didn't feel one hundred per cent. I set off on Phase C, walking him for a bit, and was sure that my competition was over. He felt okay trotting, but as I returned to the ten-minute box I had an instinct that something was wrong. I spoke to his owner Susie Cranston and to the vets, but on examining the horse they gave him the thumbs-up. So I set off on the cross-country, but it wasn't long before I realised that he wasn't right. It was an awful feeling and, when he struggled over a fence at the Lower Trout Hatchery, I pulled up. On our way back to the stables he tied up – the muscles over his back end had gone into spasm. It upset me enormously that I hadn't gone by my instinct, but when you're in the lead, and the vets have passed the horse, how do you explain an instinct to the owner? Everyone has such high expectations and you have to do your best to fulfil them.

Anyway, my disaster seemed pretty irrelevant in view of what happened later. The mood had already become sober because of the way horses were finishing when, right at the end of a seemingly endless afternoon, Caroline Pratt had a horrendous fall when her horse Primitive Control hit a fence in the water at the Lion Bridge and turned over on top of her. Her death wasn't officially confirmed until later that evening, but most people had seen it happen on the closed-circuit TV and we knew what had happened. It was terrible; it's hard to recall an unhappier day in the sport.

We were shell-shocked. Caroline was such a highly rated and respected rider, and we realised that what happened to her could have happened to any one of us. Following a dire evening full of grief and recrimination, the next afternoon we all filed into the main arena for a minute's silence. Everyone was utterly miserable. Caroline was such a dear friend and we all felt desperate for her family and owners Dick and Frances Kinsey, to whom she was a surrogate daughter. There wasn't much comfort to be had; all we could think was that Caroline had enjoyed a fantastic ride on her first horse, Call Again Cavalier, and that she had died doing the thing she was most passionate about on the horse who was dearest to her. He was going well and, for that later stage of the course, had looked one of the better runners, so there was no proof that the accident was connected with the issues raised by the riders, issues about which Caroline herself had felt strongly.

Only one good thing came out of this awful weekend, and that was that the FEI has recognised that riders must be taken more seriously if a large percentage feels strongly about something. New rules governing stronger rider representation were drawn up soon after Burghley.

I went straight on to Blenheim with Viceroy, which proved both a great cheering-up weekend for the sport and a huge personal success for me. Winning here was a massive boost to my fortunes this season – my fourth win at this event, which is a record – and exciting for Sue and Lizzie Bunn, particularly because it saw Viceroy become the first stallion to win at this level.

All year big discussions had revolved around the format of the sport and whether all events should follow the Olympic format and drop the roads and tracks and steeplechase phases, a move against tradition which once would have been considered with horror. Blenheim was the first three-day event in Britain to try the short format. For riders, it was very much a case of trial and error in relation to preparing the horse for the cross-country. Until we do more of these events – and it seems that this will be the way the sport will go now – riders won't know the best way to prepare horses. I did very little warm-up compared to what I did with Kiri at the Olympics; Viceroy isn't a puller like Kiri, who could probably have done with another half-hour in Athens and who suffered from lack of space to gallop. I have now come round to the idea that the short format, which was once anathema to us and seemed to spell the end of traditional eventing, will work, provided we are provided with a large enough warm-up area and provided the cross-country courses are designed to be influential and challenging enough, which Blenheim was.

Next stop was Necarne in Northern Ireland. Again, this was highly successful; I won the three-day event with Chamrock and the CIC (international one-day event) with Ensign. Caroline's funeral was taking place in Cheshire that week and, for those of us who would be missing it, a special service was organised in Necarne. I was asked to deliver a tribute. I've never found it a problem to stand up and address a crowd about the sport I love, but this was the hardest thing I've ever done because the words I was using didn't seem good enough. It really upset me because as I was talking about Caroline my brain was registering that my words sounded so trivial; you can't do someone like that justice in a speech. She was a very special person – and even saying that doesn't seem good enough.

My next trip was to Boekelo, which was a red-letter event for me and Mum: I was riding Ensign, the first horse we've ever owned who has run in a three-star. It was also an outing for my new lorry, in which I was giving Ruth Friend (now Mrs Edge) a lift, and what turned into an entertaining weekend inevitably began with our getting lost. I ended up having to turn my 44-foot lorry at a T-junction in Holland where there were massive great dykes in front and behind. Mum, who was travelling with me in the lorry for the first time, jumped out to direct operations but she didn't think about standing where I could see her in my wing mirrors. Thankfully I could hear her screaming and somehow avoided upending the whole lot in a ditch.

Boekelo is a big-time party event and on the Wednesday night it was my birthday. These days I am not a big drinker, but on this occasion I got well oiled. I got caught with my trousers down having a pee behind the tent and then got lost going back to my lorry. A couple of Irishmen gave me a lift; a couple of days later, sobered up, I felt mortified when I bumped into them.

Ensign finished second, which was thrilling and gave Mum and me the feeling that he could turn into a serious event horse. Bettina Hoy won on Diamond Magic but, unbelievably, she was yet again the centre of a big news story. At the start of the weekend news had broken that Ringwood Cockatoo, her Olympic horse, had failed a dope test in Athens. No one could believe this latest twist in the saga, but it did make us feel less awkward about her losing the medal and that perhaps this added justification to the decision to take away her medal. However, Bettina later appealed to the FEI and, on the grounds that the error was unintentional, was exonerated.

I am a firm believer that riders whose horses fail dope tests should be banned, without exception. We are all made aware of the banned substances and the risk of being tested, and we know that you don't use medication during a competition. I am very strict at home, to the point of neurosis. My girls know that if a horse has to have medication they must write down the details of what it has and when it is given so that I am fully aware of what might be in the system and therefore don't compete that horse until I know it is clear.

Boekelo was followed by a manic rush to ride Billy Autumn, William and Donal Barnwell's home-bred horse, in my first international jumping show, in Paris. This sounds a big deal, but it was actually quite a small competition and the trip was designed as a special girls' outing. I went with Clare Inglis, Lee Popeley and Julie Slade and we all competed while our husbands, for whom it was a busman's holiday, trained us. Billy Autumn jumped well and I got a great buzz. After a highly entertaining weekend, William and I left Lee and Clare to drive the lorry back. I was a bit concerned because neither has the greatest eyesight and I wondered if they'd be able to read the road signs. I rang them on the mobile to check progress, to find that before they'd done more than leave the showground Lee had hit a car and pushed it on the pavement!

William and I drove home through the night to get back to London in time for Monday morning and the great Olympic bus tour. We were on an open bus with the cycling team and the equestrian Paralympians. After all the fuss and anti-climax of our medals, I have to admit that this was a special day, really moving, and we were all choked when the BBC presenter Sue Barker managed to get the National Anthem played for Leslie, in front of thousands of people in Trafalgar Square.

From there we went on to Buckingham Palace where I suddenly realised that it was a real honour to be presented with our silver medals in front of so many great athletes by the Princess Royal in the presence of the Queen and Prince Philip. We may not have been on the podium in Athens, but here was something totally new and therefore memorable. Finally, after all the work, the stress and the waiting, we had an Olympic moment to savour.

My 2005 Diary

1 January. The year got off to its customary start – with me feeling jaded after a New Year's Eve party and horses to collect from all different directions. Then it's straight into the usual early fittening programme comprising endless roadwork. I admit I find it terribly tedious, even though I know it's essential.

4 January. I've taken on more and more teaching in recent years – at this time of the year my diary records endless lessons – and it's something I'd like to do even more of if only there were enough hours in the day. Today it's members of the Eridge Pony Club because I like to put something back into the branch which started me off.

14 January. I force myself to sit down and work out a programme for the horses, with the goal of a three-day event for each. It's the usual nightmare jigsaw, trying to go where each owner would like, and is always subject to change. The plan is for Supreme Rock (Rocky), who came back into work in December, to start competing at the beginning of the season; deep down, my aim with him is Badminton, but only if

I feel he is as good as he was when he won it two years previously. Primmore's Pride (Kiri) will also be aimed at Badminton, which will be his first attempt, having missed it in 2004 due to being saved for Athens. Ensign (Titch) goes to Saumur, Blue Horizon (Gucci) to Windsor for his first three-day, and Chamrock will compete at advanced level, the plan being to get him qualified for Bramham. At this stage I don't know what I'll do with Cornerman – after what happened at Burghley last year the important thing for him is to have some fun at a lower level – while for the young horses it's just a case of getting them out there competing and gaining more mileage.

16 January: An Austrian rider, Gabby, arrives for two months' training and to be an extra member of the team.

17 January: Meeting with Jamie Hawksfield of Equestrian Vision who is masterminding the latest idea for a lecture tour, Funnell Philosophy. I thought this one would be pretty straightforward – no horses, no lorries, no mass packing – just me articulating what I have learned about sport psychology, my mental approach and how I cope with competitions. But it ended up being far more time-consuming than I'd envisaged because Jamie wasn't going to allow me just to waffle on unscripted! We worked out an exact structure with bits of relevant video footage put in the right order to illustrate what I was talking about, which took ages.

18 January: Our annual meet at home for the Surrey Union Hunt. William does a great job of putting everything possible into the punch and, with all the little eats I'd prepared, I think everyone went off feeling jolly. I hadn't hunted for a while but, with the hunting ban looming (19 February), I was overcome by a strong feeling that I must get out there before it's too late. I appreciate everyone has their own view on hunting, but mine is that there are far more serious issues in the world to worry about and that we ought to be allowed to get on with our lives. I've hunted since childhood, as has William, and we feel it's a liberty issue.

I rode Polly From Poland, a grey mare who arrived back in a lorryload from William and Donal Barnwell's connection in Poland. William told me we were getting a nine-year-old bay gelding with eventing form, but when the new horse arrived it turned out to be an 11-year-old grey mare with no competition records available. The reality is that I don't think Polly had done much at all; she is now with my brother-in-law Nick Funnell for Whizz, our youngest niece.

19 January. Flew to Cork to stay with the Irish riders Trish Donegan and Mike Ryan who had arranged for me to teach some of the eventers in Southern Ireland. One major drawback with my teaching is that I find it impossible to stick to time and often over-run the day by several hours. A 45-minute lesson isn't long enough if I feel that I haven't got to the point I want to be at, if the horse isn't doing what I want, or the rider hasn't picked up on my points. The first day was, therefore, a bit of a marathon and, needless to say, when it was over I had a few jars on an empty stomach with Trish and Mike and felt decidedly ropey next day.

26 January. Great excitement: a new luxury Volkswagen Touareg 4 x 4 was delivered, part of a generous sponsorship deal for the whole Olympic team. Even though it's not mine, I feel as though I've come a long way in the last 20 years, with a brand new lorry and car outside the house.

29 January: A very special day. I'd been contacted by the Make A Wish Foundation, a charity which aims to grant the wishes of children with serious illnesses. A delightful little girl called Ellie, who is only 9, apparently dreamed of spending the day with me and my horses. She and her parents were flown over from Northern Ireland and delivered to me in a chauffeur-driven stretch limousine. We had a great day together, with lunch at the Parrot, and I put her up on Matter of Opinion (Mop) in the lunge pen. Though I was nervous, her parents were happy for Penny to ride this big young horse off the lunge, and he behaved impeccably.

I get a lot of letters nowadays from charities and children and it's an aspect I find difficult to deal with; I feel so bad because there just isn't time to help everyone.

1 February: Meeting with Jonathan Warr, the new director of the Windsor three-day event. He has devised a talent-spotting series called Quest-X, with a final at Windsor, and wants me to help promote the series and train the winner.

16 February: The horses were finally ready to go to the gallops; I'd forgotten what a beautiful setting it is, even in winter, on the estate at Arundel where I use John Dunlop's racehorse gallops.

17 February: To Greenwich with Andrew Finding, Director-General of the British Equestrian Federation, as part of London's 2012 Olympic bid. Two IOC (International Olympic Committee) members were paying a visit and I'd been asked to speak and then have lunch with them. I felt pretty daunted, but it was a relaxing lunch – slightly too relaxing, perhaps, as I was terribly conscious of not saying something silly that would in any way jeopardise the bid. I was really impressed with the plans for the equestrian site at Greenwich; the cross-country would actually be quite demanding, as it's hilly, and the whole site overlooks the Thames. It will be spectacular if it comes off. Fingers crossed.

18 February. Launch of the computer game 'Pippa Funnell and the Stud Farm Inheritance'. Promoted by Ubisoft, it's a game that has sold well in France using the show jumper Alexandra Lederman. It's now been converted into English – I'd been over to Paris in December to do the voice-over.

19 February. Mum's annual dance in aid of her Eridge horse trials. After various chaotic trips to the dance in previous years, including on a bus which got lost, this time we splashed out and hired a stretch limousine to get from our friends Duncan and Clare Inglis to the dance. Nine of us arrived quite tanked up for yet another entertaining evening. Even better, it clashed with the annual ERA ball, which I was more than happy to get out of!

20 February. Straight to BETA (British Equestrian Trade Association fair at Birmingham) with a hangover. I was mainly there to meet up with Toggi – my breeches are selling well and I'm still very involved with them and with the new product that was due to be launched at Blenheim. I was also excited that I managed to get Toggi together with Will Connell, the British team manager, and they are now the official clothing sponsors to the British equestrian team. Another change was that by this stage I had now parted with Horseware, who kindly provided me with rugs, because it makes more sense for me to link up with the Funnell rug range, which is part of Royston products, which William is involved with.

23 February. Not a moment to sit around because it was the first Funnell Philosophy evening, at Cheltenham. It was nerve-racking at first, but the feedback was positive and I was grateful to Jamie and his team for their professionalism. Drove back through the night and turned round to go to team training at Waresley Park.

24 February. Desperate weather for training – snow and sleet – but it was great to see Tracie, Kenneth and Yogi and to catch up with my team-mates after the winter.

28 February. Cross-country schooling at Tweseldown.

1 March. All-day teaching clinic in Ireland, prior to a Funnell Philosophy evening at Goff's in Co. Kildare. As usual, I went way over time with the teaching so when I arrived at Goff's my audience was already there and I had to run through them wearing my breeches and boots. They were impressed, how-ever, by my three-minute turnaround into a slightly more glamorous look. Good job I had deodorant with me.

4 March. A very sad day. Lizzie Bunn rang to tell me the dreadful news that poor Viceroy (Leroy), who has been such a fantastic and kind horse for me, has had to be put down due to severe colic. He was rushed in for major surgery but, basically, his guts never got working again. It is so sad for the Bunns because he's been a special little horse for them and, as an entire, it was a terribly unfortunate ending to his career. Any other problem and he could have been retired to a useful stud career, particularly with his Blenheim win behind him. The only good thing is that there are quite a few of his babies around now, but I was still very sad; the loss of dear friends never gets any easier.

6 March: The first event, Stilemans, with Polly and Mop. I couldn't believe it had come round so soon and wasn't sure that I was really prepared but, fortunately, there was too much frost in the ground so I couldn't go across country anyway.

8 March: Flew to Edinburgh for the final run of Funnell Philosophy.

10 March: Tweseldown. A great thrill, as I was riding Rocky across country for the first time in eighteen months. He loved it and so did I. It was a great feeling being back on him and made me realise how good he is. Kiri was also super; I'd replaced the gag bit with a Waterford fulmer and he was much easier to ride. Chamrock also went well, as did the other horses next day at Poplar Park, but this weekend wasn't about rosettes.

15 March: Taught the Potential squad. They are the Lottery-funded group expected to be the next senior team riders and I've become involved with their training, on the flatwork side. These are the type of people I enjoy teaching the most; they all have talent, dedication and enthusiasm to learn and, most importantly, are our British riders for the future.

21 March: Following a busy weekend at Aldon, I did a filmed interview with *Horse & Hound* to be shown on the big screen at Badminton and then got changed in time to be picked up and chauffeur-driven to the BBC studios in London for *A Question of Sport*. Great fun, as always; I was on Ally McCoist's team with Jade Johnston and we won!

23 March: A lecture-demo at Arena UK for Virbac, who had

kindly agreed to help out with Chamrock's running costs; this means he will now run under the ownership of Sarah Johnson and Equimax.

3 April: Belton and the most significant pre-Badminton spring run for Rocky and Kiri. Ruth came to the event to give me the benefit of her expert eye and, in swiftly correcting some bad habits, it helped me produce two very satisfactory tests so that Kiri and Rocky were first and second in the special advanced section. The organiser Stuart Buntine had made a huge effort, not only in improving the cross-country courses, but also in making the dressage and show jumping more accessible for the public and he had made a huge effort to get lots of local sponsorship and pre-event press coverage. The cross-country, designed by Sue Benson, was big, upgraded and had a few testing combinations, including a tricky corner combination three from home which caused so many problems that a crowd gathered there. I provided them with some entertainment when Rocky, who had been fantastic until that point, unbelievably put in a couple of run-outs! I wasn't worried, however; I've had unsuccessful Badminton dress rehearsals with him before and the way he felt still gave me confidence.

I tried an old Kineton noseband, that I discovered on a recent sort-out of the tackroom, on Kiri. This gave me a bit of leverage on his nose, which helped the control, and I had probably my best ever ride on him there. Oliver Townend and William Fox-Pitt went faster across country than me, but Kiri pulled out a good clear round show jumping and so we still won. I was beaming. It's great to win, but more than anything I was so chuffed at the way he went. It was a great mental boost for Badminton to have had such a good ride with no fighting.

4 April: Forty juniors arrived at 9 a.m. to spend the day with me, something I do annually for Gill Watson.

5–6 April: Rug photoshoots.

9 April: Burnham Market. I learned a new lesson: do not to try to run through a World Cup qualifier dressage test while watching the Grand National. As I was riding Ensign, mine and Mum's horse, I was perhaps a bit relaxed and didn't bother to work in properly because I so wanted to watch the race on TV. This resulted in the humiliating experience of being eliminated in the dressage for going wrong three times. Luckily, there had been some withdrawals, so the organisers let me run him in the ordinary advanced section, which we won. Chamrock also won his advanced class, so the weekend ended up better than it started.

25 April: To the gallops where, to my horror and disbelief, Rocky pulled up lame after galloping. The incident is uncannily like the last time, before Burghley 2003, but this time he was lame on the opposite foreleg. It was a very sad moment because, even without seeing a vet, at that split second I knew this would be the last time I would gallop Rocky and that I would never compete him again. The next awful job was to break the news to Emma Pitt. However, the way we all looked at it was: 'Thank God it happened on the gallops and not at Badminton'. He had only incurred a slight strain, which had been caught early. If this had happened at Badminton it would have been awful and the injury could have been far worse because adrenalin would probably have kept him going.

It can be difficult to know when to retire a horse and though mentally Rocky was telling us he was fine, physically he told us it was time to stop. I owe this horse so much for the many great moments he has given us but the blow is greatly softened by the injury happening, in a relatively minor way, at home. It's been a privilege to work with a horse of this calibre, not just for what he has won, but because he's been such a kind and easy horse to have around. He will now go and live with Emma at her new home in Northamptonshire where he will go hacking and have a lovely time.

26 April: Ruth came down for a few days and was a fantastic help. I find it amazing the difference she can make in the way a horse goes for me just by a few comments. I kept the weekend before Badminton completely free on purpose.

4–8 May: Badminton. I knew it was going to be competitive, because William Fox-Pitt had Tamarillo back in action and was bound to come close; plus there was Leslie Law, our new Olympic champion, with his two greys and Andrew Nicholson, who could have won it on Lord Killinghurst, a horse with an amazing four-star record. But I was quietly confident and very excited at the prospect of Kiri's long-awaited Badminton debut. I knew I was sitting on one of the best horses in the world and I anticipated that Badminton's flat terrain would suit him as, unlike at Athens with its downhill runs, there weren't too many places where I would have to break his rhythm.

I had been asked to be rider representative, which can be a big job if anything goes wrong but, as it turned out, my job was easy. There was no controversy, the weather was perfect and it ended up being one of the happiest weekends the sport had seen for a while. My only problem was that Kiri was at the end of the draw and, without another horse to ride, it seemed a very long, anxious wait until we got going.

I was annoyed with myself that I over-rode in the extended trot, causing Kiri to break, which lost us marks in what is usually his best pace, but he still produced a very good dressage test which left me with the optimistic feeling that there is still more exciting work to come from this horse. And we were in the lead.

Across country next day, Kiri was fantastic; he listened and kept his mind on the job. It felt a huge relief to have a good ride; in hindsight, I realised that my hairy ride on him at Athens had actually quite frightened me and I needed to have my confidence boosted. He's a big-striding, big-jumping, big horse, which is something I'll never be able to change and it will always cost us that little bit of time on the cross-country.

But because we were five points in front after dressage, we still held the lead – just – because William Fox-Pitt and Tamarillo, who thankfully showed no signs of his injury in Athens, were clear inside the time and there wasn't a show-jumping rail between us. William and I had breakfast together in the riders' canteen and joked about the situation – it seemed such a shame that we weren't at a major team championship where we would be rooting for each other to go clear. And, amazingly, we both did and so I won my third Badminton. To have done so leading from the start felt even more special.

People go on about the rivalry between William and myself but really there isn't any, we don't count who wins what; on this occasion it was just going to be my day, but another time it will be the other way around and I wouldn't begrudge that because William is probably the rider I most respect and a great friend. What was special for me, and the reason I'm so glad it was my day this time, is that Kiri will now be the only horse ever to win three traditional four-star three-day events. This was

Badminton's last year at the long format (with steeplechase and roads and tracks) and I don't see any horse now ever pulling off this feat in the future. I always thought he was a fantastic horse and now, whatever happens, he's earned a piece of history.

As usual, I was very emotional, even more so because in the space of ten minutes I'd not only won Badminton but was also having to retire Rocky officially in public, because the event director Hugh Thomas had organised for me to parade him before the prize-giving. I was in floods of tears and didn't know which way to turn.

To complete the day, I got home to find a letter telling me that I was going to be awarded the MBE in the Queen's Birthday Honours. I was overwhelmingly thrilled; what an honour! I told my husband William, somewhat nervously because it has to be kept a secret at this stage, but amazingly he kept it quiet!

9 May. Phil and Julie Middleton, our fantastic sponsors, put on a large party at their home to celebrate my Badminton win. And I heard the nice news that Kiri and I have been selected for the European Championship team at Blenheim in September. Of course I had been hoping – and expecting – for this to happen, but I never get used to the thrill of having the news confirmed. It also gives me a lot of pleasure that the four of us – me, William Fox-Pitt, Jeanette and Leslie – are going to be back together on a team, especially as it's on home ground for the first time. I just hope that's not a bad omen! It will be our fifth championship as a foursome – Jeanette's eighth on the same horse! – and in our sport that's an amazing record.

10 May. Gave up smoking! After an awful lot of big talk, William and I finally got an appointment with a hypnotist in the hope that they could help where all else had failed. It was an interesting experience and, so far, it's working. Amazing. I can't say I feel fantastically different, but my breathing is better. That evening I gave the most incoherent talk to students at the Royal Agricultural College at Cirencester. I don't know whether it was exhaustion from Badminton, the 3 a.m. bedtime the night before or the lack of nicotine. Perhaps I was still in a trance. Anyway, it was the first time I'd ever got completely lost during a public talk – those poor students must have thought I was a madwoman.

14–15 May. Chatsworth. The Germans gave notice that they would be a major threat come the Europeans; they were first, second and third in the World Cup qualifier – we Brits didn't get a look in on our home ground. Cornerman ran well to finish ninth, which made me feel that taking him to Saumur, with Ensign, was a realistic plan.

16 May. Set sail for Saumur. Both horses went well: Cornerman was sixth and Ensign eighteenth. Ensign went a lot better than his position would suggest, and was consequently listed as a reserve horse for the British squad at Blenheim.

29 May. Windsor. A win that gave me huge satisfaction for three reasons: it was Blue Horizon's first three-day event, it was my fourth win at Windsor and it was Ian and Janet McIntyre's third win here, because they owned two of my previous winners, Marshland Rubio and Burke's Boy. I just hope that Gucci goes on and gives them more success than the other horses achieved because they really deserve it. I also rode Chamrock on the British team in the Prospect Cup team contest – we didn't do terribly well, it has to be said, and that led me to re-evaluate the idea of taking him to Bramham.

William was away at the Rome Show and my big thrill of the weekend was him being in the team that won Britain's first Nations Cup in the Super League. It was a fantastic result, the show jumpers were euphoric and I was so thrilled for him.

5 June: A very happy day. With the spring three-day events over, I spend a weekend away with my husband, travelling to St Gallen in Switzerland to watch him represent Britain on the Nations Cup team there. Although the team has only finished fifth, William and Cortaflex Mondriaan are one of only three combinations in the whole competition to jump a double clear. I'm beside myself with excitement that, finally, a British team place might be within his grasp.

11 June: At last my MBE is announced – a great relief, as I'm not sure how much longer William or I can keep it to ourselves. I'm touched to get so many letters of congratulation and excited to be interviewed on Radio 4's *Today* programme. Unfortunately, my great moment becomes rather garbled, if unforgettable for listeners who know me, because when I start talking about William and I becoming the first husband-and-wife pair to represent Britain in eventing and show jumping in the same year, the interviewer says: 'I presume you're talking about William Fox-Pitt!' Alice (Fox-Pitt) was listening and got straight on to my husband, saying: 'Is there something we don't know about?'

20 June: A press conference at Blenheim to announce Volkswagen's sponsorship of the team riders and also the remaining members of our British squad at the European

Championships. It's the day after the new four-star event at Luhmühlen and the announcement that Zara Phillips will be joining the senior squad for the first time, as a result of her excellent second place there, causing predictable media excitement. Luhmühlen is won by Bettina Hoy – her long-awaited first four-star victory – and we hear that she has made it fairly clear in her victory speech that the Germans intend to thrash us at the Europeans! Certainly they may have overtaken France as our main rivals; the German riders have been doing ominously well all year and are clearly hell-bent on getting revenge for Athens.

21 June. Another great day. William's place on the British show-jumping team is announced – which means a five-day holiday for me in sunny Italy! I have written before that I intend in future to devote more time to supporting William and riding his young horses, so this result is as satisfying as anything else that has happened this year. No one has worked harder and deserves their team chance more.

As for myself, in theory the pressure should be off me – it's not an Olympic year, I've won my third Badminton and I've been a European Champion twice before. I've already said that I want to spend more time teaching up-and-coming riders in the hope that my experiences will benefit them, and I still hope to have a family. Yet I know that, come Blenheim, I will feel as nervous and as competitive as ever. Although it's been a hard road to get to the top, I now know that staying there is even harder.

Career Record

1986 Team bronze medal, Junior European Championships (Airborne II)

5th Chatsworth CCI*** (Sir Barnaby)

....

1987 Individual gold medal, Young Rider European Championships
(Sir Barnaby)

....

1988 Completed first Badminton CCI****

8th and team gold medal at Young Rider European Championships
(Sir Barnaby)

....

1989 Individual silver and team silver medals at Young Rider European
Championships (Sir Barnaby)

....

1990 5th Badminton (Sir Barnaby)

2nd British Open Championships (Sir Barnaby)

....

1991 10th Breda CCI** (Heron's Flight)

13th Bramham CCI*** (Metronome)

1st Luhmühlen CCI*** (Sir Barnaby)

2nd British Open (Sir Barnaby)

4th Burghley CCI**** (Sir Barnaby)

....

1992 Completed Badminton (Sir Barnaby)

3rd Windsor CCI** (Cartoon)

1st & 7th Bramham (Metronome & Heron's Flight)

1st British Open (Sir Barnaby)

3rd Blenheim (Cartoon)

16th Burghley (Heron's Flight)

1993 2nd Windsor (Merry Gambler)

1st Blenheim CCI*** (Metronome)

1995 1st Windsor (Designer Tramp)

1st and 8th Blenheim (Bits And Pieces & The Imposter)

1996 1st & 6th Windsor (Marshland Rubio & Rainbow Magic)

1st & 4th Achselschwang CCI** (Rainbow Magic & Supreme Rock)

4th Burghley (Bits And Pieces)

1997 9th Badminton (Bits And Pieces)

2nd Punchestown CCI*** (Designer Tramp)

Represented GB as individual at Open European Championships (Bits And Pieces)

1998 1st Hickstead Eventers' Grand Prix (The Tourmaline Rose),

4th British Open (Rainbow Magic)

5th Blenheim (Rainbow Magic)

1999 6th Badminton (Supreme Rock)

1st Punchestown CCI** (General Salute)

Team gold and individual gold medals at European Championships (Supreme Rock)

4th Achselschwang CCI** (General Salute)

5th Le Lion d'Angers CCI** (Jurassic Rising)

2000 1st Chatsworth CIC*** (Supreme Rock)

4th Punchestown CCI** (Primmore's Pride)

4th & 7th Bramham CCI*** (Jurassic Rising & Cornerman)

2nd & 4th Burgie CCI** (Viceroy & Burke's Boy)

1st Hickstead Eventers' Grand Prix (The Tourmaline Rose)

Team silver medal at Sydney Olympics (Supreme Rock)

1st Le Lion d'Angers (Primmore's Pride)

2001 2nd Saumur CCI*** (Viceroy)

1st & 4th Burgie (Teddy Twilight & Walk On Star)

11th Luhmühlen (Jurassic Rising)

1st Hickstead Eventers' Grand Prix (The Tourmaline Rose)

1st Scottish Open Championships (Supreme Rock)

4th Hickstead Speed Derby (The Tourmaline Rose)

5th Burghley (Cornerman)

4th Blenheim (Primmore's Pride)

1st Windsor (Burke's Boy)

Team gold and individual gold medals at European Championships (Supreme Rock)

2002 1st Badminton (Supreme Rock)

2nd Chatsworth CIC*** (Jurassic Rising)

1st Saumur (Jurassic Rising)

1st Bramham (Walk On Star)

2nd British Open (Primmore's Pride)

6th Burghley (Primmore's Pride)

Team bronze medal at World Equestrian Games (Supreme Rock)

1st & 4th Pau CCI*** (Cornerman & Teddy Twilight)

2nd in FEI World Rankings

2003 1st Kentucky CCI**** (Primmore's Pride)

1st & 6th Badminton (Supreme Rock & Cornerman)

1st Saumur CCI*** (Walk On Star)

3rd Bramham (Jurassic Rising)

1st Burghley & Rolex Grand Slam (Primmore's Pride)

1st & 3rd Blenheim (Jurassic Rising & Viceroy)

Team gold and individual bronze medals at European Championships (Walk On Star)

4th Le Lion d'Angers (Matter Of Fact)

1st FEI World Rankings

1st British Eventing Rankings

. . . .

2004 1st Chatsworth CIC*** (Primmore's Pride)

Team silver and individual bronze medals at Athens Olympics (Primmore's Pride)

1st Blenheim CCI*** (Viceroy)

1st Necarne Castle CCI** (Ensign)

2nd Boekelo CCI*** (Ensign)

. . . .

2005 1st Badminton CCI**** (Primmore's Pride)

6th Sammur CCI*** (Cornerman)

1st Windsor CCI** (Blue Horizon)

Selected with Primmore's Pride for European Championships

Index

Note: horses' names are denoted in italics, followed by their nicknames in brackets; names of magazines, videos and television programmes are in inverted commas.

310